MENTORING MEN FOR THE MASTER

HANDBOOK

BY DR. BILL BENNETT

Mentoring Men for the Master Handbook /
10 Absolute Life-Changers of Men; Guaranteed:
From the Book Which Cannot Lie

Copyright © 2011

ISBN-13: 978-1-935256-13-7

Published by L'Edge Press
A ministry of Upside Down Ministries, Inc.
PO Box 2567
Boone, NC 28607

DEDICATION

I lovingly dedicate this book to my inimitable companion for 55 years and very best friend, Doris, and to my three precious sons, Dr. Bill, Jr., Philip Judson, and David Palmer. My wife Doris has always been a part of the solution, never a part of the problem, throughout our long ministry. Bill, Phil and David have made me exceedingly proud because of their wonderful godly attitudes and deep devotion to Jesus Christ and His church. Each of these has inspired me to invest my life into other young guys that they may become maximum Christian men in their personal lives, their homes, their churches, and their world at large.

I also dedicate this book to the growing company of young men across the world whom I have mentored, who have been transformed by the Word of God and the power of the Holy Spirit, into powerful servants of Jesus Christ, and who are today mentoring other men themselves. Dei Soli Gloria—To God alone be the glory!

ACKNOWLEDGEMENTS

I would be guilty of gross ingratitude if I did not acknowledge the invaluable contributions of the following people in the writing of this book:

Dr. Larry McDonald, Consultant, Professor of Pastoral Ministries and Spiritual Formation, Truett – McConnell College

Mrs. Elsie Johnson, Administrative Assistant

Mr. Thad Faulk, Assistant in Mentoring

Mr. Terry Bowman, Current Mentoree

One Liners About This Book

Dr L. Russ Bush, Vice President, Southeastern Seminary says, "Bennett's experience and passion shine clearly in this volume. I can highly recommend it to those whom God has called into His Service."

Dr. Jerry Falwell says, "I urge you to purchase, read and use this book."

Dr. D. James Kennedy says, "This book is a must for anyone who is interested in being mentored or becoming a mentor himself."

Dr. Jim Henry says, "This book is a must for those who would invest their lives as 'faithful men who shall be able to teach others also.' He is a master mentor for The Master."

Dr. Adrian Rogers says, "Being mentored by Bill Bennett would be a blessing that no seminary could give."

ENDORSEMENTS:

Dr. Daniel L. Akin, President Southeastern Baptist Theological Seminary

"Bill Bennett's passion for mentoring young men to be leaders in the work of our Lord is well known and shines forth in this book. He recognizes that this was the model of Jesus and it should be our model as well. His approach is Biblical, practical and devotional. I warmly commend this work to those who have a heart to grow to be more like the Savior."

Dr. David Alan Black, Professor of New Testament and Greek Southeastern Baptist Theological Seminary

"Bill Bennett is one of my closest friends. Together for a year we met weekly for prayer and mutual encouragement. I left every meeting uplifted and challenged. I know of few men I would rather be mentored by. I hope that many join him on the 'Sunny Side of Hallelujah Avenue,' as he loves to put it!"

Dr. L. Russ Bush, Academic Vice President Southeastern Baptist Theological Seminary

"Bill Bennett has served as Campus Chaplain at Southeastern Baptist Theological Seminary for several years. His love for students and his mentoring skills have paid rich dividends. In this volume, Bennett has outlined what I call spiritual disciplines for ministry. These cover prayer and fasting, time management, evangelism, worship, physical health, money management, meditation, and Bible study. The material is structured almost like an annotated outline. It is practical, easy to read, and basic, and yet it is exactly what many ministers need as they begin and as they finish their years in ministry. Those who learn these basic disciplines, and learn to share them by mentoring others, will find strength and maturity in their walk with the Lord. We are not saved by righteous works, but the minister is surely called upon to lead by example. Bennett's experience and passion shine clearly in this volume. I can highly recommend it to those whom God has called into His service."

Dr. Jimmy Draper, Jr., President of Lifeway Christian Ministries

"Bill Bennett has spent his life in relationships and mentoring. No one does it better than he. This book will give practical strategies and guidelines for this most needed process. Mentoring is a powerful tool in passing on the passion and vision to the next generation. You will be blessed by this book."

Dr. Jerry Falwell, Founder and Chancellor Liberty University, Lynchburg, Virginia

Before his death in May, 2007 wrote, "I have known Bill Bennett for nearly 35 years. The passion of his soul for many of those years has been to build up young men in their ministries. He has done this most effectively through mentoring them and he shares the thrilling story in his new book, *Handbook for Mentoring Men for the Master*. I urge you to purchase, read and use this book."

Pastor Terry Fox, Dr. Bennett's first Mentoree Former Chairman of North American Mission Board

"Dr. Bennett, as one who had the privilege of training under your leadership, I personally know and am utilizing the tools for mentoring that you have laid out in this work. This book will have a powerful impact on those doing Kingdom business. I hope that every Pastor in America will take advantage of this anointed work."

Dr. Jim Henry, Former Pastor First Baptist Church, Orlando, Florida and former President of the SBC

"The word 'mentor' was not on my radar in early years of ministry. But, it was in the heart of Bill Bennett when the Holy Spirit placed him in my life during seminary days. Forty years later I continue to learn from him. This book is a must for those who would invest their lives as 'faithful men who shall be able to teach others also.' He is a master mentor for The Master!"

Allen Holmes, Lead Pastor, Day Star Christian Fellowship, Greensboro, NC 27410

"No one is more qualified to write this book! Dr. Bennett has pastored some of our best churches and mentored some of our best men. Now he has poured more than 50 years of knowledge and experience into this concise but powerful book. This is a must read for anyone who is serious about the gospel ministry."

D. James Kennedy, Ph.D., President, Evangelism Explosion International

"Dr. Bill Bennett was shown the effectiveness of mentoring by his initial involvement in Evangelism Explosion (see page 21). Thereafter, he began to mentor men in increasingly large numbers with great success. In his *Handbook for Mentoring Men for the Master*, he tells the thrilling story of how the Holy Spirit led him into this ministry—its Biblical basis, its message, and its methodology, and its world-wide impact through Mentoring Men for the Master, International. This book is a must for anyone who is interested in being mentored or becoming a mentor himself. "

Dr. Allen Moseley, Professor and Dean of Students, Southeastern Baptist Theological Seminary

"Bill Bennett knows how to mentor men. He has done it effectively for decades. And the proof is in the pudding—many men who are walking with God and faithfully serving God proudly refer to Dr. Bennett as their mentor. The church needs such a ministry to multiply, and for that reason I am overjoyed at the release of this book."

Dr. Paige Patterson, President, Southwestern Baptist Theological Seminary, Fort Worth, Texas

"In a day when more and more young men are coming into positions of significant leadership, churches and other organizations must realize that they bring an enormous amount of talent and energy but often little experience. Dr. Bill Bennett, whose academic preparation is matched by years in the pastorate, is a remarkable individual. I warmly recommend his *Handbook for Mentoring Men for the Master* for the development of wisdom and personal integrity in younger men."

Eddie Parrish, Dedicated Deacon, First Baptist Church, Leland, NC

"Forever grateful to be mentored by Dr. Bill Bennett"

"Several years ago, Dr. Bennett extended an invitation for me to attend his mentoring school. During my first visit to the mentoring school, I quickly realized God placed me there to become involved in a ministry which would truly challenge and help me become a better man of God. Words cannot adequately express how God is using the mentoring school to transform my life. It is evident through Dr. Bennett's actions that he has a deep desire to bring the Word of God to life and to encourage men to experience the greatness of an Almighty God. I urge you to take the time to learn from this mentoring handbook, apply the lessons to your life, and share these truths with other men. You will be forever blessed!"

Dr. Adrian Rogers, Pastor Emeritus, Bellevue Baptist Church, Memphis, TN and past President of the SBC

Before his death on November 15th, 2005, wrote, "Bill Bennett is not one who philosophizes from behind a mahogany desk. His life and impact stand for itself. The *Handbook for Mentoring Men for the Master* is a tool that I trust will be used to remind all of us of the stewardship that we have to train and encourage others. I pray that it will have wide distribution, and I am confident that it will strengthen and help those who put it into practice."

"Being mentored by Bill Bennett would be a blessing that no seminary could give."

Dr. John F. Zino, Principal Engineer, General Electric Company, Wilmington, NC

"Dr. Bennett's *Handbook for Mentoring Men for the Master* is one of the most comprehensive and systematic texts of its kind. It provides a very thorough review of all the major elements of mentoring useful for teaching, training and disciplining men at every stage of their Christian development. It is a book no man should be without."

TABLE OF CONTENTS

Chapters

Appendices

CHAPTER ONE

MENTORING

BIBLICAL BASIS FOR MENTORING

Mentoring is a new word to most persons today, but the concept of mentoring is as old as the Bible. In fact, the very word "mentor" comes to us from the ancient Greeks. "When the Greek warrior Odysseus went off to fight in the Trojan War (1184-1194 BC), he left his young son, Telemachus, in the care of a trusted guardian named Mentor. The siege of Troy lasted ten years, and it took Odysseus another ten years to make his way home. When he arrived, he found that the boy Telemachus had grown into a man–thanks to Mentor's wise tutelage.

Based on this story, we now speak of a mentor as someone who functions to some extent as a father figure (in the best sense of the term), "a man who fundamentally affects and influences the development of another, usually younger, man."[1]

Mentoring relationships are often described in both the Old and New Testaments:

In the Old Testament:

• Jethro taught his son-in-law, Moses, how to delegate (Ex. 18).

• Moses taught Joshua how to lead effectively (Deut. 3:1-8, 34:9).

• Moses groomed Caleb to lead (Num. 13; 14:6-9).

• Samuel tried to shape the character of Saul (1 Sam. 9–15).

• Samuel anointed David as king and protected him (1 Sam. 16:13).

---

[1] See Howard Hendricks and William Hendricks, *As Iron Sharpens Iron: Building Character in a Mentoring Relationship* (Moody Press, Chicago, 1995), 17-18.

- Jonathan and David mentored each other (1 Sam. 18:1-9; 19:1-7; 20:1-42).

In the New Testament:

- Barnabas taught Paul (Acts 4:36-37; 9:26-30; 11:22-30).

- Barnabas restored John Mark (Acts 15:36-39; 2 Tim. 4:11).

- Priscilla and Aquila tutored Apollos (Acts 18:1-3, 24-28).

- Paul poured his life into Timothy (Acts 16:1-3; Phil. 2:19-23; 1 and 2 Tim.).

- Paul instructed Titus (2 Cor. 7:6, 13-15; 8:17; Titus). Not only do we find examples of mentoring relationships in the Bible, but the principle of mentoring is enunciated in many biblical passages, as follows:

- "Come with us and we will do you good" (Num. 10:29). Moses to his father-in-law, Jethro.

- "He appointed twelve—designating them apostles—that they might be with Him and that He might send them out to preach" (Mk. 3:14).

- "Everyone who is fully trained will be like his teacher" (Lk. 6:40b).

- "Therefore I urge you to imitate me" (1 Cor. 4:16).

- "Follow my example, as I follow the example of Christ" (1 Cor. 11:1).

- "Join with others in following my example, brothers, and take note of those who live according to the pattern we gave you" (Phil. 3:17).

- "Whatever you have learned or received or heard from me, or seen in me, put it into practice. And the God of peace will be with you" (Phil. 4:9).

- "And the things you have heard me say in the presence of many witnesses entrust to reliable men who will also be qualified to teach others" (2 Tim. 2:2).

The "Golden Text" for mentoring in the Bible in my judgment, and the one which describes my approach to mentoring, states, *"We loved you so much that we were delighted to share with you not only the gospel of God but our lives as well, because you had become so dear to us"* (1 Thess. 2:8 NIV). Thus unlike most Bible studies, prayer meetings, discipleship training classes, and Sunday School, mentoring is a relationship, which makes it the highest and most effective expression of teaching and learning human kind has yet devised. Even Jesus, the Son of God, used this method.

MY PASSION AND PRACTICE OF MENTORING

My passion for mentoring is a long story. From my first pastorate to the present (1950–2007) I have had an extraordinary desire to help young pastors, sensing their need to have someone "come alongside" of them who would teach and encourage them. Later I observed that serious laymen also needed an "encourager" who would do the same thing for them. Thus I extended my ministry to laymen as well as the clergy.

Beginning on a small scale with one, two, or three men, I have seen my mentoring develop into a full-time ministry that has touched hundreds of lives across the world. Moreover, I have felt the hand of the Lord upon me all the way. No other ministry of mine has brought as much joy and produced such fruit for the Kingdom of God. This I say "To the praise of the glory of His grace" (Eph. 1:6).

Some of the highlights of my evolving ministry have been as follows:

I.   1975 to 1986

I instituted a summer mentoring program at First Baptist Church, Fort Smith, Arkansas. During those years God permitted me to train some men who are notable leaders in the church today.

II. 1986

God moved me, reluctantly on my part, out of the wonderful pastorate of First Baptist Church, Fort Smith, and He whispered in my ear, "The greatest ministry of" your life is ahead of you." Frankly, I was puzzled, wondering how I could have a greater ministry than the Lord had given me in Fort Smith for almost twenty years.

III. 1986 to 1988

First Baptist Church of Fort Smith graciously paid me sufficient salary to travel across the nation. I traversed the Southern Baptist Convention for 18 months in a ministry I called "Ministry of Encouragement." I ministered primarily to struggling young pastors and their wives. I spoke 56 times in 18 months. God blessed this ministry immeasurably "To the praise of the glory of His grace." This experience further revealed to me the desperate needs of pastors and their wives in the local church.

IV. 1988

I was miraculously called as pastor to Houston Northwest Baptist Church, a colossal challenge. There I continued my mentoring program, not just in the summer but throughout the year. I continued to be encouraged by the results that I saw.

V. 1993

God moved me out of this pastorate to pursue the mentoring ministry fully. I moved to my beloved home, North Carolina, that year.

VI. 1994

I was invited to teach at Southeastern Baptist Theological Seminary. Along with my teaching, I mentored as many guys as possible but without any specific structure.

VII. 1995 to 1997

I pastored Calvary Baptist, Wilmington, North Carolina, as Interim. Here I instituted mentoring with God-blessed results.

Seeing how God was blessing my mentoring ministry, a wealthy Christian business man and member of Calvary Baptist Church, approached me with these words, "If you can do what you have done with a few guys, what would you do with a thousand?" When I asked what he meant he said, "You ought to take your mentoring ministry to Southeastern Baptist Theological Seminary, and I will underwrite the expenses." Shortly thereafter, this donor and I met with Dr. Paige Patterson, President of Southeastern Baptist Theological Seminary, and Dr. Patterson immediately asked me to be Chaplain, with the expenses of this office to be paid by the aforesaid brother. This I have done for ten years with profuse joy. Dr. Patterson and I had the understanding that I would have a mentoring relationship with as many students as possible while serving as Chaplain.

IX. 2000

At this point, it became obvious that I must form an organization and incorporate under North Carolina law. This I did and formed a Board of Directors made up of nine resourceful men. The Board helps me to draw up the budget, to underwrite it and gives valuable counsel. The name of our organization was initially "Mentoring Men for the Master." Two years later, the organization became "Mentoring Men for the Master, Int'l," as we began to mentor abroad, especially in India.

X. 2002 to 2004

Alpha Ministries, Int'l of India, asked me to be General Chairman of their trustees and assist them in mentoring Indian Nationals to plant churches and preach to a billion people who have never heard the gospel. I mentored the current President of Alpha Ministries, Rev. Finny Mathews, from 1995 to the present. In November 2004, we dedicated a training center that will seat 1000 in Gujarat Province and when completed will be named in honor of my wife, Doris, and me, as requested by our governing board. This province is the center of persecution. This building will have inscribed on its side the words, "Dedicated to the Mentoring of Men for the Master in honor of Bill and Doris Bennett." We are also building dorms to accommodate

500 pastors from time to time whom we invite to come for training. Alpha's goal, with my help, is to train 100,000 pastors by 2020. My goal is to train 10,000 pastors and laymen in the USA. The thrilling thing about training Indian Nationals is that this is the only way to get the gospel to one billion Indians. India won't admit foreign missionaries. Praise the Lord for this opportunity.

The Present Status of the Ministry:

o Two schools meet weekly in Wilmington, NC – Friday 6-7 AM and Saturday 6-7 AM.

o One School at Scott's Hill Baptist Church, Wilmington, NC, Thursday, 6:30-7:30 PM.

o One school on the campus of Southeastern Baptist Theological Seminary, Wake Forest, NC in the fall and spring semesters.

o One School at Richland Creek Baptist, Wake Forest – Raleigh Area of NC.

o Regional Mentoring Schools – I conducted a school in Greensboro, NC from 2002-2004. I envision other regional schools in the near future.

o One School at First Baptist Church, Leland NC beginning September 2007.

o Special Mentoring Meetings – Increasingly I speak to men's groups and to whole churches on the principles of mentoring.

o I have taught spiritual formation and discipleship at SEBTS, in which I taught many of the disciplines I required in the Mentoring Schools.

Mentoring Men for the Master is a non-profit organization, supported entirely by the free will love gifts from individuals, churches and foundations.

The Present Staff of Mentoring Men for the Master:

1. The President

2. Administrative Assistant

3. Assistant in Mentoring.

4. Media – Publications Director

5. Outreach Director in the Raleigh Area.

The Future of Mentoring Men for the Master, Int'l.

God has already fulfilled His promise to bless this ministry beyond any ministry I have ever experienced. I am confident He will continue to "do exceeding abundantly above all that we ask or think, according to the power that worketh in us" (Eph. 3:20). My motto is that of the "father of foreign missions," William Carey, "Pray as if everything depends on God and work as if everything depends on you." This I intend to do by God's grace until the Father calls me home or Jesus comes. I expect to see hundreds of my brothers across the world mentored and thereafter to become effective mentors themselves. If I may help anyone in this glorious task, I will gladly do so, just let me know.

My ultimate goal is not just to mentor men but to mentor men who will mentor others, as commanded in 2 Timothy 2:2. I, therefore, wrote the book titled *The Handbook for Mentoring Men for the Master*, in which I set forth the basic meaning, methodology, and disciplines stressed in mentoring. The ten basic areas of mentoring are explained in this book and also much supportive material is incorporated. I use this book only as a basic outline for mentoring but also add other relevant materials. I suggest the same approach for mentors who may choose to use this book.

CLARIFYING THE NATURE OF MENTORING

The following questions reveal my own experience in mentoring which should help the reader understand the specific principles of mentoring and hopefully help him understand how to incorporate these principles into a mentoring ministry of his own.

1. What is mentoring? A relationship between a mature Christian teacher and a student in which the student learns from the life and instructions of the mature teacher. In this process the teacher not only imparts knowledge, but shares his own life also. Paul, the master mentor next to Jesus, wrote the Thessalonians that he not only gave them the gospel, but his own life, also (1 Thess. 2:8). The mentoree is expected to know and practice the disciplines prescribed by his mentor and is held accountable for the same.

2. Who qualifies as a typical mentor? A person who is called to this task, anointed by the Holy Spirit, and willing to give his time, his very soul—a big chunk of his life—to the one he is training. The mentoring relationship is a bonding of souls—a David/Jonathan repeat. The greater the bond, the more effective the process.

3. Who qualifies to be a biblical mentoree? A person, who is convinced he needs what the mentor offers, possesses absolute confidence in the mentor's integrity and abilities to help him, and is willing to give his soul and time to his mentor. Such a person will say "Any time, any place, any cost. I am ready to pay." A worthy mentoree does not have time, like his mentor, but both are willing to "make time."

4. What is the actual format of the process of mentoring?

- The mentor-mentoree meets weekly to study the disciplines required to walk with Christ on a daily basis. This study is based upon my books, *The Handbook for Mentoring Men for the Master* and *The Life and Work of the Pastor*.

- The mentor comes alongside the mentoree to hold him accountable and encourage him to be faithful in his commitments.

- The mentor asks the mentoree to accompany him to observe and at times to participate in ministry himself. I call this "on-the-job exposure."

5. What is the purpose of mentoring? The purpose of mentoring, as stated in the Scriptures, is to show one how to discipline his life by being controlled by the Holy Spirit by internalizing the Word of God that he may conform to the image of Christ (1 Tim. 4:7b; Rom. 8:29).

6. How long does the mentoring process last? In reality it will last for a lifetime if the mentor and mentoree can maintain such a relationship. I enjoyed a mentoring relationship with R. G. Lee from 1961 until his death in 1978, and with Leo Eddleman from 1959 until his death in 1992, and also with Stephen Olford from 1969 until his death in 2004. However, the time for the formal process is fixed according to the needs and availability of the mentoree. Some mentorees train for only a semester. Many train from one to four years. The most successful students continue the relationship through the years if possible.

7. Must one live in Wilmington to enroll in the formal training? The ideal would be to enroll in a class in the city where I live. However, I carry on informal partial mentoring by email, telephone, regular mail, occasional visits and prayer. My students are now scattered across the globe and increasing rapidly.

8. What are the requirements to enroll?

- Read carefully the qualifications for the biblical mentoree in question three.

- Carefully read Howard and William Hendricks, *As Iron Sharpens Iron*, based on Proverbs 27:17.

- It would be wise to ask a former mentoree if he would recommend mentoring for you.

9. Why do you recommend mentoring? Because mentoring is biblically commanded (2 Tim. 2:2; 1 Thess. 2:8; Mk. 3:14; Lk. 6:40b; 1 Cor. 4:16; Phil. 3:17; 4:9; 2 Tim. 4:10; 1 Pet. 5:3; Prov. 27:17).

- Jesus employed this method.

- Because of the alarming need.

- Because mentoring works.

- Because the Holy Spirit clearly called me into the mentoring ministry.

10. Graduate Level of Mentoring:

Our ultimate goal has always been to train men who in turn would become mentors of others (2 Tim. 2:2). Beginning in 2006, anyone who has been mentored at least two years and mastered the basic message and methods of mentoring will be invited to move to an advanced level of mentoring which will stress the mentoring of others. These students will meet monthly at "The Round Table," where they will give account of their mentoring and receive help for any problems they may be facing. In 2006, we awarded diplomas for 7 students who had met the requirements themselves for mentoring.

11. Can you cite some possible results of your mentoring? To the glory of God, I can humbly answer that our alumni who have applied themselves have benefited more than I can describe. A growing number of our students are already among the leading pastors and ministers in our nation today. For forty years I just "retailed" the gospel in churches ranging from 85 to 8000 in membership. Within the last 15 years I have been "wholesaling" the gospel to millions through the lives of young men. Some years ago, I sat in one of our greatest churches, listening to such pulpit greats as Paige Patterson, Adrian Rogers, and James Merritt. I thought, "What a ministry the pastor of this church has." Then the Holy Spirit whispered in my ear, "While sitting here, you see about 2000 persons, but at the same time you are preaching to thousands across the earth and for years to come through your mentorees" Now, listen to some representative mentorees as they give their own evaluation of their mentoring experiences:

- "Dr. Bill Bennett has been my chief mentor and incredible friend for many years." Paul Brewster, PhD, Pastor, Barlow Vista Baptist Church, Hampstead, NC.

- "I can honestly say that I use more of what Dr. Bennett taught me than anything I learned in the seminary." Rev. Robbie Brown, Georgia Pastor.

- "I would have failed in my ministry had I not learned to work hard and seek the constant infilling of the Holy Spirit under Dr. Bennett." Rev. Terry Fox, Pastor.

- "Dr. Bennett is the best example of Jesus I have ever known. His example has challenged and changed my life more than I could ever tell." Martin Graddon, Businessman, England and USA.

- "He introduced me to the wonderful Spirit-filled life. I cannot thank him enough and rejoice." Dr. Jim Henry, Former Pastor, First Baptist Church, Orlando, FL.

- "Dr. Bennett has been my constant mentor since 1995, always finding time to encourage and mentor me in many areas." Rev. Abraham Ho, Missionary to China.

- "Had it not been for Dr. Bennett's encouragement, today I would probably be out of the ministry." Rev. Allen Holmes, Pastor, Day Star Baptist, Greenville, SC.

- "Dr. Bill Bennett believed in me, loved me, and stood with me in the most trying time of my life, giving me new hope and purpose." Clint Horsley, Businessman, Wilmington, NC.

- "Dr. Bennett sensed God's call upon my life and never ceased to encourage me to launch out in faith, even before I discerned the Lord's will for my life." Tom Jaski, Church Planter.

- "I have partnered with Bill since 1995. I am an avid investor in the stock market, but the wisest investment I have ever made has been in Mentoring Men for the Master." Bob Kester, prayer/paying partner, Wilmington, NC.

- "I am what I am by the grace of God, but humanly speaking, I am what I am because of the mentoring of Dr. Bill Bennett." Rev. Aaron King, Wilmington, NC.

- "No man ever showed the love and concern for me as Dr. Bennett." Agreve Lime, Mombassa, Kenya.

- "Had it not been for Dr. Bennett, I would still be working at Harris Teeter and living out of the will of God." Rev. Tommy Lupton, Pastor, Greensboro, NC.

- "God used Dr. Bennett to show me personally what it means to live a victorious Christian life and how to minister in the power of the

Holy Spirit." Rev. Finny Matthews, President of Alpha Ministries of India, Int'l.

- "No human being has encouraged and strengthened me in ministry like Bill Bennett." Rev. Phil Ortego, Pastor, Scotts Hill Baptist Church, Wilmington, NC.

- "Bill Bennett loves young preachers more than any person I know." Dr. Paige Patterson, President of Southwestern Baptist Theological Seminary.

- "I just love this guy. He took me into his heart and began mentoring me the first time he saw me." David Pryor, Associate Pastor, High Point, NC.

- "Being mentored by Bill Bennett would be a blessing that no seminary could give." The late, Dr. Adrian Rogers, Former Pastor Bellevue Baptist Church, and Former President of Southern Baptist Convention.

- "Bill Bennett has been God's instrument and role model in my discovering the abundant life." Nathan Sanders, Noted Christian Layman and Businessman, Wilmington, NC.

- "The one thing that helps me most is to know Dr. Bennett truly loves and believes in me." Mark Smith, Youth Minister, Hickory, NC.

- "Dr. Bennett believes in me so much that I had to believe in myself. I cannot ever express how he has impacted my life and ministry and the enormous encouragement he has given my life." Rev. Sean Vernon, Youth Minister, Greensboro, NC.

- "Most of us see others for what they are; Dr. Bennett sees them for what they will become." Dr. John Zino, Principal Engineer, General Electric Company, Wilmington, NC.

JESUS—OUR MASTER MODEL FOR MENTORING

Jesus Christ was the Master Mentor of all time. In fact the plan of Jesus to build His church and evangelize the world was through the mentoring of a few men. Mentoring men was his method of winning the world to God.

In 1963, Robert E. Coleman wrote a classic titled, *The Master Plan of Evangelism*.[2] In this book, Coleman writes that Jesus spent more time with twelve men than the rest of the world combined. He described eight guiding principles Jesus used in training the twelve:[3]

- Principle #1 – Selection – Jesus did not neglect the masses, but He chose twelve to whom He gave special attention because of their willingness to learn and follow His teaching.

- Principle #2 – Association – Having called His men, Jesus made it a practice to be with them under all circumstances. Mark 3:14 asserts that He chose the twelve–*"that they might be with Him."*

- Principle #3 – Consecration – Jesus expected the men He was with to obey Him. They were not required to be smart but loyal. They were called His "disciples," meaning "learners" of His will so they could do His will.

- Principle #4 – Impartation – Jesus gave Himself away to His men. In so doing they saw His spirit and love for a lost world and caught it themselves. Christianity is more caught than taught.

- Principle #5 – Demonstration – Jesus showed the twelve how to live. This is how they learned to pray, to forgive, to suffer, to use Scripture, to win the lost and to stay in the battle.

- Principle #6 – Delegation – Eventually He let them baptize, feed the multitudes, heal the sick, etc. Coleman says, "Like a mother eagle Jesus pushed His disciples out into the world to try their own wings."[4] Eventually He inspired them to write the New Testament (2 Pet. 1:20-21).

---

[2] Robert E. Coleman, *The Master Plan of Evangelism*, reprint ed. (Grand Rapids: Revel, 2006).

[3] Ibid.

[4] Ibid., 84.

- Principle #7 – Supervision – Jesus kept check on His men. The disciples met "together with Jesus" to tell Him "what they had done" (Mk. 6:30; Lk. 9:10).

- Principle #8 – Reproduction – Jesus expected His men to reproduce. He commanded them "to go into all the world and make disciples" (Matt. 28:18-20). In His last words to His disciples, He reminded the twelve of their enormous responsibility. *"But you shall receive power when the Holy Spirit has come upon you, and you shall be witnesses to Me in Jerusalem, and in all Judea and Samaria, and to the end of the earth"* (Acts 1:8).

Indeed the disciples received the power of the Holy Spirit on the Day of Pentecost (Acts 2:4) and "went everywhere preaching the gospel."

It is believed that the gospel was preached throughout the known world. Spain was the uttermost part of the earth. While the Scriptures do not specifically say Spain was evangelized, we know Paul intended to go to Spain (Rom. 15:24), and Clement of Rome, a reliable source, records that Paul did visit Spain. Dr. James Kennedy says in his famous book, *Evangelism Explosion*, that if the early church had not been stifled by "Clericalism" in the 4th century, the gospel would have been preached to the whole world by AD 500.[5]

Will the method used by Jesus work in our day? I believe it will. Moreover I believe it is the only method that will. I say so because when I have applied this method I have seen the greatest positive results.

In 1967, I became pastor of the First Baptist Church, Fort Smith, Arkansas. This had been a church noted for its evangelism. One year the church led the Southern Baptist Convention in the number of baptisms. However, when I arrived on the scene the church had lost its evangelistic zeal. I tried to revive the church through the Sunday School, Discipleship Training, weekly visitation, Brotherhood, revival, preaching, etc., but with minimal results.

Becoming desperate, in the fall of 1969 I invited 8 faithful men to meet with me weekly and pledge to give their lives to the task of restoring

---

[5] James Kennedy, Evangelism Explosion , 4 ed. (Wheaton, IL: Tyndale, 2002), p. 5.

evangelism in the First Baptist Church. I spent 6 months with 6 men, two of the original 8 having dropped out.

For two months, we studied *The Master Plan of Evangelism* by Robert Coleman and became convinced that Jesus' method of evangelism was mentoring. At that point, I encountered James Kennedy as he lectured on evangelism in Minnesota (1969) at the U.S. congress on evangelism called by Billy Graham. He stressed that pastors must equip men to evangelize by teaching them how and then demonstrating "on the job" how to witness. I followed this plan and saw marvelous results. With this small beginning, we conducted 43 schools of evangelism from 1970–1986. The record shows we saw up to 10,000 confessions of faith. Moreover, we saw the lives of these men transformed, and with that transformation the church experienced mighty revival. I would say that the wisest single step I ever took in my ministry was to enlist these men, train them, in class and on the job, and then send them out to win others to Christ and teach them.

Believing that Jesus' method was mentoring and seeing His blessings upon ministry in evangelism, I began to mentor men. I have discovered when men are willing to be changed by internalizing the Word that God transforms them into mighty men in both character and ministry.

There are eleven basic areas in which men need mentoring:

- The Word

- Meditation

- Prayer

- Fasting

- Solitude and Silence

- Evangelism

- Worship

- Service

- Time

- Body

- Money

Lectures on the various disciplines are interspersed throughout this book with doctrinal teaching to undergird these truths, such as the doctrine of the Holy Scripture, the Trinity, Jesus Christ, the Holy Spirit, the Church, Eschatology, etc.

Also, attention is given to practical areas of ministry as needed by the students such as Baptism, Lord's Supper, Ordination, Marriage, Family Life, Ministerial Ethics and Etiquette and Staff Relations.

The material for these lectures is taken from the Bible and supplemented by my own writings as listed below:

- *Life and Work of the Pastor* [6]

- *Thirty Minutes to Raise the Dead* [7]

- *Who Really Removed the 10 Commandments* [8]

- *Book for Beginners.* [9]

[6] Dr. Bill Bennett, *Life and Work of the Pastor*, (Wilmington, NC: Copycat Printers, 1999).
[7] Dr. Bill Bennett, *Thirty Minutes to Raise the Dead*, (Nashville, Tennessee: Thomas Nelson, 1991).
[8] Dr. Bill Bennett, *Who Really Removed the 10 Commandments*, (Wilmington, NC: New Hanover Printers and Publishers, 2005).
[9] Dr. Bill Bennett, *Book for Beginners*, (Wilmington, NC: Copycat Printers, 1997).

CHAPTER TWO

HOW TO BE SAVED ACCORDING TO THE BIBLE

Only the lost can be saved, and only the saved can be mentored. Moreover, the lost person, without Christ in his heart, does not have the capacity to internalize the Word and appropriate its life changing power. Therefore, every person aspiring to be mentored should be sure that he has been saved from his sin and is a child of God. And God forbid that anyone would be deceived in believing that he could substitute mentoring for salvation. Thus we must ask, what is biblical salvation?

The Bible categorically declares that salvation is a gift as it states, *"For the wages of sin is death, but the gift of God is eternal life through Christ Jesus our Lord"* (Rom. 6:23). This means that no one deserves it, no one can earn it and no one can purchase it with money or any self efforts. But while salvation is a gift, it is not automatically given to any person. It requires the exercise of faith. God declares through His apostle, *"For by grace you have been saved by faith, and that not of yourself, it is the gift of God, not of works, lest anyone should boast"* (Eph. 2:8-9). This raises the question: What kind of faith do you and I have to exercise to be saved and know we are destined for heaven?

The Bible warns of four kinds of deceptive faith which do not and cannot save the soul:

Religious Faith – *"Not everyone who says to Me, 'Lord, Lord,' shall enter the kingdom of heaven, but he who does the will of My Father in heaven. Many will say to Me in that day, 'Lord, Lord, have we not prophesied in Your name, cast out demons in You name, and done many wonders in Your name?' And then I will declare to them, 'I never knew you; depart from Me, you who practice lawlessness!'"* (Matt. 7:21-23).

• Empty or Vain Faith – *"By which also you are saved, if you hold fast that word which I preached to you—unless you believed in vain"* (1 Cor. 15:2).

21

• Dead Faith – *"For as the body without the spirit is dead, so faith without works is dead also"* (James 2:26).

• Demonic Faith – *"You believe that there is one God. You do well. Even the demons believe—and tremble!"* (James 2:19).

In order to understand the meaning of true saving faith, we must understand two fundamental facts:

1. Saving faith always centers in the person of Jesus Christ and Him alone. We are not saved even by faith in the Bible, or in our church, or the noblest religious works. Not even by faith in the "Plan of Salvation," but by the "Man of Salvation." Salvation, in essence, is a personal relationship with Jesus Christ Himself.

Every time God instructs us how to be saved in the Scriptures, He points us squarely to the Person of Jesus Christ. Listen to these verses:

- *"But as many as received Him, to them He gave the right to become children of God, to those who believe in His name"* (John. 1:12).

- *"For God so loved the world that He gave His only begotten Son, that whoever believes in Him should not perish but have everlasting life"* (John. 3:16).

- *"He who believes in Him is not condemned; but he who does not believe is condemned already, because he has not believed in the name of the only begotten Son of God"* (John. 3:18).

- *"He who believes in the Son has everlasting life; and he who does not believe the Son shall not see life, but the wrath of God abides on him"* (John. 3:36).

- *"Nor is there salvation in any other, for there is no other name under heaven given among men by which we must be saved"* (Acts 4:12).

- *"Believe on the Lord Jesus Christ, and you will be saved, you and your household"* (Acts 16:31).

- *"For the wages of sin is death, but the gift of God is eternal life through Christ Jesus our Lord"* (Rom. 6:23).

- *"For whoever calls on the name of the Lord shall be saved"* (Rom. 10:13).

- *"He who has the Son has life; he who does not have the Son of God does not have life. These things I have written to you who believe in the name of the Son of God, that you may know that you have eternal life, and that you may continue to believe in the name of the Son of God"* (1 John. 5:12-13).

- *"Jesus said to him, 'I am the way, the truth, and the life. No one comes to the Father except through Me' "* (John. 14:6).

Now the question remains, what kind of faith must we have in the Person of Jesus?

Saving faith consists of three indispensable components:

- **The knowledge of the gospel,** namely, Christ died for our sins, was buried, and rose again (1 Cor. 15:3). It is psychologically impossible for us to believe the gospel unless we know the content of the gospel. Paul stresses the relationship between belief and knowledge when he writes, "For whoever calls on the name of the LORD shall be saved. How then shall they call on Him in whom they have not believed? And how shall they believe in Him of whom they have not heard? And how shall they hear without a preacher?...So then faith comes by hearing, and hearing by the word of God" (Rom. 10:13-14, 17).

- **The belief in the gospel we know.** The gospel must not only be known, but we must embrace it with our minds and accept it with our understanding. Many have a knowledge of the gospel who do not believe the gospel. Once I had a gentleman in a Sunday School class I taught in Houston, Texas, who attended the class every Sunday. He even thanked me profusely every Sunday for my teaching. But his wife broke the news to me that this man, her husband, was not saved and asked me to visit him in their home. I complied with her urgent request very promptly. He received me cordially; I presented the gospel fully, and asked him if he would like to receive Jesus as his personal Savior. He said, "No," whereupon I asked him "Why not?" and he said, "I do not believe the gospel." I, then, asked him why he attended my class so faithfully and acclaimed my teaching so positively. He replied, "Because while I do not believe the gospel myself, it is obvious that you do, and I love to hear you teach it."

23

I returned a second time to this man and pleaded with him to trust Jesus and he again refused, flatly saying, "I just do not believe the gospel." Alas, he died in 1999 in unbelief, even though he had heard and was knowledgeable of the gospel.

While this person possessed a knowledge of the gospel but did not believe the gospel, it is possible for one both to know and to believe the gospel and still be lost. Permit me to illustrate. Suppose I am preaching and I give the invitation for people to unite with the church and suppose the devil was here in person and comes down the aisle. He says, "Dr. Bennett, I am the devil, I want to join your church." I would tell him that I would have to ask him a few questions. "Do you really believe that Jesus is the Son of God?" The devil would answer, "Yes indeed, I believe He is the Son of God." "Do you believe that Jesus Christ was born of the virgin?" "Why I know He was born of the virgin, I heard the angel make the announcement to Mary, I was in Bethlehem the night He was born." "I want to ask you another question," "Do you really believe He arose from the dead?" "I was right there; I do not doubt that He rose from the dead." "Do you believe that one must be born again to be saved?" "No doubt about it." "Do you believe in repentance?" "Absolutely, I believe in repentance." "You know, this is a Baptist church, if you are going to join it you will need to be baptized. Are you willing to be immersed in water?" He said, "I am a great believer in immersion, I was there and saw John baptize Jesus. I would be glad to be immersed." "You understand that you are to show some faithfulness if you join this church. Are you really going to attend it, are you going to be faithful?" "I promise you that I will be absolutely faithful. As a matter of fact, I would want to sing in the choir, I would definitely want to be a deacon and I promise you I would never miss one deacon's meeting." I say, "Brothers and Sisters, you hear this testimony. Will you take him in?" "Yes sir!" But notice, there is one question I did not ask the devil—"you are a sinner and you have destroyed a lot of lives. Are you willing to turn your life over to Jesus and obey Him, and to trust Him with everything you have?" You know what his answer would be. "No, I am not going to do that. I have the knowledge of who Jesus is, I believe it in my head, but I am not going to surrender to Him. I am not really going to change my life." So it is with many who know and believe the gospel, but who refuse to surrender their lives to Jesus.

- **Trusting and surrendering to the Person of the Gospel, Jesus Christ.** Salvation is a personal surrender and relationship with Jesus Himself. Multitudes know and believe the gospel intellectually but never surrender their lives to Jesus. They possess a "head" knowledge, but not a "heart" knowledge. I say they will miss heaven by 18 inches—the distance between the heart and the head. Jesus said that many would live this life and perform many wonderful works, only to learn in the judgment that they were not saved at all. "Not every one that saith unto Me, 'Lord, Lord,' shall enter into the Kingdom of Heaven, but he that doeth the will of My Father who is in Heaven. Many will say to Me in that Day, 'Lord, Lord, have we not prophesied in Thy name, and in Thy name have cast out devils, and in Thy name done many wonderful works?'And then will I profess unto them, 'I never knew you: depart from Me, ye that work iniquity'" (Matt. 2:21-23). Evidently this multitude knew the gospel and believed in the head, but never humbled their hearts and surrendered their lives to Jesus. Don't let this happen to you.

I wish to illustrate further the importance of trusting or surrendering to the Person of Jesus Christ. Saving faith may be compared to the act of marriage. There are three stages in saving faith as there are in marriage:

a. The first stage in marriage is knowledge. The couple must know one another. So they meet and begin to date.

b. The second stage of marriage is belief. The couple must embrace each other in their hearts, believing they are meant for each other. Still there is no marriage until the third stage.

c. The couple publicly says their vows before the minister and commits themselves to each other without reservation.

So it is with saving faith. One may know and believe the gospel but he is not saved until he surrenders to the person of the gospel—Jesus Christ.

The clearest example of saving faith I know was given to me by my mother. My mother traveled 1200 miles to visit me, stayed with me one month, after which she said she needed to go home. I recommended that she fly, since the trip was long and tiring. She then said, "I don't want to fly." I asked her if she believed in airplanes. She replied, "Yes, I believe in them. I realize that you fly all over the world in them." Then I tried to reason like this, "Well, if you believe in airplanes and know that I fly on them all the time, why do you not want to fly in an airplane?" Finally, she said, "I do believe in airplanes, but I do not believe in them enough to trust my life to one of them." How great is the multitude who know and believe the gospel but refuse to invite Jesus to be the Savior and Lord of their lives. Indeed, there is growing evidence that millions of church members know and believe who have never surrendered their hearts and lives to Jesus. The SBC boasts a total membership of 16,500,000 members, but on an average Sunday only 6,000,000 can be found in church. I ask, where are the 10 million?

The question of salvation raises the question of the place of repentance in salvation. The answer is that repentance is absolutely required for one to be saved. When one truly surrenders to the Person of Jesus, he turns from his sins and trusts Him from the heart to be his Savior and Lord. But before he trusts Him, he must turn or repent of his sins. What, then, is repentance? Repentance is a revolutionary change of our minds, wrought by the Word and the Holy Spirit, concerning sin which causes us to hate sin and turn from it with all our hearts. There are really three changes in true repentance:

- **Repentance is a change which leads to a change.** The person sees sin as the destroyer of his life and soul and turns with all his heart from it to Jesus. This results in a new life lived for the glory of God.

- **Repentance is a complete change.** Repentance is not a partial turning. It is a 180 degree turn from the way one has been living.

- **Repentance is a continual change.** You have to repent only once to be forgiven of your sins and be saved (Acts 2:38). But once you have truly repented, you will repent again and again when you commit sin. You will live a repentant, broken-hearted life over your sin and failure and the sins of others. Jesus pronounced a blessing on those who do so, "Blessed are those who mourn (repent) for they shall be comforted" (Matt. 5:4).

I wish to share the most remarkable case of repentance I ever witnessed. I pastored the First Baptist Church, Fort Smith, Arkansas, for almost 20 years. God blessed me to have only one secretary for all those years—Janey Spencer. Janey was a well-nigh perfect secretary and perfect church member. She had grown up in church and came from a strong Baptist family in Oklahoma. However, in her tenth year of service, our staff was involved in a prayer meeting, when Janey cried out,—"Dr. Bennett, I am lost. I am lost." Shocked, I stopped and asked, "Janey, what do you mean?" She replied, "I mean what I say: I am lost, I am lost." I then asked, "How long have you known this?" She said, "For a very long time." "Why," I asked, "Why have you not admitted this before?" And she said, "My pride would not let me." Then I asked her to tell me what happened when she joined the church and was baptized. She then explained that she just went down with her friends when she was about six or seven. She said she believed the Bible, she loved God and Jesus as any child would, but no one ever told her she was a sinner and needed to repent. Then she put her finger on what she had done: "I went straight to the Father and by-passed the cross, and all these years I have been living a lie and pretending something I knew I was not." I asked her if she was ready to turn to the Lord and be truly saved. Then she cried unto the Lord to forgive her hypocrisy, confessed she was a lost sinner, and asked Him to save her. He did and she arose from the floor praising the Lord. The next Sunday she walked the aisle of the church, on TV, and professed saving faith in the Lord. Before this time, she had shown no love for the Word, no interest in prayer or the salvation of others. Afterwards she became a walking Bible and began proclaiming her love and joy in the Lord. A dozen times or more she came forth in the invitation and would plead to the people in these words, "Had I died before July 1977, Dr. Bennett would have preached me into heaven, but I would have gone to hell. And some of you are in the same boat as I was. Please repent and be saved."

3. How Can We Know if We Are Truly Believing This Very Moment?

We can know by two powerful witnesses:

- The Witness of the Word of God. One whole book of the New Testament was written to give the evidences of one's salvation—First John. In concluding this book, the author, John, declares *"And this is the testimony: that God has given us eternal life, and this life is in His Son…These things I have written to you who believe in the name of the Son of God, that you may know you have eternal life"* (1 John 5:11, 13). There are seven evidences of one's salvation. These evidences I call the "birthmarks" of the true believer because:

  o The true believer is **Submissive** to the Word of God (1 John 2:3-4).

  o The true believer is **Separated** from the false philosophy of this world (1 John 2:15).

  o The true believer is **Steadfast** in his profession and life (1 John 2:19).

  o The true believer is **Saved** from the power and practice of sin (1 John 3:9).

  o The true believer is **Saturated** with love for his brothers and sisters in Christ (1 John 3:14).

  o The true believer is **Sealed** with the Holy Spirit (1 John 3:24; 4:13).

  o The true believer is **Surrendered** to Jesus as His Savior and Lord (1 John 5:13).

- **The Witness of the Holy Spirit.** *"He who believes in the Son of God has the witness in himself"* (1 Jn. 5:10). *"The Spirit Himself bears witness with our spirit that we are the sons of God"* (Rom. 8:16).

The witness of the Holy Spirit is not primarily an emotional experience. The deepest work of the Holy Spirit is in the mind, not in the emotions. The witness of the Holy Spirit is the "still small voice" of the Holy Spirit speaking to your human spirit with a quiet confidence that you belong to Jesus Christ.

I plead with you before you read any further that if you have never truly trusted Jesus as your personal Lord and Savior, you may do so right now. By an act of faith, you can turn from your sins (repent) and surrender your life to Him, and He will save you. Don't look for any sign, don't expect a feeling. Trust the external witness of the Word and the internal witness of the Holy Spirit.

CHAPTER THREE

THE WONDERFUL SPIRIT-FILLED LIFE

Ephesians 5:18

God accomplishes His purposes in the believer's life by two instruments: The Word and the Spirit. "All Word and no Spirit, you dry up. All Spirit and no Word, you blow up. Combine the Word and the Spirit, you will grow up." The basis of mentoring is the "Internalization of the Word," but the Word without the Holy Spirit will not work the miracle of God's grace in the human heart. We see this very clearly in the experience of the new birth. Jesus commands that we must be born of the Water and the Spirit in order to enter the Kingdom of God (John 3:5). Water speaks of the Word of God (Eph. 5:26) and the Spirit means the Holy Spirit. It is when the Word of God and the Spirit of God come together in the heart by faith that the miracle of a new life begins.

But the new birth is but the beginning of the work of the Holy Spirit in human experience. When one repents and turns to Jesus as Lord and Savior, the Holy Spirit enters immediately and permanently into that person (1 Cor. 6:19; Rom. 8:9b). We call this His indwelling. Simultaneously, the Holy Spirit baptizes the believer into the body of Christ once and for all (1 Cor. 12:13). This is the real baptism of the Holy Spirit. All these divine acts occur at the moment one truly trusts Jesus as Lord and Savior. However, these events do not conclude the work of the Holy Spirit in the believer. Beyond these, God categorically commands through the apostle Paul that every believer be continually filled with the Holy Spirit (Eph. 5:18). The question naturally arises, why do we need to be filled (controlled) by the Holy Spirit if we already have His indwelling and His baptism. Simply for this reason: You can have the Holy Spirit, but the Holy Spirit may not have you, or to express it another way, the Holy Spirit may be present in you, but He demands to be President in you, that is, to fill or control your life. Let me bring all this truth together under three simple points:

1. **The Reasons to be Filled.** There are two main reasons:

- God commands it. *"Be filled* (literally "be being filled") *with the Holy Spirit"* (Eph. 5:18b). Please notice four facts about this command:

  o First of all, this command is in the imperative mood. This means it is not optional. To be filled is to obey God and reap His blessings; to fail to be filled is to disobey God and miss His blessings.

  o Second, this command is plural in number. This means that this command is given to every believer, not just spiritual giants, super saints, pastors, elders or deacons.

  o Third, this command is in the passive voice, which means we cannot fill ourselves but filling comes from an outside source. Our responsibility is to put ourselves in a position where the Spirit of God can control us.

  o Fourth, this command is in the present tense. Unlike the new birth and baptism of the Holy Spirit, which happens only once in a believer's life, the filling of the Holy Spirit is a repeated event. In essence, the text commands, "Be ye being filled with the Holy Spirit." Both Adrian Rogers and James Merritt, noted pastors and preachers, have said, "It is a far greater sin for a child of God not to be filled with the Holy Spirit than for a person to get drunk on alcoholic beverages."

- The demands of the Christian life require it. The demands of the Christian life cannot be met by our natural will power, but only by the supernatural power of God released in our lives. Who within his own power can "love his enemies?" (Matt. 5:44). Who in his own power can "rejoice ever more?" (1 Thess. 5:16). Who in his own power can fulfill the righteous requirements of the law? (Rom. 8:2-4).

2. **The Requirements to be Filled.** A great theologian has said, "The good things of the Kingdom of God do not belong to the well meaning but to the desperate." Candidates for the infilling must "mean business" with the Lord. The casual Christian and the average Sunday morning attendee do not qualify.

- First, you must have been born of the Holy Spirit before you can be filled.

- Second, you must desire with all your heart to be filled. Only those who "hunger and thirst...will be filled." *"Blessed are those who hunger and thirst for righteousness, for they shall be filled"* (Matt.5:6).

- Third, you must believe that God will fill you, not just can fill you.

- Fourth, you must denounce all known sin in your life. You must do more than confess sin (admit it); you must abandon it. *"He who covers his sins will not prosper, But whoever confesses and forsakes them will have mercy"* (Prov. 29:13).

- Fifth, you must dethrone self and enthrone Christ as Lord of all. This would mean that you would release your control over your life and turn it over to the living Christ.

- Sixth, you must by faith ask the Holy Spirit to fill you. *"If you then, being evil, know how to give good gifts to your children, how much more will your heavenly Father give the Holy Spirit to those who ask Him!"* (Lk. 11:13).

- Seventh, you must accept the fact that He has filled you and live with total dependence on Him saying, "Lord God, I yield control of my life to you today. Just show me what to do." This would mean that you are walking in the spirit... *"Walk in the Spirit, and you shall not fulfill the lust of the flesh"* (Gal. 5:16).

In a word, you must surrender your life to Jesus Christ as your Lord. Please notice that I did not say "commit" your life, but to surrender it. When you commit, you determine the things you will commit; when you surrender, the Lord determines the things you will surrender. Commitment would be like taking a plain sheet of paper and writing on that paper the things you would commit to the Lord and then signing your name at the bottom. Surrender would mean something entirely different. You would not write anything on the blank sheet of paper, but you would sign your name at the bottom and ask the Lord Jesus Christ to fill in the top. Be sure not to confuse surrender with the "time honored" re-dedications which take place in many churches with no continuing results. Rededications are the very opposite of surrender, as is commitment, and will never result in the filling of the Holy Spirit.

3. The Results of Being Filled:

- The person who is filled will overflow with the fruit of the Holy Spirit. *"But the fruit of the Spirit is love, joy, peace, patience, kindness, goodness, gentleness, faithfulness, self-control. Against such there is no law"* (Gal. 5:22-23).

- The person who is filled will have an intimate "Abba Father" relationship with His Father in heaven. *"For you did not receive the spirit of bondage again to fear, but you received the Spirit of adoption by whom we cry out, 'Abba, Father'"* (Rom. 8:15).

- The person who is filled will be a bold witness to the ends of the earth. *"But you shall receive power when the Holy Spirit has come upon you; and you shall be witnesses to Me in Jerusalem, and in all Judea and Samaria, and to the end of the earth"* (Acts 1:18).

- The person who is filled with the Holy Spirit will have victory over indwelling sin. *"For if you live according to the flesh you will die; but if by the Spirit you put to death the deeds of the body, you will live"* (Rom. 8:13).

- The person who is filled with the Holy Spirit will be enabled to exercise his gifts in the power of God. *"Most assuredly, I say to you, he who believes in Me, the works that I do he will do also; and greater works than these he will do, because I go to My Father"* (John 14:12).

- The person who is filled with the Holy Spirit will be powerful in prayer. *"And when they had prayed, the place where they were assembled together was shaken; and they were all filled with the Holy Spirit, and they spoke the word of God with boldness"* (Acts 4:31).

- The person who is filled with the Holy Spirit will have deep understanding of the Bible. *"But as it is written: 'Eye has not seen, nor ear heard, Nor have entered into the heart of man The things which God has prepared for those who love Him.' But God has revealed them to us through His Spirit. For the Spirit searches all things, yes, the deep things of God"* (1 Cor. 2:9-10).

- The person who is filled with the Holy Spirit will worship in Spirit and in truth. *"God is Spirit, and those who worship Him must worship in spirit and truth"* (John 4:24)

- The person who is filled with the Holy Spirit will carry out his duties in his home. (21) *"submitting to one another in the fear of God."* (25) *"Husbands, love your wives, just as Christ also loved the church and gave Himself for her."* (6:1) *"Children, obey your parents in the Lord, for this is right"* (Ephesians 5:21; 5:25; 6:1).

In a word, the Spirit-filled person will live the normal Christian life, the one God ordained for him at the time of his new birth (Ephesians 1:3).

D.L. Moody preached without the infilling for years, but one day was filled while walking the streets of New York City; then he made this statement, "You can see without eyes, hear without ears, chew without a mouth, and breath without lungs sooner than you could live the Christian life without the infilling of the Holy Spirit."

Personally, I was a defeated preacher and pastor until the Holy Spirit revealed to me, on the streets of Greensboro, North Carolina, that He was my *"Paracletos,"* (John 14:16) the one who was coming beside me, to give me the power, motivation, perseverance, all I needed to both live for Him and serve Him with great joy. Hallelujah—that was the beginning of a new day in my life, without which I believe I would have despaired long before now.

In closing, I feel impressed to share with you the testimony of the late Adrian Rogers concerning the need for the fullness of the Holy Spirit:

"I want you to imagine a man who has bought, for the first time in his life, a brand-new automobile. He's never driven before, never had an automobile, and what he does not understand is that it has an engine in it.

He is proud of the car. He invites his friends over and shows them how beautiful the paint job is, how soft the seats are. And he says, "See how nice this is, what a sleek automobile this is." But everywhere he goes, he has to push it. Sometimes when he is going downhill, he can get in and coast, but that doesn't excite him too much because he knows for every hill that he coasts down he's got to push that thing up the next hill.

While he's proud of his automobile and in some ways grateful that he has it, in other ways he secretly wishes he didn't have it. Rather than being a blessing to him, it became a burden to him. Rather than it carrying him, he has to push it.

And then somebody says, "I want to show you something. See that thing. That's called an ignition key. Put it right in there and turn it.' *Vroom!*' "What's that?" "That's a thing called the engine. Now take that lever right there and put it where it says 'D' and then press that pedal," and that automobile begins to surge forth with power." "Hey," he says, "This is wonderful, this is glorious, this is amazing. Why didn't somebody tell me before? Why didn't somebody show me about this before?"

You say, "That's foolish. Nobody could be that dumb." You're right, unless it is the Christian who does not understand the power of the Holy Spirit of God.

Many Christians don't understand that when they got saved, God put an engine in their salvation. I don't mean to speak disrespectfully about the Holy Spirit by calling Him an engine, but He is the dynamism, the power of our Christian life. Many people are somewhat proud of their Christianity, but it's almost a burden to them. Rather than it carrying them, they are pushing it. And they're just grinding out this matter of being a Christian because they have not made the discovery of the wonderful Spirit-filled life. Ephesians 5:18 has a command of God: *"And do not be drunk with wine, in which is dissipation; but be filled with the Spirit."*

When you are filled with the Spirit, it will turn the drudgery to dynamism. Rather than making your Christianity a burden, it will become an empowering blessing to you."[10]

---

[10] Adrian Rogers, *What Every Christian Ought to Know*, (Nashville: Broadman and Holman Publishers, 2005), pp. 168-169.

CHAPTER FOUR

INTERNALIZING THE WORD OF GOD

Bible intake is the most important Spiritual Discipline. Let us, therefore, consider the discipline of internalizing the Word of God. The golden text for discipline states, *"discipline yourself for the purpose of godliness"* (1 Tim. 4:7, NAS). The Spiritual Disciplines are the God-given means we are to follow in order to be godly or to be conformed to the image of Christ, which is God's purpose for every believer (Rom. 8:29).

Seven steps guide believers to internalize the Word of God.

1. We Must hear God's Word with the intent to obey it (Luke 11:28; Rev. 1:3, 2:7, 11, 17, 28, 3:6, 13, 22; Deut. 6:4; and James 1:19).

- Prepare your soul to hear the Word with the intent to obey. This should precede the hearing of the Word.

- Be sure to steadfastly attend a church where God's Word is faithfully expounded in context.

- Remind yourself that you are hearing God's Word, not the word of man. *"For this reason we also thank God without ceasing, because when you received the word of God which you heard from us, you welcomed it not as the word of men, but as it is in truth, the word of God, which also effectively works in you who believe"* (1 Thes. 2:13).

- Commit yourself to one pastor or expositor. *"My sheep hear My voice, and I know them, and they follow Me"* (John 10:27). Hearing several voices can be confusing.

2. We Must Read God's Word daily to know its overall content. Three practical rules can guide one for consistent success in Bible reading.

- Make time each day. Try to meet at the same place and time.

- Devise a Bible reading plan so you won't run out of material. Do you realize that tape-recorded readings of the Bible have proven that you can read through the entire Bible in seventy-one hours? The average person in the United States watches that much television in less than two weeks. In no more than 15 minutes a day you can read through the Bible in less than a year's time. Only five minutes a day takes you through the Bible in less than three years. And yet the majority of Christians never read the Bible all the way through in their whole life. So we are back to the idea that it's primarily a matter of discipline and motivation. It's no wonder that those who simply open the Bible at random each day soon drop the discipline.

- Find one word, phrase, or verse to meditate on each time you read.

3. We Must Study God's Word to know the depths of its meaning.

If reading the Bible can be compared to cruising the width of a clear, sparkling lake in a motorboat, studying the Bible is like slowly crossing the same lake in a glass-bottomed boat. The motorboat crossing provides an overview of the lake and a swift, passing view of its depths. The glass-bottomed boat of study, however, takes you beneath the surface of Scripture for an unhurried look of clarity and detail that's normally missed by those who simply read the text. As author Jerry Bridges put it, "Reading gives us breadth, but study gives us depth."[11] Why do so many Christians neglect the study of God's Word? R. C. Sproul said it painfully well: "Here then, is the real problem of our negligence. We fail in our duty to study God's Word not so much because it is difficult to understand, not so much because it is dull and boring, but because it is work. Our problem is not a lack of intelligence or a lack of passion. Our problem is that we are lazy."[12]

4. We Must Memorize in order to have fuel for meditation and for use in our ministries.

Many Christians look on the spiritual discipline of memorizing God's Word as something tantamount to modern-day martyrdom. Ask them to memorize Bible verses and they will react with about as much eagerness as a request for volunteers to face Nero's lions.

---

[11] Quoted in Donald Whitney, *Spiritual Disciplines for the Christian Life*, (Colorado Springs, Colorado, 1991), p. 31.
[12] Ibid. p. 32.

How come? Perhaps because many associate all memorization with the memory efforts required of them in school. It was work, and most of all it was uninteresting and of limited value. Frequently heard, also, is the excuse of having a bad memory. But what if I offered you one thousand dollars for every verse you could memorize in the next seven days? Do you think your attitude toward Scripture memory and your ability to memorize would improve? Any financial reward would be minimal when compared to the accumulating value of the treasure of God's Word deposited within your mind.

"When Dawson Trotman, founder of the Christian organization called the Navigators, was converted to faith in Christ in 1926, he began memorizing one Bible verse every day. He was driving a truck for a lumber yard in Los Angeles at the time. While driving around town he would work on his verse for that day. During the first three years of his Christian life he memorized his first thousand verses. If he could memorize over three hundred verses a year while driving, surely we can find ways to memorize a few."[13]

Here are a few steps in memorizing Scripture.

- Disabuse yourself of the myth that you can't memorize.

- Memorize one verse at a time.

- Continue to review the verses that you have memorized until they are etched in your psyche.

- Use the Scripture you've memorized in prayer, conversation, writing, teaching, counseling, preaching, telephoning, etc.

- Be selective by memorizing verses on important teachings of the Bible.

- Depend upon the Holy Spirit, the One who brings the Bible to the believer's remembrance. *"But the Helper, the Holy Spirit, whom the Father will send in My name, He will teach you all things, and bring to your remembrance all things that I said to you"* (John 14:26).

---

[13] Donald Whitney, *Spiritual Disciplines for the Christian Life*, (Colorado Springs: NavPress, 1991), 40-41. For an excellentbiography on Dawson Trotman see Betty Skinner, *Daws: A Man who Trusted God* (Colorado Springs: NavPress, 1993).

- Keep up the process.

- Give God the glory.

What are the benefits of Internalizing of the Word?

- Builds your faith – *"So then faith comes by hearing, and hearing by the word of God"* (Rom. 10:17).

- Keeps you from sin – *"Your word I have hidden in my heart, that I might not sin against You"* (Ps. 119:11).

- Repels the Devil – *"Therefore submit to God. Resist the devil and he will flee from you"* (James 4:7).

- Gives divine guidance – *"Your testimonies also are my delight And my counselors"* (Psalm 119:24).

- Enhances preaching, teaching, counseling, witnessing, etc. *"But the Helper, the Holy Spirit, whom the Father will send in My name, He will teach you all things, and bring to your remembrance all things that I said to you"* (John 14:26).

- Imparts incredible joy – *"Your words were found, and I ate them, And Your word was to me the joy and rejoicing of my heart;…"* (Jer. 15:16).

- Increases one's credibility and authority – *"And so it was, when Jesus had ended these sayings, that the people were astonished at His teaching"* (Matt. 7:28).

- Fills you with the Holy Spirit – *"Let the word of Christ dwell in you richly in all wisdom, teaching and admonishing one another in psalms and hymns and spiritual songs, singing with grace in your hearts to the Lord"* (Col. 3:16).

- Assures success in all you do – *"This Book of the Law shall not depart from your mouth, but you shall meditate in it day and night, that you may observe to do according to all that is written in it. For then you will make your way prosperous, and then you will have good success"* (Josh. 1:8). See also Psalm 1:1-3 and James 1:25).

5. We Must Meditate for deeper understanding of the Word and food for our soul. A good example would be that of a cow chewing the cud.

The cud is a mouthful of previously swallowed food regurgitated from the first stomach of cattle and other ruminants back to the mouth, where it is chewed slowly a second time. Likewise meditation is regurgitating the spiritual food that we have memorized and receiving great nourishment for our souls.

6. We Must Make an Application of the Truth to show its value.

- Pray it through.

- Dialogue with God.

- Rely upon God

7. We Must Be Motivated in Knowing that Internalizing the Word is the one and only secret God gives for success in our spiritual lives.
There is a specific connection between success and the practice of meditation on God's Word (Jos. 1:8; Ps. 1:1-3; James 1:25). We must remember that the prosperity and success the Lord speaks of here is prosperity and success in His eyes and not necessarily in the world's. True success is promised to those who meditate on God's Word, who think deeply on Scripture, not just one time each day, but at moments throughout the day and night.

Internalizing the Word includes four simple steps:

- **Know** the Word in your head by diligent study.

- **Stow** the Word in your heart by memorization and meditation.

- **Show** the Word in your life by obeying its teachings.

- **Sow** the Word in your world by witnessing.

No Spiritual Discipline is more important than the intake of God's Word. Nothing can substitute for it. There is simply no healthy Christian life apart from a diet of the milk and meat of the Scripture. The reasons for this are obvious. In the Bible God tells about Himself, and especially about Jesus Christ, the incarnation of God. The Bible unfolds the law of God to us and shows us how we've all broken it. There we learn how Christ died as a sinless, willing substitute for breakers of God's Law and how we must repent and believe in Him to be right with God. In the Bible we learn the ways and will of the Lord. We find in Scripture how to live in a way that is pleasing to God as well as best and most fulfilling for ourselves. None of this eternally essential information can be found anywhere else except in the Bible. Therefore, if we would know God and be godly, we must know the Word of God intimately.

THE VALUE OF SCRIPTURE MEMORIZATION AND MEDITATION

Jesus Christ openly declared that our spiritual existence depends upon every word of God when He stated, *"man shall not live by bread alone but by every word that proceedeth from the mouth of God"* (Matt. 4:4). Where are the words of God written? In the Bible. The Apostle Peter's last word to us is "to grow in the grace and knowledge of our Lord Jesus Christ" (2 Pet. 3:18). But how are we to grow? Growth in the Lord is called sanctification, the life-long process by which we become more and more like Jesus, fulfilling God's purpose for every redeemed person; *"for whom He did foreknow, He did predestinate that he be conformed to the image of Christ"* (Rom. 8:29). Jesus Himself said sanctification comes by the Word of God. His last prayer for every Christian was *"Sanctify them in Thy truth; Thy Word is truth"* (John 17:17).

However, for the Word to "sanctify" or make me like Jesus it must enter into me. How does the Word of God enter us? It enters through our minds to change our hearts and ultimately to change our character and lifestyle into His likeness. Thus we should meditate on every verse that comes from the mouth of God. As we meditate deeply our understanding grows. But to meditate we need to memorize. It is almost impossible for one not to meditate on Scripture which he has memorized; and it is almost impossible to meditate on Scripture he has not memorized. Thus, there is no more useful discipline than the continual process of memorizing and meditating on the Scriptures.

- **By memorization and meditation**, a lifetime of reflection is now available through ongoing review—while driving on long trips, while walking on the beach, conversing with friends, hearing the great hymns, sharing in small groups, reflecting during the night time or early rising.

- **By memorization and meditation,** we are armed to hate sin and to determine to fight it vigorously.

- **By memorization and meditation,** we are able to withstand in the moment of temptation through "the sword of the Spirit, which is the Word of God" (Eph. 6:18).

- **By memorization and meditation,** the young can keep their purity. How can a young man keep his life pure? By living according to your Word. "I have hidden your word in my heart that I might not sin against God" (Ps. 119:11). It is alledged that Spurgeon wrote on the flyleaf of his Bible: "This book will keep you from sin, or sin will keep you from this book."

Andrew Davis states, "the word sanctifies us by transforming our entire worldview from secular to heavenly: 'Do not be conformed any longer to the pattern of this world, but be transformed by the renewing of your mind. Then you will be able to test and approve what God's will is—his good, pleasing, and perfect will.'" (Rom. 12:2) The "renewing of your minds" happens by the flow of Scripture through them like a pure river. As this river flows through your mind constantly, you will see things more and more the way God does, if you are a child of God…for "we have the mind of Christ." (1 Cor. 2:16) This gives us more and more wisdom to deal with this world."[14]

- **By memorization and meditation** on Scripture, the Scripture becomes a treasure trove for the growth of you and the church. "The Scripture memorizer will be used mightily by God to teach and encourage other Christians, with an apt word from the perfect Word of God: "Let the word of Christ dwell in you richly as you teach and admonish one another with all wisdom" (Col. 3:16) How better can you obey Colossians 3:16 than by Scripture memorization? The "word of Christ" will indeed "dwell in you richly" as you memorize it, and then work it over in your mind through meditation. Then you will most certainly be useful to God to "teach and admonish" another brother or sister. Scripture builds the Church to its final doctrinal and practical maturity (Eph. 4:13-16), and God uses those who memorize it to do this building in a powerful and eternally fruitful way."[15]

---

[14] Andrew Davis, *The Value of Scripture Memorization*, First Baptist Church, Durham, NC website.
[15] Ibid.

- "**Finally, the memorization** of Scripture enables us to bless lost people with a powerful and vivid presentation of the gospel of salvation. 'Faith comes from hearing the message, and the message is heard through the word of Christ.' (Rom. 10:17) Those who memorize Scripture obey Peter's command in this regard: 'Always be prepared to give an answer to everyone who asks you to give a reason for the hope that you have' (1 Pet. 3:15). The 'preparation' Peter had in mind is best done by memorizing Scripture. Remember that it is Scripture which is 'able to make you wise for salvation through faith in Christ Jesus' (2 Tim. 3:15). The evangelist who stores up Scripture on the life of Christ, for example, can vividly retell the miracle stories to a generation which is Biblically illiterate, which knows very little about the life of Christ. That person can also give the theology of salvation from Paul's epistles, if he has memorized from those books. In short, Scripture memorization makes one a much more powerful and effective evangelist,"[16] preacher, teacher, and witness.

- There are other benefits of memorization and meditation:

  o Comfort during trials and bereavement.

  o Power and wisdom for counseling.

  o The development of heavenly mindedness.

  o The manifestation of the fruit of the Spirit.

  o Conviction over indwelling sin.

  o Increase of faith as *"faith comes by hearing and hearing by the Word of Christ"* (Rom. 10:17).

  o It saves the preacher much time in sermon preparation, weddings, funerals, writing, etc.

  o It enhances your ability to effectively communicate God's word to your audiences.

  o It raises the confidence of your hearers in your message.

---

[16] Ibid.

CHAPTER FIVE

MEDITATE ON THE WORD BOTH DAY AND NIGHT

THE LOST ART OF THE 21ST CENTURY

The lost art of the twenty-first century is meditation. Americans are masters when it comes to activities—entertainment, planning, and going. But meditation—forget it. For some reason we have the mistaken idea that meditation is day dreaming. It is time spent in thinking about nothing, humming some religious melody, reflecting upon the good old days—just plain wasting time which we could spend having fun. Yet meditation is not just letting our minds drift here and there with no purpose. But it is pondering and reflecting upon specific truths found in a verse or passage of Scripture—slowly, piece by piece, allowing our minds to dig deeply into a word, phrase, idea, command, warning, or principle, with the purpose of gaining insight for great living and for others with whom we may share.

For example, let us delve into a well known verse, Proverbs 3:5-6 which states, *"Trust in the Lord with all thine heart: and lean not unto thine own understanding. In all thy ways acknowledge Him, and He shall direct thy paths."* Consider four practical steps as we meditate upon these two verses:

1. Focus on the key words in the verse: Trust" in the "Lord," "Lean"not on your "own understanding," "acknowledge" God in *all* your ways. Ask yourself, "Am I really trusting all my problems and concerns to the Lord—my family, my finances, my church, my nation, my present, past, and future?"

Think of the warning "Lean not unto your own understanding" and think of the many ways you have tried to work things out for yourself. I have one grandson. At twelve he was going on twenty-five. He lived far away. I tried to stay in touch by email and telephone and occasional visits. I suggested books. Nothing worked. Then the Lord said to me, "You can't change him, but I can if you will quit leaning to your own understanding and start praying." I did and today the boy is completely changed.

2. Compare the two verses with other Scriptures. For example, Psalm 37:4-5; Philippians 4:6-7; Isaiah 41:10,13; 1 Peter 5:7 and Matthew 11:28-30.

3. Relate the verses to your present circumstances. Suppose you are restless and uneasy. Suppose you are struggling over paying your bills. Over a rebellious child? Name these problems to the Lord. And ask "Am I ready to rely on God, or will I keep trying to work things out?" Am I ready to trust God or do I really enjoy my worry?" A Christian doctor had this question emblazoned in big letters on the wall of his study, "Why pray when you can worry?"

4. Finally, use prayer as a follow-up, remembering this eternal truth: When you work, you work; but when you pray God works. Dial God's telephone number, *"Call unto me and I will answer and will show you great and mighty things which you never dreamed of before."* (Jer. 33:3).[17]

THE IMPORTANCE OF MEDITATION

There is no way to walk intimately with God and have His blessings upon our lives and ministry except through meditation. This is what God says in Joshua 1:8; Psalm 1:2-3; James 1:25. Meditation is far more than reading the Bible and praying. Meditation is to quiet your heart before the Lord, to focus entirely on Him and His Word, to listen to His voice, and to ask Him questions and hear His reply, and not to rush but spend the time in quiet to get through to God. What are the results?

- A quiet heart.

- A sense of confidence.

- A sense of direction.

---

[17] As I recall I received some of my insights on meditation from Charles Swindoll, but I cannot locate the reference.

- The purification of our hearts.

- A growing hunger for God.

- An enlargement of the greatness of God.

- A deep sense of joy.

- Holy optimism.

- The revelation of the meaning of His Word.

- A sense of expectancy.

- The diminution of our problems.

The final result of meditation is God's kind of success and prosperity in our lives and ministry. Without meditation, the opposite occurs: frustration, anxiety, uncertainty, failure, being in a rut, etc.

CHAPTER SIX

PRAYER

HOW TO HAVE A MEANINGFUL TIME WITH THE LORD

We have got to understand that the best way to experience spiritual power, direction, and purpose is to have a meaningful time with God daily.

The number one priority in the life of a true disciple should be having a meaningful time with God daily. If nothing else gets done in your day, this must get done.

Seven guidelines for having this meaningful time:

- **A Special Time** —"The first guideline to having a meaningful time with God daily is to have a special time that you meet with Him. It is your most important appointment, and you need to make and keep it daily. Ask yourself right now, "What time am I going to meet with God every single day for the rest of my life?" Since this is the number one priority in the life of a true disciple, I believe that your appointment with God should take place before anything else in your life.

Your time with God should take place before you read the newspaper each day. It should take place before you turn on the television to watch your favorite newscast. Since a meaningful time with God is imperative for you to have a vital relationship with God, then the priorities of your day should reflect this truth. The moment you wander around the house or leave for work or school in the morning without having a meaningful time with God, you make yourself vulnerable to attacks from the enemy."[18]

---

[18] Dr. Ronnie Floyd, *How To Pray*, (Nashville: Word Publishing, 1999). p. 33.

"Some of you may protest, "I am not a morning person.' Even if you are not a morning person by nature, it is still important for you to make your time with God the first thing every day. When you meet with God, it shows you depend upon Him. When you do not, it shows you depend upon yourself. If you are going to be involved in effective praying—talking to God and listening to what He is saying—then you must set aside a time for this to happen, or else it will probably not happen."[19]

I have a time set aside for God. I meet God for a private devotion at 3:00 or 3:30 every morning. Yes, the Holy Spirit is awake at this time.

- **Sufficient Time** – There is a place for short, even an– "arrow" prayer. Jesus often prayed one sentence. But if you have a meaningful time with God, you must take some time. Jesus chided His disciples for not praying one hour. I recommend you begin with thirty minutes, move to one hour, and often you will need to tarry longer. Jesus commanded persistence in prayer if we expect to get answers (Matt. 7:7; Luke. 11:8). Persistence means time. How do you think God feels when we give Him no more than 2, 3, 4, 5 or 10 minutes in prayer? How much time are you praying daily?

- **A Special Place** —"Places are important to God. All through Scripture, we read various accounts of God's activity, and often the place of the activity receives special attention. If you are going to have a meaningful time with God every day, then set aside a special place to meet with Him. This special place needs to be somewhere you enjoy. It needs to be somewhere private. The fewer interruptions you have, the easier it is for you to have a meaningful time with God.

I meet with God every morning in my study at home. This is my special place to be with Him. He has been so real to me in this place. He has spoken to me through His Word. He has built me back up when I have been discouraged. He has put me back together when I was broken. Yes, it is a special place—not because of the color of the room, the beauty of the desk, or the books on the shelves. The thing that makes it really special is that is where God and I hang out together."[20]

---

[19] Ibid. p. 34
[20] Ibid. pp. 34-35

- **A Special Plan** —"If you do not have a plan to meet with God and pray, then you probably will not do either one. If you are going to have a meaningful time with God daily, you need to develop a game plan. Every day is game day for the Christian. There are no off days or off seasons. In order to be ready for your game day every day, you need to follow a plan when you meet with God."[21]

  I have used several prayer plans. I began with the Lord's Prayer, then the *One Year Bible*,[22] the Acts, then one chapter each day, Monday through Friday. Sometimes I combine plans. "Just remember this, if you do not plan to pray, you will not pray. In order to be an effective prayer warrior, you need to plan to meet with God daily."[22]

- **A Special Book** —"The special book that you need to read is a compilation of sixty-six smaller books...This book is called the Bible. The Bible is essential for your life. It needs to be studied. It needs to be memorized. It needs to be read daily. There is no way that you can have a meaningful time with God without reading the Bible daily. The Bible is the main way God speaks to you. The Bible is His love letter to you. God's Word is intended to be a lamp for our feet and a light for our path. This kind of guidance is possible when you read it and study it during a daily time with Him."[23] It is by hearing the Bible that faith arises in our hearts (Rom. 10:17).

- **A Special Spirit** – A special time, a sufficient time, a special place, a special plan, a special book—none of these will result in a meaningful time with the Lord unless you possess a special spirit. What is that spirit? A broken spirit and a contrite heart. This is the sacrifice God requires. This is the sacrifice He honors (Ps. 51:16-17). God dwells in only two places: in heaven and in a humble heart (Is. 57:15). He dwells through the Holy Spirit, the mediator of Jesus to the humble spirit. But He mediates only with the humble spirit. "God resists the proud but gives grace to the humble" (1 Pt. 5:5 and James 4:6).

---

[21] Ibid. p. 35
[21] For example, see *One Year Bible: The New International Version* (Wheaton, IL: Tyndale, 1986).
[22] Dr. Ronnie Floyd, p. 36
[23] Ibid. p. 36

You must have His effectual indwelling to have a meaningful time with the Lord, and you have it only if you approach Him with a repentant and broken heart.

- **A Special Hunger for God** – We know it is God's will for us to have a hunger for Him (Matt.5:6 and John 7:37). If you don't have a hunger, you can pray and He will give it to you according to I John 5:14. What sends you to the refrigerator day and night? Hunger for food. Hunger for God will also send you to Him to pray daily.

TEN REQUIREMENTS FOR ANSWERED PRAYER

1. To Get Your Prayers Answered, you must pray in Jesus's name (John. 15:16).

When you pray in the name of Jesus, you are praying to the God who manifests Himself in Jesus. You are not praying to Allah or Buddha or some pantheistic force. Pastor Bob Russell was asked not to pray in Jesus's name at a civic event. He ended his prayer "in the name of the Lion of Judah." After praying he thought to himself, "I am so clever, how smart I am." Then the Lord convicted him that he was shrewd but was a coward. "Jesus said, if you are ashamed of me and my words, I will be ashamed of you."[24]

• When you pray in Jesus name you are praying to the only way to God. This is clearly stated in 1 Timothy 2:5, *"For there is one God and one Mediator between God and men, the Man Christ Jesus."*

2. To Get Your Prayers Answered, you must pray according to God's will.

When you pray in the name of the Lord, you are submitting your will to His will. You are acknowledging that if both parties don't agree, you want God's will to prevail. Bob Russell states, "We don't dictate to God what He is supposed to do. As Jesus Himself prayed in Gethsemane, so we should pray, 'Not my will, but Yours be done.' "[25]

---

[24] Adapted from Bob Russell, *When God Answers Prayer* (West Monroe, LA: Howard, 2003), 45-46.

[25] Bob Russell, *When God Answers Prayer* (West Monroe, LA: Howard, 2003), p. 48.

3. To Get Your Prayers Answered, you must pray with dependence upon the Holy Spirit.

Romans 8:26 is a special promise. *"Likewise the Spirit also helps in our weaknesses. For we do not know what we should pray for as we ought, but the Spirit Himself makes intercession for us with groanings which cannot be uttered."* Often we really don't know what to pray for, but when you sincerely pray in Jesus's name, the Holy Spirit intercedes for you. He knows you better than you know yourself. He brings your heart and God's heart together to make something happen that is agreeable to both parties.

4. To Get Your Prayers Answered, you must pray in faith.

Mark 11:24, James 5:15 and Hebrews 11:6 all speak of the importance of faith. The Apostle James says that when we pray, we must believe and not doubt (James 1:6-8). Does that mean that if you have any doubts, your prayers will not be answered? No. In Mark 9:20-24 a father requested of Jesus that He heal his son and Jesus replied, *"If you can believe, all things are possible to him who believes,"* The man replied, *"but Lord help my unbelief."* Jesus did not refuse to help the man because he had doubts. He proceeded to heal the man. God does not require perfect faith, but sincere faith.

5. To Get Your Prayers Answered, you must be righteous in your lifestyle.

Read James 5:16 and consider the following.

- You must have right relations with God — *"Behold, the LORD's hand is not shortened, That it cannot save; Nor His ear heavy, That it cannot hear. But your iniquities have separated you from your God; And your sins have hidden His face from you, So that He will not hear"* (Is. 59:1-2).

- You must have right relations with your fellow man — *"If someone says, "I love God," and hates his brother, he is a liar; for he who does not love his brother whom he has seen, how can he love God whom he has not seen? And this commandment we have from Him: that he who loves God must love his brother also"* (1 John 4:20-21).

"Therefore if you bring your gift to the altar, and there remember that your brother has something against you, leave your gift there before the altar, and

go your way. First be reconciled to your brother, and then come and offer your gift" (Matt. 5:23-24).

If you are at odds with another Christian, if you are at odds with God, you are not ready to pray. Go and make things right with your brother and then pray. Confessing your sins does not mean spilling your guts to everyone or airing your dirty laundry in public. Warren Wiersbe offered words of wisdom:

"We must never confess sin beyond the circle of that sin's influence. Private sin requires private confession; public sin requires public confession. It is wrong for Christians to hang dirty wash in public, for such confessing might do more harm than the original sin."[26]

6. To Get Your Prayers Answered, you must pray fervently.

"Confess your trespasses to one another, and pray for one another, that you may be healed. The effective, fervent prayer of a righteous man avails much" (James 5:16).

"Therefore I say to you, whatever things you ask when you pray, believe that you receive them, and you will have them" (Mark 11:24).

Just mumbling some words with no passion and sometimes half asleep will not be honored by God.

Permit me to give you three practical suggestions for praying with greater fervency.

- Kneeling. It is nearly impossible to sleep when on your knees and harder for your mind to wander.

- Pray aloud. When you pray aloud, you impress your spirit and keep your focus.

- Fast. Fasting demonstrates your seriousness. Fasting reminds you that spiritual things are more important than physical things.

7. To Get Your Prayers Answered, you must persist in prayer.

Luke 11:5-8 and Matthew 7:7: *"And He said to them, "Which of you shall have a friend, and go to him at midnight and say to him, 'Friend, lend me*

---

[26] Quoted in Russell, pp. 51-52.

three loaves; for a friend of mine has come to me on his journey, and I have nothing to set before him'; and he will answer from within and say, 'Do not trouble me; the door is now shut, and my children are with me in bed; I cannot rise and give to you'? I say to you, though he will not rise and give to him because he is his friend, yet because of his persistence he will rise and give him as many as he needs." "*Ask, and it will be given to you; seek, and you will find; knock, and it will be opened to you.*" The words ask, seek and knock are in the present tense which means keep on asking, seeking and knocking. Russell states, "Don't quit praying just because your prayers aren't answered on the first request."[27] Jesus said, "*Men ought always to pray and not give up*" (Luke 18:1). Remember that God's delays are not His denials but a display of His grace. Isaiah 30:18 says "*Therefore the LORD will wait, that He may be gracious to you; And therefore He will be exalted, that He may have mercy on you. For the LORD is a God of justice; Blessed are all those who wait for Him.*"

8. To Get Your Prayers Answered, you must pray with boldness.

You are invited to pray boldly in Hebrews 4:16. Russell says he memorized the words of John Newton regarding asking largely of God, "Thou are coming to a King, large petitions with thee bring, for His grace and power are such, none can ever ask too much."[28] It is alleged that D. L. Moody prayed for $50,000 when the pastor had suggested $5, and Moody received $50,000.

9. To Get Your Prayers Answered, you must incorporate thanksgiving into your petitions. "*Be anxious for nothing, but in everything by prayer and supplication, with thanksgiving, let your requests be made known to God; and the peace of God, which surpasses all understanding, will guard your hearts and minds through Christ Jesus*" (Phil. 4:6-7).

10. To Get Your Prayers Answered, you must abide in God's Word

"*If you abide in Me, and My words abide in you, you will ask what you desire, and it shall be done for you*" (John. 15:7)

"*One who turns away his ear from hearing the law, Even his prayer is an abomination*" (Prov. 28:9).

---

[27] Ibid. 63.
[28] Ibid., 67.

Prayer must not be left to convenience, our feelings or our moods. The command of our Lord is to pray continually (Luke. 18:1) and persistently (Luke 18:5-12). He Himself prayed several hours per day before the light of day (Mark 1:35). I believe every believer should also pray continually, persistently, and prior to daybreak if possible.

One fact is well attested: No one will ever have a powerful prayer life unless he plans it. Left to convenience and feelings, you would do well to pray two hours per week.

Consider the following "Personal Prayer Plan."

1. Step One: Read the Bible.

- Before you begin to read, bow your head, be quiet for a moment and clear your mind.

- Then pray this prayer, "Dear Father, speak to me through your Word today."

- Use the *One Year Bible* or some systematic plan.

- Now take your time.

- You may want to write meaningful verses in your notebook.

2. Step Two: The four "Talking Principles" begin with the letters ACTS:[29]

Adore or praise the Lord. Praise is your adoration for Him who loves you so much.

Confess. Sin clogs the lines of communication between you and God. Claim the promise of 1 John 1:9 which says, *"If we confess our sins, He is faithful and just to forgive us our sins and to cleanse us from all unrighteousness."* Also Proverbs 28:13, *"He who covers his sins will not prosper, But whoever confesses and forsakes them will have mercy."*

---

[29] Bill Bright, *The Coming Revival*, (Orlando, Florida: Newlife Publications, 1995) p. 188.

Thanksgiving. Thanksgiving is verbal expression to God for all He has done for you. Be specific. *"In everything give thanks; for this is the will of God in Christ Jesus for you"* (1 Thess. 5:18).

Supplication. This is petition and intercession.

- Focus your prayer on personal needs (petition).

- Stand in the gap between God and the person for whom you pray (intercession).

- One may also use the Lord's Prayer.

3. Step Three: Weekly Prayer Calendar. In order not to miss important objects of prayer, you will need to organize your prayer according to the days of the week.

The following is an example:

Sunday – World Missions, Evangelism, Missionaries. Your praying is part of your vital involvement in world evangelization And Jesus came and spoke to them, saying, *"All authority has been given to Me in heaven and on earth. Go therefore and make disciples of all the nations, baptizing them in the name of the Father and of the Son and of the Holy Spirit, teaching them to observe all things that I have commanded you; and lo, I am with you always, even to the end of the age. Amen"* (Matt. 28:18-20).

Monday– United States of America, The President, your Congressman, Senators, Mayor, Governor, etc. You are to "pray for all men in authority" (1 Tim. 2:1-2), regardless of whether you agree with them or not. *"Therefore I exhort first of all that supplications, prayers, intercessions, and giving of thanks be made for all men, for kings and all who are in authority, that we may lead a quiet and peaceable life in all godliness and reverence."*

Tuesday – The lost, unchurched, lost people in China, India, the Middle East, and around the world (Rom 10:1). *"Brethren, my heart's desire and prayer to God for Israel is that they may be saved."*

Wednesday– Friends.

Thursday– Christian Leaders of the nations and world.

Friday – Relatives.

Saturday – Local churches and pastors.

There are two Urgent Categories of Prayer: **1) Urgent Current Needs** – There are always immediate critical needs that require daily prayer; and **2) Continuing Needs** – There are always critical needs which never cease to be needs, such as prayer for your children by name, for the Holy Spirit's infilling, for the boldness to witness daily.

4. **Step Four: Journal.** I say to my students "Anything worth speaking is worth writing down." Also, anything worth praying is worth writing down. I regret that I have not done this through the years. My nervousness, mobility, and unending labors have prevented this. Also, I have depended on my God-blessed memory, but no mind can recall everything. I have a friend, Ronnie Floyd, who closes his prayer time by writing a one-page letter to God. This letter records his main burdens of that day and also the joy of answered prayer.

5. **Step Five: Pray it through.** Some years ago the word circulated that if one asked God more than once he was showing his lack of faith. This teaching is totally contrary to the teaching of Jesus. Jesus commands us "to ask and keep on asking." "Seek and keep on seeking." "Knock and keep on knocking" (Luke 11:9 and Matt. 7:7). Jesus illustrates this truth by telling of an unwilling neighbor who gave his friend bread simply because he kept on asking, seeking and knocking. Woodrow Kroll goes to the heart of the matter when he states, "If persistence was the key to the unwilling heart of a neighbor, how much more effective will persistence be to the willing heart of God."[30]

How long should you pray through? Ronnie Floyd says to pray until one of the following three things occur, and I agree: 1) Until you know it is not God's will; 2) until God answers your prayer; or 3) until God releases you.[31]

---

[30] Quoted in Ronnie Floyd, *How to Pray*, (Nashville, Tennessee: Word Publishers, 1955), p. 106.
[31] Ibid. pp. 106-109

PRAYER BUSTERS AND HOW TO BUST THEM

If you are not getting your prayers answered, you should ask three questions:

- Are my prayers right?

- Is the timing right?

- Am I right?

If constantly your prayers are not answered, it is not likely that your prayers are wrong or that the timing is wrong. The major problem is probably you. So let's look at twelve prayer busters and how to bust the prayer busters:

The first prayer buster is **lostness**. Without a personal relationship with the Father, you cannot pray. Rom. 10:13 says,... *"whoever calls on the name of the LORD shall be saved."* and in John 14:6, *"Jesus said to him, 'I am the way, the truth, and the life. No one comes to the Father except through Me.'"* So it's clear that no man or woman comes to the Father except through Jesus. The answer is to get truly saved.

The second prayer buster is **prayerlessness**. Jesus said, *"Ask and it shall be given"* (Matt. 7:7). James spells it out further, *"You have not because you ask not"* (James 4:2). The answer is to begin praying and keep on praying no matter your discouragements.

The third prayer buster is **half-praying**. Jesus said not only to "ask" but to "seek" and to "knock." Sometimes you can receive an answer by merely asking, but in most cases you must also "seek" and then "knock." I arise early to first ask; then I seek; and then I go to my office to knock. The answer is more time in prayer each day.

The fourth prayer buster is **heartless praying**. Just saying words is not praying. Prayer is passion, conviction, urgency and feeling (James 5:17-18 and Mark 11:24). The answer is to surrender to the Holy Spirit.

The fifth prayer buster is **unconfessed sin**. (Is. 59:1-2 and Ps. 66:18). The answer is true confession, not just naming your sins, but naming them personally and specifically and turning from them in the power of God (Prov. 28:13). "Lord, forgive me of my many sins" is a cop out.

You must name your sins one by one and specifically, "Lord, I backbited Hazel Snodgrass today. I repent and ask your forgiveness and cleansing."

Broken Relationships *"Therefore if you bring your gift to the altar, and there remember that your brother has something against you, leave your gift there before the altar, and go your way. First be reconciled to your brother, and then come and offer your gift"* (Matt. 5:23-24). John states, *"If you say you walk in light and hate your brother you are still in darkness"* (1 John 2:9). The answer is to seek reconciliation. It may not be possible but we must try. *"If it is possible, as much as depends on you, live peaceably with all men"* (Rom. 12:18).

Mistreating Your Spouse (1 Pet. 3:7). The answer is to obey Eph. 5:25 which says, *"Husbands, love your wives, just as Christ also loved the church and gave Himself for her."*

Uncaring Attitude Toward The Oppressed (Prov. 21:13). *"Whoever shuts his ears to the cry of the poor will also cry himself and not be heard."* The answer is to ask forgiveness and repent and start helping the oppressed.

Stingy Heart (Luke 16:11). *"Therefore if you have not been faithful in the unrighteous mammon, who will commit to your trust the true riches?"* The answer is to start tithing and giving as a way of life. Claim the promise of Luke 6:38. *"Give, and it will be given to you: good measure, pressed down, shaken together, and running over will be put into your bosom. For with the same measure that you use, it will be measured back to you."*

Bad Motives (James 4:3). *"You ask and do not receive, because you ask amiss, that you may spend it on your pleasures."* Many good prayers go unanswered because of their selfish motives. The answer is to check your prayers by four questions:

- Does this prayer glorify Jesus Christ?

- Does this prayer help carry out the Great Commission?

- Does this prayer build the local church?

- And does this prayer build the kingdom and help me spiritually?

Hostility Toward The Word Of God (Prov. 28:9). *"One who turns away his ear from hearing the law, Even his prayer is an abomination."* The answer is to search your soul to see if you are saved. Repent. Get back under the water. Read it. Hear it on every occasion possible, internalize it and obey it.

Unbelief. (Heb. 11:6). *"But without faith it is impossible to please Him, for he who comes to God must believe that He is, and that He is a rewarder of those who diligently seek Him."* The answer is a steady dose of the Word, answered prayer, and close contact with those walking in victory.

Do you have to be sinlessly perfect? No, but Psalms 66:18 must be taken seriously, *"If I regard iniquity in my heart, The Lord will not hear."* In 1981 Doris and I were asked by the International Mission Board of the SBC to go to Thailand to minister to our missionaries. Upon arriving we learned that the President of the Thai Convention, Brother Bonkramp, had terminal cancer. After two days of praying we felt led, at his invitation, to pray for his healing, and anoint him with oil. We did so in faith and, believing God had directed us to do so, but at the same time doubting that he would live at that point. About a year later, we were surprised when he appeared at our church to attend our annual clinic on evangelism. When asked him how he was doing, he exclaimed victoriously, "After you prayed for me, I was healed." So God honored our prayer, not because our faith was perfect, but it was earnest, sincere and obedient.

CHAPTER SEVEN

FASTING

YOU HAVE NOT BECAUSE YOU FAST NOT

FUNDAMENTAL FACTS ABOUT FASTING[32]

1. What is Fasting?

Donald Whitney defines biblical fasting as "a Christian's voluntary abstinence from food for spiritual purposes."[33] However, fasting applies to more than food. Richard Foster defines fasting as "the voluntary denial of a normal function for the sake of intense spiritual activity."[34] So then, fasting does not always deal with the abstinence from food. Sometimes we may need to fast from involvement with other people, the media, the telephone or sleep. This allows one to become more absorbed in a time of spiritual activity. Martyn Lloyd-Jones concurs with this wider definition of fasting.[35]

2. Does Jesus Expect Believers to Fast?

Jesus' words at the beginning of Matthew 6:16-17 state, *"And when you fast...But when you fast."* This clearly implies that He expects His followers to fast. Whitney indicates that "by giving us instructions on what to do and what not to do when we fast, Jesus assumes that we will fast."[36]

---

[32] For a more comprehensive study on fasting see Bill Bennett, *How to Commence, Continue, and Conduct a Biblical Fast* (Wilmington, NC: Mentoring Men Publications, 2006).

[33] Donald Whitney, *Spiritual Disciplines for the Christian Life* (Colorado Springs: NavPress, 1991), 152.

[34] Quoted in Whitney, *Spiritual Diciplines for the Christian Life*, (Colorado Springs: NavPress, 1991) p. 152.

[35] Ibid. p. 152.

[36] Ibid., 154-155.

3. How Long Should We Fast?

Whitney answers this by saying "it is up to you and the leadership of the Holy Spirit."[37] He then gives examples in the Bible of fasts that lasted.

- One day or part of a day (Judges 20:26; 1 Samuel 7:6; 2 Samuel 1:12, 3:35; Nehemiah 9:1; Jeremiah 36:6).

- One night fast (Daniel 6:18-24).

- Three day fasts (Esther 4:16; Acts 9:9).

- Seven day fasts (1 Samuel 31:13; 2 Samuel 12:16-23).

- Fourteen day fast (Acts 27:33-34).

- Twenty-one day fast (Daniel 10:3-13).

- Forty day fasts (Deuteronomy 9:9; 1 Kings 19:8; Matthew 4:2).

- Fasts of unspecified lengths (Matthew 9:14; Luke 2:37; Acts 13:2, Acts 14:23).[38]

4. What are the Purposes for Fasting?

Whitney states, "There's more to a biblical fast than abstaining from food. Without a spiritual purpose for your fast it's just a weight-loss fast. You'll be just like the man who told one writer on fasting, 'I've fasted on several occasions; and nothing happened. I just got hungry." Whitney condenses the purpose for fasting into ten categories.[39]

- To Strengthen Prayer – "Whenever men are to pray to God concerning any great matter,' wrote John Calvin, 'it would be expedient to appoint fasting along with prayer.'"[41]

---

[37] Ibid., 156.
[38] Ibid. 156.
[39] Ibid. p. 157.
[40] Ibid. pp. 157-170.
[41] John Calvin, *Institute of the Christian Religion*, ed. John T. McNeil, trans. And indexed by Ford Lewis Battles (Philadelphia, PA: Westminister, 1960). Vol. 2, p. 1242.

- To Seek God's Guidance – Paul and Barnabus fasted before they appointed elders in the churches (Acts 14:23). The church at Antioch fasted and prayed before sending forth the first missionaries to other countries (Acts 13:1-5).

- To Express Sorrow and Grief (Judges 20:26).

- To Seek Protection (2 Chron. 20:3-4).

- To Express Repentance (1 Samuel 7:6 and Joel 2:12).

- To Humble Oneself Before God (1 Kings 21:27-29).

- To Express Concern for the Work of God (Nehemiah 1:3-4).

- To Minister to the Needs of Others (Isaiah 58:6-7).

- To Overcome Temptation – Jesus fasted "forty days and forty nights while being tempted in the wilderness" (Matthew 4:2).

- To Express Devotion to God (Luke 2:37).

5. What is the Reward for Fasting?

Whitney summarizes this by stating, "before we fast we must have a purpose, a God-centered purpose. But even at our best we do not deserve what we desire, nor can we force God's hand. Having said that, however, let's balance that truth with the incontestable promise of Jesus in Matthew 6:17-18, *"But when you fast, put oil on your head and wash your face, so that it will not be obvious to men that you are fasting, but only to your Father, who is unseen; and your Father, who sees what is done in secret, will reward you."* God will bless a biblical fast by any of His children. And whether or not you receive the blessing you hope for, one thing is sure: If you knew what God knew, you would give yourself the identical blessing that He does. And none of His rewards are worthless."[42]

---

[42] Donald Whitney, *Spiritual Disciplines for the Christian Life* (Colorado Springs: NavPress, 1991), p. 170.

CHAPTER EIGHT

SILENCE AND SOLITUDE: BE STILL AND KNOW I AM GOD

SILENCE AND SOLITUDE FOR THE PURPOSE OF GODLINESS

The discipline of silence can be defined as the voluntary and temporary abstention from speaking in order to pray, memorize, meditate, think, write, or reflect.

1. Ten Reasons for Silence.

- To follow the example of Jesus (Mark 1:35 and Luke 4:42).

- To encounter God in worship (Habakkuk 2:20; Zephaniah 1:7; and Psalm 46:10).

- To hear the voice of God – Elijah on Mt. Horeb (1 Kings 19:11-13.)

- To wait on God in utter dependence (Psalm 62:1-2, 5-6).

- To find strength (Isaiah 30:15).

- To bear the yoke of God (Lamentations 3:25-28).

- To be physically and spiritually renewed (Mark 6:31). As the famed old preacher, Vance Havener, used to say, "you must go apart or fall apart."

- To recover spiritual perspective – Billy Graham was urged by Chuck Templeton to renounce the Bible. Billy sought the Lord in solitude and was established on the impregnable rock of an infallible Bible.

- To seek God's will (Luke 6:12-13).

- To learn to control the tongue (James 1:26; Ephesians 4:29; Proverbs 10:19; and Proverbs 18:21).

2. Suggestions for Silence and Solitude.

- Arise before day (Mark. 1:35).

- Retreat to a center, lodge, cabin, the country, or the mountains.

- Find a quiet place—up a tree, haystack, hideaway, your car, or house behind your house.

- Improvise – Susanna Wesley, mother of 19 children, one of whom was John Wesley, pulled her apron over her head and read her Bible and prayed underneath it.

- Use special times—long drives, walking on the beach, or jogging. I jog two to four miles daily and it seems short because I often quote and meditate on the Scriptures.

CHAPTER NINE

TIME: YOU HAVE TIME TO DO ALL THAT GOD REQUIRES TIME MANAGEMENT

Busyness is the greatest enemy to having a meaningful time each day with the Lord; therefore, you must learn to manage your time so you will have time to pray.[43] God gives us all the time we need to do all He requires us to do. However, He has not given us time to do what He requires if we also do what satisfies our selfishness, our pride, our laziness and our materialistic appetites. Many justify not praying by saying "I don't have time to pray." But how can you say that you don't have time to do the most important thing in the Christian life? You don't have time to pray if you are not willing to turn off the television, to get out of bed, and you are not willing to crucify your flesh and live like a man or woman of God. But you do have sufficient time to do what God requires, what pleases Him, and what blesses your life abundantly and above measure.

IF YOU WOULD MANAGE YOUR TIME:

1. You must obey the fourth commandment, *"Remember the Sabbath Day to keep it holy."*

2. You must engage in future decision making, that is, you must decide beforehand that you will do those things which God specifically requires in His Word.

How? Look at your time and schedule essential things. For example, I decided fifty years ago that when Sunday came along, I would attend Sunday School and Church and tithe my income. I don't wait until Saturday night to make that decision.

---

[43] This section is taken from Bill Bennett, *Manage Your Time Or Time Will Manage You* (Wilmington, NC: New Hanover Publishing and Printing 1999).

- Make time to pray daily.

- Make time to read your Bible daily.

- Make time to attend your church regularly.

- Make time to tithe weekly.

- Make time to witness.

- Make time to work.

- Make time to love your family.

3. Learn to use every minute of your time.

4. Control the television in your home.

5. Limit your time on the computer (the internet).

6. Learn to say "No."

7. Learn the miracle of prayer and time management. Jesus had only 1200 days to do His ministry, yet He ministered to thousands of people. He had time for individuals. He spent all night with them. He never missed church (Luke 4:16). He never failed to tithe (Matthew 23:23). He was never in a hurry. He was never late.

THE DISCIPLINED USE OF TIME

Godliness is the result of a disciplined spiritual life. But the heart of a disciplined spiritual life is the discipline of time and the discipline of money. The clock and the dollar are such factors in all of life that their roles must be considered in any serious discussion of Godly living.

If we are going to be like Jesus, we must see the use of our time as a Spiritual Discipline. Having so perfectly ordered His moments and His days, at the end of His earthly life Jesus was able to pray to the Father, *"I have brought you glory on earth by completing the work you gave me to do"* (John 17:4). As with Jesus, God gives us both the gift of time and work to do during that time.

1. Time is a Divine Gift

- God created all time.

- Time belongs to God.

- Time is precious because it is "the stuff life is made of."

2. God Has Loaned Us Time

- Time allotted is brief. The Psalmist promises seventy years for an average life, and it is much more for many, *"Seventy years are given us! And some may even live to eighty. But even the best of these years are often emptiness and pain; soon they disappear and we are gone"* (Ps. 90:10). Suppose you live seventy years, you would have only 25,500 days or 613,200 hours, or 36,792,000 minutes, or four billion seconds. Sounds like a lot, but it is brief compared to eternity.

- ALL Time on this earth will end for us (John 14:1; Heb. 9:27).

3. God has given us all the time we need to do what He requires.

4. God has given us time to do all the things He requires, but not the selfish things we desire.

I hear people say, "I just don't have time to go to church." Oh yes they do, but they don't have time to go to church and go pleasure seeking every weekend. I hear a lot of people say, "I don't have time to pray." And you don't have time to pray if you are not willing to turn off the television, if you are not willing to get out of bed, and if you are not willing to crucify your flesh and arise as a man or woman of God—no, you don't have time. But you have sufficient time to do what God requires and what pleases God. This is a wonderful truth.

5. God has revealed most of the things He requires in our allotted time.

- Accept the Lord

- Obey the fourth commandment

- Pray

- Study the Bible

- Attend Church

- Tithe

- Witness

- Work

- Love our family and neighbor

- Attend School

6. Learn to use every minute wisely.

How are we to do this? We have to look at our time and schedule these things, and then we need to protect this time with our lives. Fifty seven years ago I decided that when Sunday came, I would attend church. Every Christian ought to decide that he will be in church unless there is an emergency that he cannot handle. I also decided that I would tithe my money every Sunday and I have tithed it every Sunday. You will be amazed when you make tithing a priority, which many of you have, but most of you have not even to this day, how the money will be right there. When you discipline your life to give, you say that you are going to do it, the money is there. Also, when you decide that you are going to pray, there will be time. When you decide you are going to witness, you will find the time. The Holy Spirit will bring it to pass in your life—I see it all the time. Have you done that? If we don't take life that seriously, we are going to squander it in piddling, being disorganized, and being pulled by every force around us.

I have done much of my internalizing of the Bible in airports and on airplanes. I carry a Bible on my person all the time. The greatest messages that I have ever preached were given to me, as I got closer to heaven on those big planes. If you don't learn to use your time, you'll waste your vital time. Men of God who travel tell me they listen to tapes, that they pray, that they memorize the Bible as they travel. Time is precious. Do not waste it. You say, "Can't I ever relax and have a coffee break?" Yes, but that is all some people do. Corporate people tell me that they almost go crazy over the coffee breaks. I am not against that, but the coffee break is not the issue. There is something else. The issue is not to squander your time on trivialities.

7. Control the TV and Internet.

Americans are spending 30 hours out of 168 per week watching television. You say, "Can't we ever watch television?" Not much. I watch FOX News and Billy Graham occasionally—but I don't watch television programs much. If you spend 30 hours watching television, you have messed up, and you cannot succeed in time management. If you watch television much, and also stay on the internet, you will have to neglect your total spiritual discipline. Let us be the children of eternity. Let us live above these things and live like the children of light and not the children of darkness.

8. Learn to say "No."

You cannot let others set your agenda, especially those who are disgruntled. The late Adrian Rogers said it better than anyone I've ever heard when he said, "The Pastor who is always available is no good when he is available."

I cannot go to every meeting. God has told me to protect certain times to be with my family, to win the lost, to pray, to study, etc. and to sanctify them unto Him. Sometimes I have to say "No." You must do the same thing. You cannot always socialize. You cannot always go on that outing. You cannot always go to the mall. You cannot always do these things if you are going to serve God and manage your time. You must have the guts and discipline to say, "No."

9. Set a daily agenda and trust God.

Let me give you a testimony: I can but share it for the blessing it will be in your life. I don't believe that there is a day in my ministry that I don't have about three or four times more than I can possibly do, humanly speaking. I go to my study, and I make an agenda, and the first thing I put on it is: GTWTF (Get In Touch With The Father). I list on a paper 25 to 50 things that I have to do that are humanly impossible for any man to do within a day. To visit the hospitals, to meet with the staff, to meet with a family in trouble, to meet with the little child to talk about salvation, some administrative problem, some committee meeting, long-distance telephone calls, many e-mails, twenty-five letters—that is the routine of my life. Impossible, but I do it. And I do it with joy. You say, "What are you talking about?" I am talking about the miracle that God gives His people. God does not require of you and me what we cannot do in a given day if we really pray. He will give us wisdom in multiplying our time, and He will show us a way to do it better and with joy, when we really pray. Absolutely!

10. Learn the Miracles of Prayer.

The greatest factor in time management is consistent, fervent, continual, believing prayer. Jesus proved it. He had but 1200 days to do His ministry—only three years. He ministered to thousands of people. Yet He had time for individuals, and He spent whole nights with them. He was never in a hurry, but He was never late. He never missed church one time (Luke 4:16). He never failed to tithe His money (Matt. 23:23).

11. Time lost cannot be regained.

There are many things you can lose but then regain. Many a man has declared bankruptcy, only to amass an even greater fortune later. Time is different. Once it is gone, it is gone forever and can never be regained. God has offered you this time to discipline yourself for the purpose of Godliness. Jesus said in John 9:4, *"As long as it is day, we must do the work of him who sent me. Night is coming, when no one can work."* The time for the works of God, is now, and limited, while it is "day." For each of us "night is coming," and none of us is a Joshua who can stop the sun and lengthen his or her day (Jos. 10:12-14). If you misuse the time God offers to you, He never offers that time again.

12. We must give an account to God for the use of our time.

Jonathan Edwards suggested living each day as if at the end of that day you had to give an account to God of how you used your time. Deciding to discipline yourself to use your time for the purpose of godliness is not a matter for delay and deliberation. Each hour that passes is another for which you must give an account.

If there are any regrets in Heaven, they will only be that we did not use our earthly time more for the glory of God and for growth in His grace. If this is so, this may be Heaven's only similarity with hell, which will be filled with agonizing laments over time so foolishly squandered.

13. Above all, God has given us time to be saved.

But not forever—salvation is always in the present tense (2 Corinthians 6:2; Joshua 24:15). God's clock says "now." The devil's clock says "tomorrow."

A young man came to the great Gladstone, Prime Minister, of England and said, "May I lay my life before you and get your reaction?" The great statesman said, "Yes." He said that he planned to go to college and study law. And Gladstone asked, "What then?" He said, "I intend to be admitted to the Bar of England." "What then?" "I intend to go to the House of Lords." He said, "What then?" "I intend to do great things for my nation." "What then?" "I'll probably get married and have a family." "What then?" "I'll probably retire one day." "What then?" "I guess I'll die someday." And the great prime minister said, "What then?" He said that he had never thought that far ahead. The great statesman looked him in the eyes and said, "You are a fool, go home and think life through."[44] We are going to die one day. Christian, you are going to answer for the way you use your time.

Are you using it wisely? Lost person, today is your day to use the time to receive Christ.

Where to Begin Time Management

1. Discover how you are using your time now.

2. Discover how you are wasting your time and stop it.

3. Do those things God requires in His Word.

4. Lengthen your day by going to bed early and getting up early.

5. Take common sense steps to save time. For example, control telephone calls and answer letters promptly.

6. Use the remaining time to do those things not specifically required by God but necessary in your situation. Make a daily agenda of these things.

7. Pray and trust God for a miracle.

---

[44] Louis Evans, *Youth Seeks A Master*, (Westwood, N.J.:Fleming H. Revell Company, 1951) pp. 76-77.

8. Always believe that God gives time for all He requires.

9. Live your life in the light of eternity and suddenly you will discover that half the things you have been doing, you will not even want to do. The things which have seemed important to you will appear foolish, petty, and trivial.

CHAPTER TEN

EVANGELISM: MAKING EVANGELISM
A LIFESTYLE

EVANGELISM IS DISCIPLINE[45]

Paul states, *"Discipline yourself for the purpose of godliness"* (1 Timothy 4:7 NAS). Godliness requires that we discipline ourselves in evangelism as well as in Bible intake, prayer, etc. The main reason most people don't witness for Christ is three fold: 1) Fear 2) Business 3) and Scriptural ignorance. Yet nothing is as exhilarating as sharing Jesus.

What is Evangelism? Evangelism is to present Jesus Christ in the power of the Holy Spirit to lost people, in order that they may realize they are lost in sin, repent and trust Jesus Christ as Lord and Savior, and serve Him as their King in the fellowship of His Church.

1. Evangelism is demanded.

The Risen Christ commanded it in five great commission passages.

- Matthew 28:19-20

- Mark 16:15

- Luke 24:47-49

- John 20:21b

- Acts 1:8

---

[45] For further reading on the discipline of evangelism see Larry S. McDonald, *Rethinking the Gift of the Evangelist: Reflection on C. Peter Wagner's Teaching*, Journal of the American Society for Church Growth, 10 (Fall 1999): 15-28.

Some Christians believe that evangelism is a gift and the responsibility of only those with that gift. They appeal to Ephesians 4:11 for support: *"It was he who gave some to be apostles, some to be prophets, some to be evangelists, and some to be pastors and teachers."* While it is true that God gifts some for ministry as evangelists, He calls all believers to be His witnesses and provides them with both the power to witness and a powerful message. Every Christian is called to be a witness, but only a few witnesses are called to the vocational ministry of an evangelist. Just as each Christian, regardless of spiritual gift or ministry, is to love others, so each believer is to evangelize whether or not his or her gift is that of evangelism.

2. Evangelism is a debt every Christian owes.

Paul states, *"I am debtor both to the Greeks and to the Barbarians; both to the wise, and to the unwise. So, as much as in me is, I am ready to preach the gospel to you that are in Rome also. For I am not ashamed of the gospel of Christ: for it is the power of God unto salvation to every one that believeth; to the Jew first, and also to the Greek"* (Rom. 1:14-16).

3. Evangelism is a delight.

If I knew the sure cure for cancer, could I withhold sharing it with others? Everyone loves good news. One great evangelist said evangelism is one beggar telling another beggar where to find bread. It is rescuing a soul from hell. James says, *"Let him know, that he which converteth the sinner from the error of his way shall save a soul from death, and shall hide a multitude of sins"* (James 5:20).

4. Evangelism is dynamite.

The gospel is the power that produces salvation—the dynamite of God to everyone who believes (Rom. 1:16). Many cop out on witnessing because they lack Bible knowledge and training. But no amount of preparation equips us to witness unless we are filled with the Holy Spirit. When one is filled, he can't keep from witnessing. Acts 1:8 says the inevitable result of the infilling is witnessing.

5. Evangelism is dividends.

- In this life, *"I pray that you may be active in sharing your faith, that you will have a full knowledge of all the good things that we have in Christ"* (Phil. 1:6 NIV) and *"He that winneth souls is wise"* (Prov. 11:30).

- In eternity, *"And they that be wise shall shine as the brightness of the firmament; and they that turn many to righteousness, as the stars for ever and ever"* (Dan. 12:3).

6. Evangelism is a discipline.

Evangelism should be a natural outflow of the Christian life. We should all be able to talk about what the Lord has done for us and what He means to us. But evangelism is also a discipline in that we must discipline ourselves to get into the context and practice of evangelism, that is, we must not just wait for witnessing opportunities to happen. If we leave it to our feelings, time and convenience, we will find ourselves doing very little in winning the lost.

Evangelism should be a *lifestyle* but to be effective, it must be planned also.

- Set aside, that is, sanctify specific times to witness each week.

- Visit specific individuals for whom you have prayed and cultivated relationships.

- Discipline yourself to be with unbelievers, whether at lunch, golfing, fishing, etc.

- Ask people how you can pray for them, even before you grace the food at a restaurant.

  o On Monday's, ask "How was church yesterday?" That opens a religious conversation.

  o Ask College students, "Would you like to be a success? Then share with them the 3 Q's of success-IQ, PQ, SQ. Suppose your student's name is Bill. I would say, "Bill, it is obvious that you have the two main traits to make you a success. You undoubtedly have IQ or Intelligence Quotient, you have PQ or Personality Quotient, but to be a success, you also must have the SQ or Spiritual Quotient. By this, I mean you have to have a personal relationship with God through Jesus Christ." From this discussion, I receive various reactions and respond accordingly etc. This approach has been very effective with most individuals.

- Get with co-workers on off hours.

- Team up with another witness and prayer warrior.

- Work out a definite plan for presenting the whole gospel. For example, use the model of Evangelism Explosion or F.A.I.T.H.

- Pray constantly for the lost by name. Secure a "soul book" in which to record a prospect list.

- Pray constantly to be in love with Jesus and be soul minded.

Consider this paraphrase of 1 Corinthians 13. "Though I speak with the tongues of scholarship, and though I use approved methods of education, and fail to win others to Christ, or to build them up in Christian character, I am become as the moan of the wind in a Syrian desert. And though I have the best methods and understanding all mysteries of religious psychology, and though I have all biblical knowledge, and lose not myself in the task of winning others to Christ, I become as a cloud of mist in an open sea. And though I read all Sunday School literature, and attend Sunday School conventions, institutes, and summer school, and yet am satisfied with less than winning souls to Christ and establishing others in Christian character and service, it profiteth nothing. The soul-winning servant, the character-building servant, suffereth long and is kind; he envieth not others who are free from the servant's task; he vaunteth not himself, is not puffed up with intellectual pride. Such a servant doth not behave himself unseemingly between Sundays, seeketh not his own comfort, is not easily provoked. Beareth all things, believeth all things, hopeth all things. And now abideth knowledge, methods, the Message, these three: but the greatest of these is the Message."[46]

The more we love Jesus and others, the more we will tell of Christ and His saving message. But we must discipline ourselves to do this. May we discipline ourselves to live so that we can say with the Apostle Paul, *"I do all this for the sake of the gospel, that I may share in its blessings"* (1 Cor. 9:23).

---

[46] As quoted in Ernest C. Reisinger, *Today's Evangelism: Its Message and Methods* (Phillipsburg, NJ: Craig Press, 1982), pp. 142-143.

EVANGELIZING CHILDREN

Two errors should be avoided in winning children to Christ. First, children can be evangelized too early. The head of Child Evangelism Fellowship once insisted that children should be evangelized from three to five years of age. The idea of a three-year old child understanding the gospel enough to repent and trust Jesus as Savior and Lord is most unlikely. Sara Pierpoint, wife of Jonathan Edwards, was saved at three years of age, but this is the exception rather than the rule. Second, children can be evangelized too late. Statistics show that the vast majority of persons are converted prior to their thirteenth birthday. I am greatly concerned if a child reaches the age of fifteen and has not made a genuine profession of faith.

When, then, should children be evangelized? The answer is: at the age of accountability. A Jewish boy submitted to the bar mitzvah at age twelve, indicating the age of accountability in the Bible. William Hendricks defines the age of accountability as "the moment of grace when one is brought to a decision for or against Christ."[47] Delos Miles wrote that "infants are safe in God's care until they become capable of responsible decision-making."[48] However, when a child reaches the age of accountability, he is responsible for turning to Christ, lest he be eternally lost, and it is the responsibility of his guardians (parents, teachers, pastors) to lead him in that direction. The Holy Spirit can and does convict children of sin, reveals Christ savingly to them and works the miracle of regeneration in their hearts. At the age of nine, the Holy Spirit did all three in my heart.

The most definitive passage on the conversion of children in the New Testament is found in Matthew 18:1-14. Dr. Roy Fish, Professor of Evangelism, Southwestern Baptist Theological Seminary, deduces six principles from this passage:

1. Conversion does occur on the level of a child. *"Except you be converted and become as little children, you will by no means enter the kingdom of heaven."* (Matthew 18:2)

---

[47] William Hendricks, *Age of Accountability in Children and Conversion* (Nashville: Boardman Press, 1970), 97.

[48] Delos Miles, *Introduction to Evangelism* (Nashville: Broadman and Holman Publishers, 1983), 325.

2. Humility already belongs to the child. The older we become, the more proud we become.

3. A little child can believe in Jesus. Jesus used the word "believe" to describe little children in verse 6—the same word as appears in John 3:16 (*pisteuo*).

4. Jesus says to cause a child to stumble concerning salvation is a grievous sin. Parents, beware of treating with indifference the interest of your child in being saved. A parent should be cautious in dealing with his child, but he should not be unbelieving concerning the real possibility of the wonderful work of the Holy Spirit in the life of his child.

5. Jesus says that young children should be sought for him as a shepherd seeks his sheep.

6. Finally, Jesus says it is the Father's will that no child should perish. The word perish is the same word as appears in John 3:16, meaning to be separated from God in hell forever (*apollumi*). In using this word, Jesus is saying that a child who has reached the age of accountability should be saved, and if he or she is not and dies, he is just as lost as an adult.[49]

What are guiding principles in dealing with children about their salvation? Dr. Alvin Reid, Professor of Evangelism at Southeastern Baptist Theological Seminary, lists seven insightful principles in dealing with children in his valuable book, *Introduction to Evangelism*.

1. Deal with each child individually.

2. Avoid asking questions that require a yes or no answer.

3. Consider the child's religious background.

4. Do not use fear as a primary motivation.

5. Explain the gospel on the level of the child.

6. Affirm the child regardless of his level of comprehension.

---

[49] As quoted in Alvin L. Reid, *Introduction to Evangelism* (Nashville: Broadman and Holman, 1998), 248-249.

7. Distinguish between the internal experience of conversion and the external expressions associated with it. For example, children tend to equate salvation with baptism.[50]

[50] Ibid., 250-253.

CHAPTER ELEVEN

THE BODY: REMEMBER YOUR BODY IS WHERE GOD LIVES

TAKING CARE OF ALL OF YOU

Obesity was the number one killer in America in 2006. Also the number one killer of the children of God. Of all religious groups, Baptists are the fattest! What is the answer to this devastating problem? The discipline of the total person. The Bible speaks loud and clear about "Taking Care of all of You" (I Cor. 6:19-20; I Cor. 9:26ff).

1. Taking Care of Your Body:

- Eat Right. Eat in Moderation. If you feel a need to eat till you are full, the famous psychiatrist Frank Minirth suggests you try the following:

    o Stock up on raw vegetables. They're filling, nourishing, and they won't put on fat.

    o Eat more slowly. Psychologically if we'd just eat more slowly and wait before taking that second helping, we'd feel better with less. Fast eaters actually consume more than they need because they don't give their bodies time to feel full.

    o Don't keep lots of junk food around. If it's not there, you can't eat it!

    o Make a treat a treat. Give yourself a bonus on occasion so that a special treat is really something special. That way it never loses its great taste.[51]

---

[51] Frank Minirth, *You Can* (Nashville: Nelson, 1994), 87-88.

Minirth also observed: "God never intended food to become a compulsion for any of us. The cycle can be broken, but it must be approached the same way it began, step by step, little by little. Take it a day at a time and you will succeed."[52]

- Above all, eat breakfast. Why? Minirth states, "Researchers have repeatedly proven that breakfast is the most important meal of the day. Why? Because at breakfast—literally "breaking the fast"—we get the nourishment that sustains us through most of the day. What we eat at lunch and dinner really doesn't benefit us until the day is almost over."[53]

- Get the right amount of sleep. "Some people need more; some need less. The key is consistency."[54]

- Have a physical checkup at least once every two years.

- Exercise. "Choose an exercise routine that fits you and that you can fit in your daily schedule."[55]

- Flee from sexual sins. The Bible says, *"Run away from sexual sin! No other sin so clearly affects the body as this one does. For sexual immorality is a sin against your own body. Or don't you know that your body is the temple of the Holy Spirit, who lives in you and was given to you by God? You do not belong to yourself, for God bought you with a high price. So you must honor God with your body"* (1 Cor. 6:18-20 TLV). There is a sense in which sexual sin destroys a person like no other, because it is so intimate and entangling, corrupting on the deepest human level. But Paul is probably alluding to venereal disease, prevalent and devastating in his day and today. No sin has greater potential to destroy the body, something a believer should avoid at all cost.

- Avoid Internet pornography like a plague.

---

[52] Ibid., 88.
[53] Ibid., 85.
[54] Ibid., 90.
[55] Ibid., 89.

2. Taking Care of Yourself Emotionally:

Solomon said *"As a man thinketh in his heart, so is he"* (Proverbs 23:7). How we think about God, ourselves, others, our lives, yourselves is the key to our behavior.

- Memorize Scripture as Minirth explains:

  o Sharpens your mind and concentration.

  o Teaches you to think logically and redemptively.

  o Raises your capacity to learn and stay alert.

  o Helps us to combat the lies of the world, the flesh, and the devil.

There are multitudes of falsehoods out there from 'I'm worthless', 'God can't love me like He loves others' to 'some sins just can't be overcome.' As we memorize Scripture we are exposed to God's truth. Isaiah said, God's Word [His truth] never returns void without accomplishing what it was sent out for"[56] (Is. 55:11).

- Learn to love everybody. Through love we reach out, give, share, care, open our hearts to others, become vulnerable and sacrifice. In fact love makes possible every positive trait of Christian character.

- Especially love those who won't love you even when you love them. Paul states the Christian approach in 2 Corinthians 12:15, *"And I will very gladly spend and be spent for you, though the more abundantly I love you, the less I be loved."* Every minister must do this.

- Learn to Laugh. *"A merry heart doeth good like a medicine"* (Proverbs 17:22). Arnold Glasgow says "Laughter is a tranquilizer with no side effects."[57]

- Overcome your fears by letting God love you. *"There is no fear in love; perfect love casts out fear"* (I John 4:18). How is this so? When we know the omnipotent God loves us, we realize there is nothing that can overcome us. We may even be killed in this world, but we know we have a permanent home in the next.

---

[56] Ibid., 93-94.
[57] Ibid. Quoted in Minirth, p.97.

- Learn not to worry. *"I have learned in whatsoever state I am therewith to be content"* (Phil. 4:11). How? Learn to pray, to praise, and refuse to entertain worry, think worry, believe worry, tolerate worry, talk worry or write worry. *"And we know that God causes all things to work together for good to them who love God, to them who are the called according to His purpose"* (Rom. 8:28).

- Give everyone, including yourself, a break. Don't require perfection from your friends, family, your spouse, your children, your boss, your parents or yourself.

- Give problems time.

- "Watch carefully how you allow yourself to be entertained."[58] Television is the major source of our modern lifestyle. I urge you to assess your television viewing habits. Are you throwing your life away by watching sitcoms and soaps? A capital "T" followed by a "V" spells victim. Don't become a victim in front of the boob tube.

3. Taking Care of Yourself Spirituality.

I see a very troubling condition among Christians today: Many are talking about being Christians but are doing little to live like Christians. To such Paul gives this sobering word, *"They profess they know God; but in works they deny Him, being abominable, and disobedient, and unto every good work reprobate"* (Titus 1:16). Someone told me that a leading Rabbi said some years ago, "We Jews deny Christ by our teaching, but you Christians deny him by your living." It is alleged that Mahatma Gandhi looked Billy Graham in the eye, and said, "Mr. Graham, I will become a Christian when I see a Christian." What is the trouble? One serious trouble is that the average Christian is prayerless. A recent survey shows he prays only three minutes per day and the average pastor only seven minutes. Another problem is biblical illiteracy. Most Christians don't even know they are to "internalize" the Word, and when most are confronted with this need, they seem to think it is only for the super-spiritual and refuse to do so.

However, I believe the most serious problem among Christians is their failure to understand the seriousness of sin. Most professing believers

---

[58] Ibid., 103.

certainly believe that Jesus Christ paid the penalty for their sins on the cross and they are forgiven. But they to do not believe Jesus broke the power of sin and that they do not have to continue to practice and live in sin. Yet Scripture makes it crystal clear that when we came to Christ we were united in His death to sin and made alive to God through the Lord Jesus Christ. After stating this truth in Romans 6:1-10, Paul then says, *"Likewise reckon ye also yourselves to be dead indeed unto sin, but alive unto God through Jesus Christ our Lord. Let not sin therefore reign in your mortal body, that ye should obey it in the lusts thereof. Neither yield ye your members as instruments of unrighteousness unto sin: but yield yourselves unto God, as those who are alive from the dead, and your members as instruments of righteousness unto God. For sin shall not have dominion over you: for ye are not under the law, but under grace"* (Rom. 6:11-14).

The results of thinking we must sin are devastating. For example, the foremost problem in our churches today is the unforgiveness and bitterness of professing Christians toward their fellow Christians. Yet many Christians live in this state, either believing God will understand or that he cannot overcome such an attitude.

So if you would take care of yourself spiritually, you must claim the victory of Christ over all sin in your life. Until you do, you have not taken care of yourself spiritually. How do you do this? You cannot do so alone, so God in His graciousness has given the Holy Spirit to us to enable us to crucify indwelling sin. This glorious truth is stated in Romans 8:13. Let us look carefully at this verse. *"For if you live according to the flesh you will die; but if by the Spirit you put to death the deeds of the body, you will live."*

There was a man who had an old dog-named Skipper. Skipper began to have so many health problems that the vet advised the owner that he was going to have to be put to "death." The man became very agitated and said, "but I can't do that. I love him too much. I am too attached to him. I just can't do that." The vet said, "Oh, but don't you see? That's my job. You don't have to do it. I will take care of it for you. But it is your responsibility to give me permission" My friend agreed. The vet removed Skipper out of his life. In the same way, you should repent of persisting sin and give the Holy Spirit permission to remove it from your life. He will.

What is your Skipper? Are you going to continue to try to tolerate him? You do so at the risk of your spiritual life. Give the Holy Spirit permission to take him to the place of execution today.

MEN, YOU CAN OVERCOME SEXUAL LUST! BUT HOW?

The great area of struggle for men is in the area of sexual lust. It is truly "Every Man's Battle." Before proceeding, we need to understand the meaning of some crucial words.

Definition of Terms:

- Lust (*Epithumia*) – a burning desire to have sexual gratification, so intense that one overlooks the consequences.

- Adultery – sexual relations with someone other than your spouse. "Thou shalt not commit adultery"—this commandment covers not only the physical act but the mental thought (Matt. 5:28).

- Fornication – sexual relations with another before marriage.

- Pornography – (*porneia* + *graphe*) – immoral writings or pictures.

- Source of lust – from the heart, not from the devil (James 1:14-15 and Matthew 15:19).

- Seriousness of pornography – In the mind of a wife, pornography is a "second" woman. Therefore, in the mind of God, it is the ultimate sin (Prov. 6:32-33, 1 Cor. 6:18 and Galatians 5:21).

- Enduring Results – Proverbs 6:31ff.

- The Enemy – not sex but lust.

- Men look at pornographic material and women allow themselves to be pornographic. Monies expended by Americans for pornography every year amount to billions of dollars—at least 500 times more than monies given to missions to other countries.

History

Arnold Tonybee, foremost authority on the rise and fall of civilizations, writes that 21 civilizations have risen and fallen and a major factor in the fall of all 21 was sexual immorality. America will soon become the 22nd fallen civilization if things continue as they are. In 1953, Hugh Hefner published his first edition of Playboy Magazine with the naked body of Marilyn Monroe on the front cover. By this, he announced to our nation that there should be no restriction on sexual expression—that people had the right to have sex with children, animals, etc. The playboy philosophy has permeated our culture until today "It is sex o'clock in America, even in our living room every day."

Men, You Can Overcome Sexual Lust

Note the following points from Matthew 5:27-30:

- Do not commit physical adultery.

- Do not commit mental adultery.

- Take radical action to prevent mental adultery—preventive and corrective.

Warren Wiersbe comments on this passage when he states, "Sexual impurity begins in the desires of the heart. Again, Jesus is not saying that lustful desires are identical to lustful deeds, and therefore a person might just as well go ahead and commit adultery. The desire and the deed are not identical, but, spiritually speaking, they are equivalent. The "look" that Jesus mentioned was not a casual glance, but a constant stare with the purpose of lusting. It is possible for a man to glance at a beautiful woman and know that she is beautiful, but not lust after her. The man Jesus described looked at the woman for the purpose of feeding his inner sensual appetites as a substitute for the act. It was not accidental; it was planned.

How do we get victory? By purifying the desires of the heart (appetite leads to action) and disciplining the actions of the body. *"And if thy right eye cause thee to fall, pluck it out and cast it from thee; for it is profitable for thee that one of thy members should perish, and not that thy whole body should be cast into hell. And if thy right hand cause thee to fall, cut it off and cast it from thee; for it is profitable for thee that one of thy members should perish, and not that thy whole body should be cast into hell."* Obviously, our Lord is not talking about literal surgery; for this would not solve the problem in the heart. The eye and the hand are usually the two "culprits" when it comes to sexual sins, so they must be disciplined. Jesus said, 'Deal immediately and decisively with sin! Don't taper off—cut off!' Spiritual surgery is more important than physical surgery, for the sins of the body can lead to eternal judgment. We think of passages like Colossians 3:5 and Romans 6:13; 12:1-2; 13:14."[59]

TEN SPECIFIC WAYS YOU CAN HAVE VICTORY OVER LUST

These ways are predicated on the fact that you have a personal relationship with Jesus Christ because of the new birth (2 Cor. 5:17). You must consciously and constantly appropriate the enabling power of the indwelling Christ. A literal translation of Phil. 4:13 is "I am a match for all circumstances through the One whose inflow of power keeps enabling me."

You must also *know, reckon* and *yield* your physical body to the fact that you do not have to say "yes" to lust. You are already "dead" to it through Christ's power in His death and resurrection. Read carefully Romans 6:1-6, 11 and 12-14. Don't ever adopt Flip Wilson's theology, "The devil made me do it." The source of lust is in your heart and you are responsible for it (James 1:13-15 and Matt. 15:19). Having taken advantage of the source of your victory over lust, you will be able to take ten actions to overcome lust:

1. Guard Your Lifestyle Constantly. In 1 Thessalonians 4:3 "immorality" includes all forms of sexual sin such as adultery, fornication, homosexuality, lesbianism, sodomy, bestiality, pedophilia and internet pornography. One must understand the kinds of temptation:

- Tempting time of day.

- Tempting places.

---

[59] Warren Wiersbe, *New Testament Bible Exposition Commentary*, vol. 1 (Colorado Springs: Victor, 1989), 24.

- Tempting people. Be careful whom you talk with, go to lunch with, socialize with and spend time on the phone with.

- Tempting kind of music.

- Tempting kinds of movies, including PG's. God's answer is to "flee sexual immorality" (1 Cor. 6:18). Especially note that "sexual immorality" in 1 Thessalonians 4:3 is the Greek word porneias, where we get our word pornography.

2. Guard Your Eyes. Job did this when he confessed, "I have made a covenant with my eyes that I will not look lustily upon a woman" (Job 31:1). Have you done this? Job did not say he would not ever look upon a woman but that he would not look upon a woman with the intent of adultery. The Pharisees tried to keep from looking at a woman, walking around blinded, stumbling and hitting objects until they were called "the bruised and bleeding Pharisees." At the same time they were guilty of adultery in the heart. To make the commandment clear: Men, do not allow your eyes to have any gratification except for your wife. Don't fantasize. Stay out of chat rooms talking to men or women. Don't even hint of sex with others (Eph. 5:3).

3. Guard Your Mind, Hands, and Feet. Remember you can commit adultery in your thoughts. Apply 2 Corinthians 10:5 which states, *"Do not allow any lustful thoughts to fixate in your mind, but take every thought captive in obedience to Christ."* Every man ought to take that verse seriously. Do you know that victories are won or lost in the mind? Jesus says it all starts in your mind. You never commit the act of adultery or fornication until it is first committed in your mind. Many men who brag about not committing physical adultery are committing it in their minds.

Here are some practical tips on guarding your mind:

- Learn the lies of Satan. He says, "It doesn't hurt to look," "It's not cheating as long as you don't meet face to face," "It's ok if you don't go too far," "It does not hurt my marriage." Don't kid yourself. Ninetyeight percent of women consider mental adultery as a "second woman." Many divorces are caused by mental adultery.

- Destroy the tapes of past sexual sins. Men often hit the play button several times a day or week replaying the tapes of past sins. Sincerely turn to Jesus and pray, "Lord, I've been hitting the play button and I want you to yank it out so I will not revisit it." He will hear and answer you.

4. Renew Your Mind Constantly by Internalizing the Word. Note the importance of constant memorization and meditation upon the Word (Romans 12:2 and Psalm 119:9, 11).

5. Don't Believe the Devil's Lie. He states, "The sexual grass is greener on the other side." Seventy percent of second marriages fail.

6. Guard Your Heart. Note Jesus did not say "Out of the Internet, a naked woman, a movie, etc. but out of the heart proceedeth adultery and fornication" (Mark 7:21).

- Have a meaningful time daily with the Lord (Psalm 27:4; Luke 18:1). Begin your day with the Lord and you will have Him when you need Him in that tempting situation.

- Obey the great commandment (Matt. 22:37). Ponder the truth that sexual sins are against God primarily. Thus, when tempted to commit adultery, Joseph asked the question, "How can I do this wicked thing and sin against God?" (Genesis 39:9).

- Do the right things in spite of your feelings. Many believe that a relationship has to be right because it feels right. This is false. Feelings can never be the standard. Only the Word of God is to be the standard.

7. Love Your Spouse for Who She is Today, not when you married her or what you may want her to become (Ephesians 5:25).

8. Make Yourself Accountable to Somebody in the area of internet pornography.

- Call pornography what it is, adultery.

- Genuinely repent and receive God's forgiveness.

- Receive the forgiveness of your wife if possible.

- Get a "Big Dog" filtering system and give the code to your wife or some other person.

- Don't be on the internet in the absence of your wife or late at night.

- If losing the battle with sexual lust, check out the website "covenanteyes.com." It is recommended by Promise Keepers and Focus on the Family. This program will send your accountability partner every week the sites you have visited or use "covenant eyes" designed just for "Mentoring Men for the Master."

- Or get rid of the internet in your home. Jesus commanded us to take radical action to avoid physical and mental adultery (Matthew 5:29).

9. Do Not Pack A Lunch For Lust In Your Life. My mother used to pack my lunch for school, making provision for my food. In Romans 13:14, Paul commands us to *"cloth ourselves with the Lord Jesus Christ and do not make any provision for the flesh."* Many men, including some of you, pack lunches for lust. For example, some plan lunch with their secretary, meet her at certain spots, telephone her regularly, send her emails, have "spiritual" Bible studies and attend "spiritual" socials with her.

C. S. Lewis tells of a "ghost of a man" who was afflicted with sexual lust and it was personified by a red lizard on his shoulder that would whisper in his ears often and he struggled back and forth and one day an angel appeared to this man and said, "I will show you how to kill the lizard." And the ghost of a man said, "I don't want to let him go and I want to let him go." He wrestled many days and came to the end of his wits and said to the angel, "I am ready." And the angel touched the lizard of lust and turned it into a white stallion. This man, who was a ghost of a man, became a real man, mounted the stallion, and the stallion carried him to heaven.

Now that is C. S. Lewis' brilliant way of showing how that which was our downfall, sexual lust, can become our access to glory with a touch of God's grace through Calvary and the Holy Spirit's victory in our lives. That is what needs to happen to some of you men and to some of you women. You need to let the Lord Jesus convert the red lizard into a white stallion. It can happen; but it can only happen when you admit your sin, come clean and call it what God calls it, get accountable about it, receive His forgiveness, move forward without the guilt, deal with it with your spouse, get an accountability partner, take drastic action, throw yourself upon the mercy of the Lord, and seek His grace. Then you will find victory over this sin in your life.

10. Take Drastic Action Now. A family in California took a young mountain lion into their home, fed it from the bottle as a member of the family and thought they had fully domesticated the animal. One day the parents returned home to find that the mountain lion had killed their four year old son and eaten half of him. Men, you can keep on hiding your lust, keeping it from your wife, suppressing it and thinking you have tamed it, but like the mountain lion, it will destroy you one day unless you destroy it. You can be sure that *"your sin of sexual lust will find you out"* (Num. 32:23).[60]

[60] David L. Allen, "How to Have Victory Over Sexual Lust," sermon preached at Macarthur Blvd. Baptist Church, Dallas Texas, 2004.

CHAPTER TWELVE

WORSHIP: ENCOUNTERING GOD'S HOLINESS AND OUR SINFULNESS BECOMING GODLY THROUGH THE DISCIPLINE OF WORSHIP

Worship is the highest activity of the soul. Authentic worship is the closest you and I will ever come to heaven in this life. Heaven will be the everlasting preoccupation of the redeemed in worship to the Lamb of God (Revelations 4 & 5). But if we expect to worship there, we must begin here. In fact our days on this earth should be a rehearsal for heaven. This raises very pertinent questions. What is true worship? What are the requirements of true worship? What are its results? What are our responsibilities in worship?

1. WHAT IS TRUE WORSHIP?

- **Worship is focusing on the worthiness of God.** The word *worship* comes from the Anglo-Saxon word *weorthscype*, which later became *worthship*. To worship God is to ascribe the proper worth to God, to magnify His worthiness, or better, to approach and address God as He is worthy. As the Holy and Almighty God, the Creator and Sustainer of the Universe, the Sovereign Judge to whom we must give an account, He is worthy of all the worth and honor we can give Him and then infinitely more. Notice, for instance, how those around the throne of God in Revelation 4:11 and 5:12 addressed God as "worthy" of so many things. The more we focus on God, the more we understand and appreciate How worthy He is. As we understand and appreciate this, we can't help but respond to Him. Just as an indescribable sunset or a breathtaking mountaintop vista evokes a spontaneous response, so we cannot encounter the worthiness of God without the response of worship.

- **Worship is an encounter with the Living God through the Holy Spirit.** The best example is Isaiah 6. Isaiah saw God by faith. He saw himself. He repented. He was cleansed, and he surrendered to serve the Lord. But worship is more than focus and more than encounter.

- **Worship is loving God with all our hearts, mind and strength.** Consider the analogy of a wedding anniversary. Mine is on July 19th. Suppose on this day I bring home a dozen long stemmed roses for Doris. When she meets me at the door I hold out the roses, and she says, "Oh Bill, they're beautiful. Thank you," and gives me a hug. Then suppose I hold up my hand and say matter-of-factly, "Don't mention it, it's my duty."

What happens? Is not the exercise of duty a noble thing? Do not we honor those we dutifully serve? Not much. Not if there's no heart in it. Dutiful roses are a contradiction in terms. If I am not moved by a spontaneous affection for her as a person, the roses do not honor her. In fact, they belittle her. They are a very thin covering for the fact that she does not have the worth or beauty in my eyes to kindle affection. All I can muster is a calculated expression of marital duty. The real duty of worship is not the outward duty to say or do the liturgy. It is the inward duty, the command—*"Delight yourself in the Lord!"* (Psalm 37:4).

- **Worship is the practical offering of our lives to God.** The Bible says, "Offer your bodies as living sacrifices, holy and pleasing to God—this is your spiritual act of worship" (Rom. 12:2). Why does God want your body? Why doesn't he say, "offer your spirit"? Because without your body you can't do anything on this planet. In eternity you will receive a new, improved, upgraded body, but while you're here on earth, God says, "Give me what you've got!" He's just being practical about worship.

You have heard people say, "I can't make it to the meeting tonight, but I'll be with you in spirit." Do you know what that means? Nothing. It's worthless! As long as you're on earth, your spirit can only be where your body is. If your body isn't there, neither are you.

2. WHAT ARE THE REQUIREMENTS OF TRUE WORSHIP?

- **Worship must be done in Spirit.** John 4:24 says, *"God is Spirit and His worshipers must worship in spirit and in truth."*

- **Worship must be in truth** (John 4:24). Before we can worship in Spirit and in truth we must have within us the One whose name is the Holy Spirit and the *"Spirit of truth"* (John 14:17). He lives only within those who have come to Christ in repentance and faith. Without Him true worship will not happen. Having the Holy Spirit residing within does not guarantee that we will always worship in spirit and truth, but it does mean we can.

  o To worship God in spirit is to worship from the inside out. It means to be sincere in our acts of worship. No matter how spiritual the song you are singing, no matter how poetic the prayer you are praying, if it isn't sincere then it isn't worship, it's hypocrisy.

  o The balance to worshiping in spirit is to worship in truth. We are to worship according to the truth of Scripture. We worship God as He is revealed in the Bible, not as we might want Him to be. We worship Him as a God of both mercy and justice, of love and wrath, a God who both welcomes into Heaven and condemns into hell. We are to worship in response to truth. If we don't we worship in vain. We need to realize that unless the heart is plugged in, there's no electricity for worship.

- **Worship must possess: two Biblical ingredients.**

  o **A sense of awe** –"When we come into the presence of the King of kings and the Lord of the presidents, our appropriate response is one of wonderment and reverence."[61] Illus: My visit to the White House – I was invited to the East Room of White House, to attend a briefing on energy given by the President of the United States. All of us who were invited to the meeting remained seated until the President entered the room. But the moment he entered, everyone stood in respect because we knew we were in

---

[61] Bob Russell, *When God Builds a Church* (West Monroe, LA: Howard, 2000), 43.

the presence of the President of the United States—much more should we stand in awe when in the presence of our holy God.

o **A sense of joy** - Awe in the presence of God doesn't rule out a sense of gladness. Biblical worship is characterized by an overwhelming sense of joy in the hearts of God's people. Not only was the early church filled with a sense of awe (Acts 2:43), they also *"broke bread in their homes and with glad and sincere hearts, praising God and enjoying the favor of all the people"*[62] (Acts 2:46-47).

3. WHAT ARE THE RESULTS OF TRUE BIBLICAL WORSHIP?

- **The Consciousness of God's Holiness**
  Isaiah 6:1 —*"In the year that King Uzziah died, I saw the Lord sitting on a throne, high and lifted up, and the train of His robe filled the temple."*

- **The Conviction of our sinfulness**
  Isaiah 6:5 —*"Woe is me, for I am undone! Because I am a man of unclean lips, And I dwell in the midst of a people of unclean lips; For my eyes have seen the King, The LORD of hosts."*

- **The Comfort of His cleansing**
  Isaiah 6:6-7 – *"Then one of the seraphim flew to me, having in his hand a live coal which he had taken with the tongs from the altar. And he touched my mouth with it, and said: 'Behold, this has touched your lips; Your iniquity is taken away, And your sin purged.'"*

- **The Commitment of our will to serve Him**
  Isaiah 6:8 -*"Also I heard the voice of the Lord, Saying: 'Whom shall I send, And who will go for Us?' Then I said, "Here am I! Send me."*

Evangelism is a by-product of authentic worship. I read of a Baptist who visited a Quaker Church with a friend. There was complete silence for a time. The Baptist brother did not understand the extended quietness and turning to his Quaker friend asked, "When does the service begin?" He replied, "The service will begin when the worship is over." Amen.

---

[62] Ibid., 44.

4. WHAT ARE OUR RESPONSIBILITIES IN WORSHIP?

"Discipline yourself (in worship) for the purpose of godliness" (1 Tim. 4:7b NASB). To worship God throughout a lifetime requires discipline. Without discipline, our worship of God will be thin and inconsistent. Worship can't be diagramed or calculated, for it is the response of a heart in love with God. And yet, we also must be able to think of worship as a discipline, a discipline that must be cultivated just as all relationships must be to remain healthy and grow. People become like their focus. We emulate what we think about.

- **Develop the habit of assembling with other believers weekly where the primary purpose is worship** (Heb. 10:25 and Luke 4:16). There is an element of worship in Christianity that cannot be experienced in private worship or by watching worship. There are some graces and blessings that God gives only in the "meeting together" with other believers.

- **Develop the habit of worshiping privately.** "There is no way," says the Welsh Baptist, Geoffrey Thomas, "that those who neglect secret worship can know communion with God in the public services of the Lord's Day."[63] "If you cannot worship the Lord in the midst of your responsibilities on Monday, it is not very likely that you are worshiping on Sunday!" said A. W. Tozer. He also said, "If you do not know the presence of God in your office, your factory, your home, then God is not in the church when you attend."[64] Let's not fool ourselves. Worship is not a once-a-week event. We can't expect worship to flow from our lips on the Lord's Day if we keep it dammed up in our hearts throughout the week. The waters of worship should never stop flowing from our heart, for God is always God and always worthy of worship. But the flow of worship should be channeled and distilled at least daily into a distinct worship experience.

- **Set specials times to worship.**

---

[63] Quoted in, Donald Whitney, *Spiritual Disciplines for the Christian Life*, (Colorado Springs, Colorado: Navepress, 1991), p. 87.
[64] A.W. Tozer, *Whatever Happened to Worship?* (Camp Hill, Pennsylvania: Christian Publications, 1985), pp. 122-123.

- **Set special places to worship.** A vital part of worship is relationship. The person who roams from church to church misses these vital relationships.

- **Make sure that you do not substitute religious form for real worship.** Russell states, "Worship is more than just singing a few songs, performing a few rituals, and enduring a sermon. We come to experience the presence of God, to acknowledge His authority in our lives, and to worship Him as our Creator."[65] The prophet Amos said, *"I hate, I despise your religious fests; I cannot stand your assemblies. Even though you bring Me burnt offerings and grain offerings, I will not accept them. Though you bring choice fellowship offerings, I will have no regard for them. Away with the noise of your songs! I will not listen to the music of your harps. But let justice roll on like a river, righteousness like a never-failing stream!"* (Amos 5:21-24).

- **Keep your "hands clean" and your "hearts pure"** (Psalm 24:6 and Matt. 5:23-24).

- **Get counsel from those who are growing in private and public worship.**

- **Remember that worship is not something we do one hour a week, but a lifestyle we offer to God.** (Romans 12:1-2).

---

[65] Ibid., Russell, p. 40.

CHAPTER THIRTEEN

SERVICE: IF YOU WOULD BE GREAT

THE DISCIPLINE OF SERVICE FOR THE

PURPOSE OF GODLINESS

1. Every Christian Is Expected To Serve (Psalm 100:2; 1 Cor. 15:58). There are six motives for serving.

- Motivated by obedience (Matthew 4:10).

- Motivated by gratitude (1 Samuel 12:24).

- Motivated by gladness (Psalm 100:2).

- Motivated by forgiveness – Isaiah served not because he felt guilty but because God had taken away his guilt (Isaiah 6:1-8).

- Motivated by humility (John. 13:12-16).

- Motivated by love (1 John 5:3).

2. Every Christian Is Gifted To Serve. 1 Peter 4:10 says: *"As each one has received a gift, minister it to one another, as good stewards of the manifold grace of God."* This verse says two things:

- If you are a Christian you definitely have a spiritual gift.

- God's purpose in giving you that gift is for you to serve others in His kingdom.

3. Serving Is Often Hard Work. (Colossians 1:29; 1 Corinthians 15:58).

4. Serving Is A Satisfying and Fulfilling Work. Jesus said that His serving God was so meaningful that it was like food (John 4:34).

5. Serving Requires Discipline.

- Time

- Inconvenience

- Prayer

- Persecution

- Criticism

- Hard Work

- Consistency

- Persistency

6. Serving Will Be Rewarded. God sees and knows your service to Him and He will never forget it (Hebrews 6:10; Galatians 6:9). Also, serving is the hallmark of greatness in the Kingdom of God (Matthew 20:26).

SIX CRITICAL KEYS IN KNOWING AND EXERCISING YOUR SPIRITUAL GIFTS

Various schemes have been advanced to show us how to discover and exercise our spiritual gifts. Romans 12 is the real answer to this question when interpreted in its contextual setting. These verses give us six guidelines:

1. You must make an unconditional presentation of your total being to the Holy Spirit. It must be voluntary, decisive and wholly (holy) (Rom. 12:1). To sacrifice a part of an animal in the Old Testament was unthinkable. For a Christian to pretend to give the Lord a part of his life—the convenient part—is an abomination, a form of blasphemy. I read somewhere that Wilbur Chapman the great evangelist asked William Booth, "Mr. Booth, would you tell me the secret of your life and why the Lord has used you so." Booth did not have to search for an answer. "God has had all there was of me. Other men have had greater brains and greater opportunities than I, but from the day that I had a vision of what God could do with poor old London, I made up my mind that God would have all there was of William Booth." Have you ever given God all there is of you?

2. You must undergo a definite separation from the thinking of this world. Paul states, *"do not be conformed to this world"* (Rom. 12:2a).

3. You must also experience a radical transformation of your mind. Paul says, *"be ye transformed by the renewing of your mind"* (Rom. 12:2b). You are more than spirit, you are mind and soul. Mind and soul is that part of you which thinks, imagines, remembers, and wills. You may want to do right in your heart, but your mind stops it. I tell you your mind must undergo a radical change through the internalization of God's Word. What you are is what you think, and what you think is what goes into your mind, and is ultimately what you will do. *"for as one thinketh in his heart, so is he…"* (Proverbs 23:7)

4. You must make a thoughtful evaluation of your gifts. *"I would say to every one of you not to estimate himself above or below his real value, but to make a sober rating of himself, in accordance to the degree of faith God has apportioned him"* (Rom. 12:3). Avoid two great errors: 1) sinful exaggeration, and 2) false humiliation.

5. Having done these four things, you will enjoy a thrilling participation in the exercise of your gifts in the body. (Romans 12:4ff). Knowing our gifts, we can know God gives us grace to exercise them, and we can do so with great joy and confidence.

- It is thrilling to know we have an indispensable function in Christ's body. "No one is indispensable," someone said. Paul says the opposite in 1 Corinthians 12. He says every member with his gift is indispensable to the well being of the whole body. Of course, the man who feels he is indispensable and must run the show has made himself unusable in the body.

- It is thrilling to know the God who gives us the gift equips us to exercise it.

- It is thrilling to know God is using me to build up the Body of Jesus in the world.

- It is thrilling just to exercise your gift. There is fulfillment, challenge, and a sense of belonging, and of being linked with Jesus in the great task of redemption.

- The thrill does not diminish. It increases the more I exercise the gift in the power of the Holy Spirit.

6. Finally, these five actions will produce a glorious harmonization in the body of Christ. Let's suppose we are having dinner at church. Somebody drops the dessert on the floor. Let's see how different people would react:

- If you had the gift of prophecy you'd say, "That's what happens when you are not careful."

- If you had the gift of mercy you'd say, "Don't feel badly, it could have happened to anybody."

- If you had the gift of serving you'd say, "Oh, let me clean it up."

- If you had the gift of teaching you'd say, "The reason it fell is, it was too heavy on one side."

- If you had the gift of exhortation you'd say, "Next time let's serve the dessert with the meal."

- If you had the gift of giving you'd say, "I'd be happy to buy a new dessert."

- If you had the gift of administration you'd say, "Jim, would you get the mop? Sue, please pick it up. Mary, help me fix another dessert."

The most beautiful and functional organization on earth is the local church where each member is exercising his or her gifts—thereby creating the real "Body of Christ" in the world—until everyone who observes the church will see Jesus ministering through His body. It is God's purpose that His church be the reincarnation of Jesus on earth.[66]

---

[66] This section was adapted from a sermon tape by the late Dr. Adrian Rogers,"Five Principles for Discovering Your Spiritual Gifts," 10/05/03.

CHAPTER FOURTEEN

MONEY: MANAGE YOUR MONEY FOR THE GLORY OF GOD

GOD'S FIVE LAWS OF SUCCESSFUL MONEY MANAGEMENT

Did you know Jesus said more about money than on any other subject? In fact one third of His teaching concerned material matters. Why? Jesus' answer is the most enlightening word in the Bible about money when He stated, *"He that is faithful in that which is least is faithful in that which is much"* (Luke 16:10). Jesus makes the point that that which is least is money and that which is much is spiritual things.

In simple English, Jesus is saying "Money is very important because it is a test—God's test of a person's spiritual relationship to God." In fact, Jesus declares that if a person is faithful in managing his money he will be faithful in spiritual things and if unfaithful in money, he is unfaithful in spiritual thing's. Furthermore, He asserts that if one is unfaithful in the use of mammon (money) God cannot trust him with spiritual riches. The result, of course, is spiritual disaster. Therefore, I appeal to you, "Manage your money God's way or money will murder you spiritually." But how should we manage money?

The Bible teaches that God has five laws for successful money management:

LAW # I – Secure your money righteously. Money is "filthy lucre." No, money is neither moral nor immoral. But it becomes tainted if earned immorally.

- Money should not be earned in violation of your character.

- Money should not be earned when it injures other persons. For example, cheating, selling drugs, alcohol, or the lottery.

- Money should not be earned to the neglect of family, church, and devotion.

- Money should not be earned to fulfill your greed.

- Money should not be earned by crooked investments.

- Money should not be earned by the desecration of the Lord's Day.

LAW # 2 – Save your money–realistically.

- Don't spend all you make. Save some for the uncertainties of the future. The wisdom of Solomon says, *"Go to the ant, you sluggard! Consider her ways and be wise, which, having no captain, overseer or ruler, provides her supplies in the summer, and gathers her food in the harvest"* (Prov. 6:6-8)

- Save 10% of what you make for unexpected and emergency needs. But do not hoard your money. Invest your money in souls for heavenly reward or in the judgment your money will *"eat your flesh like fire"* (James 5:3). This means that your failure to use your riches for God and others will cause you the keenest remorse. When your eyes see the cruelty of your selfishness and greed (costly jewelry, elegant clothing, extravagant homes, high-priced cars, and huge bank accounts) it will be a hellish experience. James 5:1-5 says, *"Come now, you rich, weep and howl for your miseries that are coming upon you! Your riches are corrupted, and your garments are moth-eaten. Your gold and silver are corroded, and their corrosion will be a witness against you and will eat your flesh like fire. You have heaped up treasure in the last days. Indeed the wages of the laborers who mowed your fields, which you kept back by fraud, cry out; and the cries of the reapers have reached the ears of the Lord of Sabaoth You have lived on the earth in pleasure and luxury; you have fattened your hearts as in a day of slaughter."*

LAW # 3 – Spend your money responsibly. You are as responsible for the 90 % as you are for the 10%.

- Stay out of debt.

- Do not engage in credit buying.

- Do plastic surgery, "cut up your credit cards."

- Avoid impulse buying.

- Avoid ego spending.

- Live within your income.

- Remember, you can buy all kinds of things on credit, but none of it is yours until you pay for it. Purchasing something, when you know you can't pay for it, is stealing.

- Be guided by this economic principle: "If your outgo exceeds your income, your upkeep will be your downfall."

LAW # 4 – Share your money redemptively. Jesus said, *"Do not lay up for yourselves treasures on earth, where moth and rust destroy and where thieves break in and steal. But lay up for yourselves treasures in heaven, where neither moth nor rust destroys and where thieves do not break in and steal"* (Matthew 6:19- 20). How can you lay up treasures in heaven? We do this by spending our money on things which are going to heaven. Stocks, bonds, and money are not going to heaven—only redeemed souls. How can we get souls into heaven?

- Start with the tithe. The tithe is 10% off the top given to God weekly through the storehouse, that is, the local church to pay the expenses of the churches incurred in winning the lost (Malachi 3:10; 1 Corinthians 16:2; and Leviticus 27:30).

- Give *"as God has prospered you"* (1 Corinthians 16:2). Everyone is commanded to tithe (Malachi 3:10, Matthew 23:23), but many should give more. You rob God in offerings as well as tithes (Malachi 3:8) if you do not give *"as God has prospered."*

- Especially invest in areas of direct missions. For example, Mentoring Men for the Master has a goal to train 10,000 pastors and laymen in America.

- Alpha Ministries, Int'l., has a goal to train 100,000 national pastors in India. Ministries which are making an impact for the kingdom of God are worthy of your support.

- Pay your way to the mission field.

LAW # 5 – Send your money—before you. You can't take it with you, but you can send it on before you. How? You can send it before you by using your money to get people into heaven. This is precisely what Jesus commands us to do and promises an incredible reward in heaven for those who do. Jesus said, *"I say unto you, make friends for yourself by the use of your unrighteous mammon so that when you check out, they will welcome you into everlasting habitations"* (Luke. 16:9). This is the teaching of our Lord. By the wise investment of material possessions, we can have part in the eternal blessing of men and women. We can make sure that when we arrive at the gates of heaven, there will be a "welcoming committee" of those who were saved through our sacrificial giving and prayers. These people will thank us saying, "It was you who made it possible for me to be here."

CONCLUSION

I can say all that I have said above in one statement: God is measuring you and me by the way we secure our money, the way we save our money, the way we spend our money, the way we share our money, and the way we are sending our money ahead.

- Are you securing your money *righteously?*

- Are you saving your money *realistically?*

- Are you spending your money *responsibly?*

- Are you sharing your money *redemptively?*

- Are you sending your money *before you?*

CHAPTER FIFTEEN

MENTORING YOUR WIFE[67]

Any man who is serious about mentoring and serious about having a godly home that is filled with relationships that honor the Lord will eventually come to the realization that the Bible commands him to mentor his wife. "Mentor my wife?" you say. "Yes, mentor your wife!"

In Ephesians 5 and 6 the apostle Paul gives us very specific instructions on what the relationships inside our homes are supposed to look like in order that we might have godly homes and God-honoring interaction with each other inside of the home.

Mentorees who wish to be obedient to God and to become mentors themselves understand that according to the Scripture, we must start in our own homes with our own wives. If we cannot do this, I do not believe that we can honestly say that we are prepared to mentor anyone. When I realized that my wife's spiritual condition was my responsibility under God, I began to mentor my wife and my home was completely changed and revolutionized as I began to do what the Bible commands us to do.

In order for you to begin mentoring your wife you must first meet three crucial criteria.

- You must be born again, saved, converted, regenerated, a new creation (John 3:3 and 2 Corinthians 5:17).

- You must be controlled by the Holy Spirit, and the Word of God (Ephesians 5:18 and Colossians 3:15-16).

- You must be willing to emulate Christ in His role as servant leader (John 13:14-15).

---

[67] For further reading see Larry S. McDonald, "Shepherding the Pastor's Wife," DMin dissertation (Jackson, MS: Reformed Theolgocial Seminary, 1986).

If you meet these criteria, you are ready to begin mentoring your wife. Let us look at Ephesians 5:25-27 and please note the instruction from the Scripture on how we are to mentor our wives.

- In verse 25 we are told to serve our wives sacrificially. Christ sacrificed Himself for the church, so you must also sacrifice and put your wife's needs above your own.

- In verse 26 we are told to serve our wives *sanctifyingly* with the Word.

  o What does it mean to sanctify your wife with the Word? It means at least five things.

    • Read the Bible with your wife.

    • Study the Bible with your wife.

    • Internalize the Bible with your wife.

    • Discuss the Bible with your wife.

    • Show her how to apply the Bible in life.

  o What are the results of sanctifying your wife with the Word?

    • Your wife will be purified ("not having spot or wrinkle").

    • A spot is something that is caused from the outside, it is external. Just as Jesus protects the church from the outside corruption of the world, so you will protect your wife from the external forces of this sinful world when you sanctify her with the Word of God.

    • A wrinkle is caused internally. It is the outward manifestation of internal decay. Just as Jesus protects us from the internal forces of sin and self by washing us with the Word, so you will protect your wife when you sanctify her with the Word of God.

- Serve your wife *selflessly* (Eph. 5:28-29). The Scripture says that Jesus nourishes and cherishes the church because it is His body. By giving His life for the church, He has selflessly esteemed us above Himself. If we are going to emulate Him and love our wives just as He loved the church, then we must also take on this two-fold responsibility of nourishing and cherishing our wives. For just as He delivered His bride from the dangers of sin, death, and Hell, so you must provide for, protect, preserve, and love your bride, giving her comfort and security through your warm and tender affection.[68]

---

[68] This chapter was contributed by my Assistant in Mentoring, Michael Thad Faulk, who shares his wonderful experience in mentoring his wife.

CHAPTER SIXTEEN

ATTITUDE—NOT APTITUDE—IS THE ISSUE

Phil. 2:3-11

The mentoree's attitude, not his aptitude, is the major factor in his being successfully mentored. What then is the attitude a mentoree needs? Paul answers this when he states,

"Let nothing be done through selfish ambition or conceit, but in lowliness of mind let each esteem others better than himself. Let each of you look out not only for his own interests, but also for the interests of others. Let this mind [attitude] be in you which was also in Christ Jesus, who, though existing in the form of God, did not consider equality with God, something to cling to, but made Himself of no reputation, taking the form of a bondservant,and coming in the likeness of men. And being found in appearance as a man, He humbled Himself and became obedient to the point of death, even the death of the cross. Therefore, God also has highly exalted Him and given Him the name which is above every name, that at the name of Jesus every knee should bow, of those in heaven, and of those on earth, and of those under the earth, and that every tongue should confess that Jesus Christ is Lord, to the glory of God the Father" (Phil. 2:3-11).

Notice the key phrase,"Let this attitude be in you which was in Christ." Here is the foremost need of every mentoree—the mind or attitude of Christ. If mentorees have this attitude, it will solve all their other problems—from a feeling of inadequacy to memorizing Scripture and unwillingness to discipline one's life. But what is the attitude of Christ? Paul goes on to describe four characteristics of the attitude of Christ:

1. The attitude of Christ was the ATTITUDE OF SELFDENIAL. Note the words, "Though existing in the form of God, He did not consider His equality with God something to cling to, but made Himself of no reputation or emptied Himself."Before coming to earth, Jesus was the

owner, and ruler of the universe—the praise and glory of heaven. Perfect in His Person, His privileges, His power, His possessions. The Bible declares that though Jesus was rich in eternity, He became poor on this earth that He through His poverty would make us rich (2 Corinthians 8:9 and Matthew 8:20). How poor was He? He was born in a stable, lived as a peasant, and was buried in a borrowed tomb. He was too poor even to own a donkey. When He died, He had no property to leave but only peace (John 14:27). And just think—He did all this willingly in order to serve the redemptive purposes of God—dying a criminal's death on the cross for wretched sinners like us.

2. Not only did He have the attitude of self-denial, but an ATTITUDE OF SUBMISSION. Jesus submitted Himself entirely to His Father's will—not His own. Consider the following words of Jesus:

- "My meat is to do the will of Him who sent me and finish His work" (John. 4:34).

- "For I have come down from heaven, not to do My own will, but the will of Him who sent me"(John. 6:38).

- "I do not seek My own will but the will of the Father who sent Me" (John. 5:30).

How different our world would be if there were a spirit of submission among all Christians. But we have a spirit of rebellion rather than submission:

- We need to be submissive in the area of personal choices. For example in abortion.

- We need to be submissive in marriage (Ephesians 5:22).

- We need to be submissive in the work place (Ephesians 6:5ff).

- We need to be submissive in the church (Hebrews 13:17).

Two women were fussing and fighting in the church at Philippi. Paul was telling them they could solve the problem by being submissive or having the same mind in the Lord (Philippians 4:2).

3. But Jesus also had the ATTITUDE OF SERVICE. Jesus never asked anyone to serve Him, He always served others (Matthew 20:28). The disciples were disputing who was greatest in the kingdom, and He states "... but whoever desires to become great among you, let him be your servant" (Matthew 20:26).

Do you realize the last time we see Jesus serving in this world that He is on His knees, performing the work of a slave, washing His disciples' feet, including Judas, the traitor? Not one disciple would get up and wash the disciples' feet. How surprised they were when Jesus arose from the table, laid aside His robe, and girded Himself with the garment of the slave—a towel—and washed the disciples' feet. Jesus asked, "Do you know what I have done to you? You call Me Teacher and Lord, and you say well, for so I am. If I then, your Lord and Teacher, have washed your feet, you also ought to wash one another's feet" (John. 13:12-14).

Why hadn't they already washed their feet? Because they did not have the attitude of serving but of being served.

Statistics tell us that 10% of church members do 100% of the serving and 20% give 80% of the money. "If the average car had as many dysfunctional parts as the average church, it would not run downhill."

4. Finally, Jesus went far beyond self-denial, submission, and serving, to one of–SUPREME SACRIFICE. The Scripture says, "He became obedient unto death," even going so far as actually to die a criminal's death on the cross. The time came when Jesus could have gone back to heaven, but He set His face steadfast for Jerusalem to be crucified (Luke 9:51). Peter forbade Him to go and Jesus said to Peter, "Get behind me, Satan" (Matthew 16:23).

- On that cross Jesus became sin for us, but He prayed "...Not my will but thine be done" (Matthew 26:39).

- He was cast into outer darkness, into torments like hell, forsaken by His Father, crying out, "My God, My God, why hast Thou forsaken Me?" (Matthew 27:46; Mark 15:34).

Many Christians are willing to serve, if it costs them nothing. At a religious festival in Brazil, a missionary saw a sign which read, "Cheap Crosses." And he thought, "That's what most Christians are looking for today—cheap crosses." My Lord's cross was not cheap. Why should mine be?

Thank God for a few in our rising generation who dare to sacrifice for Christ. "A church council was planning the annual "Youth Sunday" program, and one of the youth suggested that the teenagers serve as ushers, lead in prayer, bring special music. One of the teens stood up and said, 'Quite frankly, we're tired of being asked to do little things. We'd like to do something difficult this year, and maybe keep it going all year long. The kids have talked and prayed about this, and we'd like to work with our trustees in remodeling that basement room so it can be used for a classroom. And we'd like to start visiting our elderly members each week and taking them cassettes of the services. And, if it's OK, we'd like to have a weekly witness on Sunday afternoons in the park. We hope this is OK with you.' "[69]

Thus, we have seen the primary need of mentorees and all Christians is to have the mind of the Christ so they will think and act like Christ.

But a question remains, How does one get such an attitude? Paul answered when he made this loving appeal to every born again individual, "I beseech you therefore, brethren, by the mercies of God, that you present your bodies a living sacrifice, holy, acceptable to God, which is your reasonable service. And do not be conformed to this world, but be transformed by the renewing of your mind, that you may prove what is that good and acceptable and perfect will of God" (Rom. 12:1-2). Notice the transformation comes by a changing of the mind or attitude. If you would have the "attitude" of Christ, it must be changed supernaturally, for naturally it is self-seeking, unsubmissive, self-serving, and unsacrificial to the core. How can it be changed? By internalizing the Word of God:

- We must know the Word in our heads by diligent study.

- We must stow it in our hearts by memorization and meditation.

- We must show it in our lives by obeying its teaching.

- Then we can sow it in our world by our witness.

---

[69] Warren Wiersbe, *The Bible Exposition Commentary*, Vol. 2 (Colorado Springs: Victor, 2001), 76.

When a mentoree possesses the attitude of self-denial, of submission, of service and sacrifice, he will be willing to discipline his body, mind, and spirit and allow his mentor to hold him accountable for the acts required of him. So the basic issue in being mentored is not one's aptitude but his attitude.

APPENDIX ONE

Victory Pledge

I am too anointed to be disappointed,
I am too blessed to be depressed,
I am too chosen to be frozen,
I am too elected to be rejected,
I am too inspired to be tired,
I have more to shout about than to pout about,
And I have more to sing about
Than complain about.

APPENDIX TWO

Pledge to my Bible

This is my Bible.
It is God's inerrant word.
It is my most valuable earthly possession.
I will, therefore, make it a lamp unto my feet and a light
unto my path, and I will hide its words in my heart that I
might not sin against God.

The Bible is God talking to me personally.
I will, therefore, listen to it carefully and obey it fully.
And I will endeavor to internalize it in my life by doing
four things:

- I will Know it in my head by diligent study;

- I will Stow it in my heart by memorization and meditation;

- I will Show it in my life by obeying its teachings; and

- I will Sow it in my world by witnessing.

Hereafter I will never be the same, never, never, never!
In the name of Jesus, for His honor and glory, both now and
forever more,
Amen.

APPENDIX THREE

10 VITAL SIGNS OF A HEALTHY MENTOREE

Vital signs help medical professionals quickly assess the physical health of patients under their care. Ten (10) vital signs help Mentors assess the spiritual health of mentorees under their care. Please diagnose your spiritual health on the basis of the following "Vital Signs." In the physical realm, a patient may possess a perfect score; however, in the spiritual realm, the mentoree will always find room to improve. The important factor, however, is that he is showing continuing growth in all areas, and is determined to improve in areas where he is the weakest. Are there areas of your life in which you need and desire to improve? Determine today how you can become a healthier mentoree during this semester. May I suggest that you prayerfully set a goal in those areas in which you need to show improvement this semester. So on a scale of 1 to 10 (10 being the highest) estimate your present state and the state you are determined to be at the end of the semester. Enlist an accountability partner if you need one and Thad and I are available to "come alongside" you for the calling.

1. Are you spending 15 minutes daily to internalize the Word of God? (Psalm 119:11)

Beginning Score _____ End Goal _____.

2. Are you seeking to have a meaningful time daily with the Lord? (Psalm 27:4)

Beginning Score_____ End Goal _____

3. Are you consciously surrendering to the Holy Spirit each day that He may fill (control) you and use you? (Ephesians 5:18)

Beginning Score _____ End Goal _____

4. Are you a member of a local church and contributing faithfully to its ministry? (Hebrews 10:25)

Beginning Score_____ End Goal_____

5. Are you inter-relating with at least one or more persons in order to share your life with them? (1 Thess. 2:8)

Beginning Score _____ End Goal _____

6. Are you seeking to win people to Christ regularly? (Philemon 1:6 NIV)

Beginning Score_____ End Goal _____

7. Are you investing your money redemptively with God, beginning with the tithe? (2 Cor. 9:6-11)

Beginning Score _____ End Goal_____

8. Do you exercise your physical body in a definite regimen at least 3 days per week? (1 Cor. 9:26-27)

Beginning Score _____ End Goal_____

9. Are you wholeheartedly devoted to the care of your family, especially your spouse? (1 Timothy 5:8)

Beginning Score _____ End Goal _____

10. Are you careful not to sin but when you do, do you instantly confess it, repent of it, and receive Christ's cleansing? (1 John 1:9)

Beginning Score_____ End Goal_____

Total Beginning Score _____Total Goal End_____

APPENDIX FOUR

VERSES ON THE IMPORTANT TEACHINGS OF

THE BIBLE

1. God-Breathed Word
2 Timothy 3:16-17
1 Peter 1:20-21
Hebrews 4:12
Psalm 19:7

2. Bible Intake
Psalm 119:9, 11
Psalm 119:105
Matthew 4:4
1 Peter 2:2
Job 23:12

3. Greatness of God
Psalm 145:3
Isaiah 40:28-31
Romans 11:36
1 Timothy 6:16

4. The Trinity
Matthew 3:16-17
Genesis 1:26
2 Corinthians 13:14
Ephesians 1:3-14

5. Relationship with God
Philippians 3:8-10 CEV
Jeremiah 9:23-24a
Mark 12:30-31

6. Worship
John 4:24
Psalm 95:6
Isaiah 6:1-8
Matthew 4:10

7. Prayer
Jeremiah 33:3
Matthew 7:7-11
Luke 11:13
Matthew 6:16

8. Creation
Genesis 1:1-2
John 1:1-3
Colossians 1:16-17

9. The Devil
John 8:44
James 4:7
1 John 4:4
Luke 10:19

10. Home
Psalm 127:1
Proverbs 12:7
Joshua 24:15c

11. Marriage
Genesis 2:24-25
Hebrews 13:4
Ephesians 5:22, 25

12. Children and Youth
Ecclesiastes 12:1
1 Timothy 4:12
Proverbs 22:6
Lamentations 3:27

13. Sin
Ezekiel 18:4
Isaiah 59:1-2
Roman 3:23

14. Unpardonable Sin
Mark 3:28-29

15. Temptation
James 1:13-14
1 Corinthians 10:13

16. Worldliness
1 John 2:15-17
Romans 12:2

17. Pride
Daniel 4:37b
Proverbs 16:18
James 4:6
1 Peter 5:5

18. Alcohol
Proverbs 20:1
Ephesians 5:18
1 Thessalonians 5:22
Isaiah 5:11

19. Homosexuality / Lesbianism
Leviticus 18:22
Romans 1:26-27
1 Corinthians 6:9-11
Jude 1:7
Hebrews 13:4

20. Divorce
Malachi 2:16
Matthew 5:32
Matthew 19:9
1 Corinthians 7:10-15

21. Tongue – Gossip
Proverbs 10:19
Proverbs 18:21
Psalms 39:1
James 1:26
James 3:5,8

22. Virgin Birth
Luke 1:35
Isaiah 7:14
Matthew 1:23

23. Who Jesus Is
John 1:14
Philippians 2:9-11
Colossians 2:9-10

24. What Jesus Did
Matthew 1:21
Isaiah 53:4-6
Leviticus 17:11
Galatians 6:14
Hebrews 9:22
1 Peter 1:18-19

25. The Resurrection of Christ
Romans 1:4
1 Corinthians 15:20
Romans 14:9
Philippians 3:10

26. Repentance
2 Peter 3:9
2 Chronicles 7:14
Luke 13:3, 5
Isaiah 55:7

27. Faith
Hebrews 11:6
Romans 10:17
Romans 14:23b
Ephesians 2:8-9
James 2:26
Hebrews 11:1

28. Grace
Ephesians 2:8-9
Genesis 6:8
Romans 5:20b
2 Corinthians 9:8
Titus 2:11-14

29. New Birth
Ezekiel 36:26
John 3:3,5
2 Corinthians 5:17
1 Peter 1:23

30. Justification
Genesis 15:6
Romans 3:20
Romans 3:24
Romans 5:1

31. Adoption
Ephesians 1:5
Romans 8:15
Galatians 4:4-5

32. Righteousness
Isaiah 64:6
2 Corinthians 5:21
Philippians 3:9
1 Corinthians 15:34

33. Perseverance of the Saints
Psalm 37:24
1 John 2:19
1 John 3:9 ESV
2 Peter 2:21-22

34. Assurance of Salvation
1 John 5:13
John 10:28
John 5:24

35. Sanctification
1 Thessalonians 5:23
Hebrews 12:14
1 Thessalonians 4:7
Titus 2:11-14
Romans 6:1-14

36. Glorification
1 John 3:2-3
Romans 8:30
Philippians 1:6
Philippians 3:21

37. The Holy Spirit
John 14:16-17
John 16:7-11

38. Life in the Spirit
Ephesians 5:18-20
Galatians 5:16-22
Hebrews 13:5

39. The Church
Matthew 16:18
1 Peter 2:9
Romans 12:4
1 Corinthians 12:26-27
Hebrews 10:25

40. Soul-winning / Missions
Proverbs 11:30b
Luke 14:23
Matthew 28:18-20
Acts 1:8
Luke 24:47-49
John 20:21
Matthew 4:19

41. Baptism
Matthew 3:15-17
Matthew 28:19
Acts 2:38
Romans 6:3-5

42. Lord's Supper
Luke 22:19-20
1 Corinthians 11:26-32

43. Discipleship
John 8:31-32
Luke 14:26
Luke 9:62
Mark 8:35

44. Mentoring
1 Thessalonians 2:8 NIV
2 Timothy 2:2

45. Tithing
Malachi 3:8-10
Matthew 23:23
Leviticus 27:30

46. Service
Psalm 116:12
Hebrews 6:10
Matthew 10:42
Matthew 5:13-16
Ephesians 2:10

47. Revival
2 Chronicles 7:14
Psalm 85:6
Habakkuk 3:2
Acts 3:19

48. Church and State
Matthew 22:21
Romans 13:1-7

49. Healing
James 5:14-16
Psalm 107:20
Proverbs 4:20-22

50. Death
Psalm 116:15
Hebrews 9:27
Philippians 1:21
Revelation 1:18
Revelation 21:4

51. Hell
Luke 16:19-31
Psalm 9:17
Revelation 21:8

52. Heaven
John 14:1-3
Revelation 21:4
1 Peter 3-5
Philippians 1:21-23

53. Rapture
1 Thessalonians 4:16-18
1 Corinthians 15:51-58

54. Second Coming
Matthew 24:36
Matthew 24:44
Acts 1:11
Revelation 19:11-20

55. Judgment Seat of Christ
2 Corinthians 5:10
Romans 14:12
1 Corinthians 3:11-15

56. Great White Throne Judgment
Revelation 20:11-15

57. Love
John 13:35
1 John 4:7-8
Matthew 5:44
1 Corinthians 13:1-13

58. Joy
Nehemiah 8:10
Philippians 4:4
Romans 14:17
John 15:11

59. Peace
Philippians 4:6-7
Isaiah 26:3
Romans 5:1
John 16:33
Isaiah 48:22

60. Anger
James 1:19-20
Ephesians 4:31
Proverbs 15:1

61. Dealing with Sin
1 John 1:8-9
1 Corinthians 10:13
Romans 6:11-13
Galatians 6:1-2
James 4:7-8
Ephesians 6:10-12

62. Depression
Psalm 42:5
Lamentations 3:19-23
2 Corinthians 1:8b-9
Isaiah 43:1b-2
Psalm 34:17-18
2 Corinthians 4:8-10

63. Guilt
Romans 8:1-2
Psalms 51:9-10
Proverbs 28:13
Psalms 32:1-2
2 Corinthians 7:10
James 5:16

64. Perfectionism
Galatians 3:3
Psalms 127:1-2
Ephesians 2:8-9
Ecclesiastes 2:10-11
2 Corinthians 12:9
Luke 10:40-42

65. Patience
Luke 21:19
2 Peter 3:9
James 5:8

66. Comfort
Hebrews 13:5
Isaiah 41:10, 13

67. Money / Stewardship
Deuteronomy 8:18
Luke 12:15
1 Timothy 6:17-20
James 5:1-5
Psalm 37:25

68. Sex / Sexual Purity
Proverbs 6:32
Exodus 20:14
Matthew 5:28
Song of Solomon 2:7 HCSB
2 Timothy 2:22
Job 31:1
1 Thessalonians 4:3-5
Ephesians 5:3 NIV

69. Faithfulness
Revelation 2:10c
1 Corinthians 4:2
1 Corinthians 15:58

70. Self-Discipline
2 Timothy 1:7
1 Timothy 4:7b NASB
Hebrews 12:11 NASB

71. Thanksgiving
Psalm 103:1-5
Ephesians 5:20
1 Thessalonians 5:18

72. Stress / Anxiety
Psalm 118:5-6
Matthew 11:28-30
Psalm 73:26
Philippians 4:6-7
2 Corinthians 4:16-18
1 Peter 5:6-7

73. Knowing God's Will
Proverbs 16:9
Proverbs 3:5-7
Jeremiah 29:11-13
Romans 12:2
Isaiah 30:21
1 John 5:14-15

74. Self-Image
Psalms 139:13-14a
1 Samuel 16:7b
Jeremiah 9:23-24a
Philippians 2:3-5
1 Peter 3:3-4

75. Suffering
Romans 5:2b-5
1 Peter 4:12-13
1 Peter 1:6b-7
2 Corinthians 1:3-4
James 1:2-4
James 1:12

76. Forgiveness
Ephesians 4:32
Matthew 6:12, 14-15

APPENDIX FIVE

Some Accountability Questions Used in MMM

1. Have you spent quality and quantity time with the Lord this week?

2. Can you honestly write "Christ" in the following blank, "For me to live is _____" ? (Phil. 1:21).

3. Have you chosen some action recently that you knew made you unpopular with your peers but which pleased God?

4. Have you chosen an action to please man, which you knew displeased God?

5. Can you name a sin of which you really repented in recent days?

6. Are you obeying Ephesians 4:29?

7. Do you "obey and submit" to those the Lord has placed over you? (Heb. 13:17).

8. Do you resent being told you are wrong or do you receive it gratefully and repentantly?

9. Name one way you have significantly been changed by mentoring.

10. Do you really believe Luke 6:38 and see it working in your life?

11. Would you like to hear that something bad has happened to someone you know?

12. Have you sacrificed time and money and denied yourself of something in order to serve someone else?

13. Are you dwelling with your wife according to understanding (1 Peter 3:7)? Are you living with your wife in an intelligent, kind and patient consideration of her great unlikeness to you? (1 Peter 3:7).

14. If your answer to question thirteen is negative, do you realize the spiritual devastation it is causing you?

15. Have you lied, exaggerated, added to, or taken away from the truth within the last week?

16. Is the kingdom of God more important to you than making money?

17. If God granted you one request what would you choose?

18. If you knew Jesus was coming today, is there some act, attitude, habit you would quit?

19. Have you told or listened to a dirty joke this week?

20. Have you done something this week that you do not want your wife to know?

21. Have you been sexually pure? This includes your hands, eyes, and your mind.

22. Have you shared your faith or invited anyone to church recently?

23. Do you give your ministry your best and do you serve for God's glory not your own?

24. Did you put your family first after God this week?

25. Are you faithfully tithing through your church each week?

26. Are you willing to discipline yourself though it requires you to deny creature comforts?

27. How's your relationship with your spouse (or person you're seeing regularly)?

28. How's your relationship with your children?

29. What temptations are you facing today and how are you dealing with them?

30. How has your thought life been this week?

31. Which is more important to you: your wife's spirit and soul or her body?

32. With whom have you shared the gospel during the past week?

33. Name one way you loved your wife this week which reflected the way Christ loved the church.

34. Name one thing you avoided this week to keep you from sinning.

35. Name one person you ministered to this week at some sacrifice.

36. How much quiet time have you spent with the Lord this week?

37. Are you reading five chapters in the NT each week?

38. Name one thing you denied yourself in order to serve Jesus and people.

39. Have you bragged about one good thing in your life this week?

40. Name one way you may have used your hands, feet, eyes or mind to fulfill some lustful desire.

41. Name one place you have been which stimulated your temptation.

42. Name one person you have seen, telephoned or contacted that you should not have done this week.

43. Have you worshiped truly and biblically recently?

44. Is there any area of your life not under the Lordship of Christ?

45. Do you keep your promises, dates and appointments to a "T"?

46. Are you monitoring your eyes continually?

47. Are you repenting when these accountability questions point out a sin you are committing?

APPENDIX SIX

10 Scriptural Imperatives For

Continuing Spiritual Growth

(The 10 I's)

1. Internalizing the Word – Joshua 1:8; James 1:18-25

2. Infilling of the Holy Spirit – Ephesians 5:18

3. Intimacy with the Father – Psalm 27:4

4. Intentional Involvement in the World Mission of Christ – Matthew 28:18-20

5. Interrelating with others to share your life – (Mentoring) - 1 Thessalonians 2:8

6. Investing your money redemptively with the Lord, beginning with the tithe to your church –Matthew 6:19-20

7. Identification with, support of, and service in a local church – Hebrews 10:25

8. Intense devotion to one's family, especially his wife - Ephesians 5:25

9. Intentional discipline of the physical body – 1 Corinthians 9:27

10. Instant repentance and cleansing from all sin – Psalm 51:17.

APPENDIX SEVEN

A TIME TO LAUGH –BIBLE TRIVIA

Ecless. 3:4

Dr. Bill Bennett

Q. When did Baptists have their beginning?
A. In Genesis 14 when Abraham said to Lot, "You go your way and I'll go mine."

Q. What was Eve's Telephone number in the Garden?
A. Adam-812

Q. What is the most appropriate verse in the Bible pertaining to the Nursery?
A. "They shall not all sleep, but they shall all be changed." (1 Cor. 15:51)

Q. Who was the most successful doctor in the Bible?
A. Job – he has the most patients.

Q. What did Noah say to his two sons fishing off the ark?
A. Go easy on the bait, sons, we only have two worms.

Q. Where is tobacco mentioned in the Bible?
A. In Genesis, where it says Rebekah lighted off a camel.

Q What is the only state mentioned in the Bible?
A. Arkansas – Genesis says Noah looked out the "Arkansaw."

Q. Where is medicine mentioned in the Bible?
A. Exodus, which says God gave Moses two tablets.

Q. Who was the straightest person in the Bible?
A. Joseph – Pharaoh made him a ruler.

Q. Why couldn't they play cards on the ark?
A. Because Mrs. Noah sat on the deck.

Q. Who was the smallest person in the Bible?
A. Simon Peter – the Bible says he slept on his watch.

Q. Why is it wrong to play marbles?
A. Because Jesus said, "Marble ye not."

Q. The oldest man who ever lived died before his father did. Who was this?
A. Methuselah. Enoch, his father, was raptured to heaven and never died.

Q. Why do we know Nero was a Christian after all?
A. Because of the hymn, "Nero My God To Thee."

Q. Where is tennis mentioned in the Bible?
A. In Genesis where it says Joseph served in Pharaoh's court.

Q. What plant did Noah want to keep off the ark?
A. Leeks.

Q. What was the name of Noah's wife?
A. Joan of Ark.

Q. Where is the US Postal Service mentioned in the Bible?
A. Genesis, where it says, "'God made all creeping things."

Q. Who spoke the very day he was born?
A. Job – he "cursed the day he was born."

Q. What is the favorite verse of an old maid?
A. If any man will, let him come unto me.

Q. How do we know Paul was probably not a Southern Baptist?
A. Because he did not keep count of his baptisms.

Q. Why have some assumed that Corinth was a Southern Baptist Church?
A. Because it was divided 4 ways.

Q. What is the difference between Methodists and Baptists?
A. Methodists teach falling from grace and Baptists practice it.

Q. What is the difference in pastors and deacons?
A. Pastors are paid for being good; deacons are good for nothing.

Q. What is the biblical proof that Jesus was a Baptist?
A. Because he asked a Baptist, John, to baptize him.

Q. What did Adam and Eve do after leaving the garden?
A. They raised Cain.

Q. When is Jesus coming again?
A. According to the Bible, "when He gets good and ready."

Q. Where was Jesus going when he was 20 years old?
A. Into 21.

Q. What is the favorite verse of dentists?
A. Psalms 81:10 —"Open your mouth wide and I will fill it."

Q. Did the Media ever give Jesus any trouble?
A. Yes, Mark's gospel says the people could not see Jesus because of the press.

Q. What kind of man was Boaz before he married?
A. He was Ruthless.

Q. What do they call pastors in Germany?
A. German Shepherds.

Q. Who was the greatest financier in the Bible?
A. Noah – He was floating his stock while everyone else was in liquidation.

Q. Who was the greatest female financier in the Bible?
A. Pharaoh's daughter – She went down to the bank of the Nile and drew out a little prophet.

Q. What kind of motor vehicles are in the Bible?
A. Jehovah drove Adam and Eve out of the garden in a Fury. David's Triumph was heard throughout the land. Honda, because the apostles were all in one Accord.

Q. Who was the greatest comedian in the Bible?
A. Samson, because he brought down the house.

Q. What excuse did Adam give to his children as to why he no longer lived in Eden?
A. Your mother ate us out of house and home.

Q. Who was the biggest sinner in history?
A. Moses. He broke all 10 commandments at once.

Q. Which area of Palestine was especially wealthy?
A. The area around Jordan. The banks were always overflowing.

Q. Who was the greatest babysitter mentioned in the Bible?
A. David – He rocked Goliath to a very deep sleep in a second.

Q. Which Bible character had no parents?
A. Joshua, son of Nun.

Q. Who was the fastest runner in history?
A. Adam – He was first in the human race.

SELECTED BIBLIOGRAPHY

Akin, Daniel. A Theology of the Church, Nashville, Tennessee: B & H. Academic, 2007.

Arn, Win and Charles Arn. The Masters Plan for Making Disciples: Every Christian an Effective Witness through an Enabling Church, 2nd ed. Grand Rapids: Baker, 1998.

Barna, George. Growing True Disciples: New Strategies for Producing Genuine Followers of Christ. Colorado Springs: WaterBrook, 2001.

Biel, Bob. Mentoring: How to Find a Mentor and How to Become One, Lake Mary, Florida: Aylen Publishing, 1196, 2005.

Boa, Kenneth, Conformed to His Image, Grand Rapids, Michigan: Zondervan, 2001.

Boice, James Montgomery. Christ's Call to Discipleship. Grand Rapids: Kregel, 1998.

Bruce, A. B. The Training of the Twelve: Timeless Principles for Leadership Development, 2 ed. Grand Rapids: Kregel Classics, 2000.

Clinton, J. Robert. The Making of a Leader: Recognizing the Lessons and Stages of Leadership Development. Colorado Springs: NavPress, 1988.

Coleman, Robert E. The Master Plan of Discipleship. Grand Rapids: Revell, 1998.

_____. The Master Plan of Evangelism, reprint edition. Grand Rapids: Revell, 2006.

Due, Carson. Mentoring Leaders: Wisdom for Developing Character, Calling, and Competency. Grand Rapids: Baker, 2005.

Egeler, Daniel.Mentoring Millennials: Shaping the Next Hero Generation. Colorado Springs: NavPress, 2003.

Eims, LeRoy. The Lost Art of Disciplemaking. Grand Rapids: Zondervan, 1998.

Engstrom, Ted W.ÄThe Fine Art of Mentoring: Passing on to Others What God has Given to You. Brentwood, TN: Wolgemuth and Hyatt, 1989.

Foster, Richard, The Challenge of the Disciplined Life, New York, N. Y.:Harper Collins Productions, 1985

Forman, Rowland, Jeff Jones, and Bruce Miller. The Leadership Baton: An Intentional Strategy for Developing Leaders in Your Church. Grand Rapids: Zondervan, 2004.

Henrichsen, Walter A. Disciples are Made, Not Born. Victor, 2002.

Hendricks, Howard and William Hendricks. As Iron Sharpents Iron: Building Character in a Mentorong Relationship. Chicago: Moody, 1999

Houston, James M.The Mentored Life: From Individualism to Personhood. Colorado Springs: NavPress, 2002.

Hull, Bill. The Disciple-Making Pastor: The Key to Building Healthy Christians in Today's Church. Old Tappan, NJ: Revell, 1988.

_____. New Century Disciplemaking: Applying Jesus' Ideas for the Future. Grand Rapids: Revell. 1997.

Jeremiah, David. God in You: Releasing the Power of the Holy Spirit in Your Life, Sisterd, Oregon: Multnomah Publishers, 1998.

Jones, Timothy K. Finding a Spiritual Friend: How Friends and Mentors Can Make Your Faith Grow. Nashville: Upper Room, 1998.

Kellemen, Robert W. Spiritual Friends: A Methodology Of Soul Care And Spiritual Direction. Crown Point, IN: Rpm Books, 2004.

_____. Soul Physicians: A Theology of Soul Care And Spiritual Direction, rev. ed. Crown Point, IN: Rpm Books, 2005.

Kroll, Woodrow, When God Doesn't Answer, Grand Rapids, Michigan: Baker Books, 1997.

McNeal, Reggie. A Work of Heart: Understanding How God Shapes Spiritual Leaders. Jossey-Bass, 2000.

Minirth, Frank, You Can, Nashville, Tennessee: Thomas Nelson Publishers, 1994

Moon, Gary W. and David G. Benner, eds. Spiritual Direction and the Care of Souls: A Guide to Christian Approaches and Practices. Downers Grove: InterVarsity, 2004.

Ogden, Greg. Transforming Discipleship: Making Disciples a Few at a Time. Downers Grove: InterVarsity, 2003.

Petersen, Jim. Lifestyle Discipleship: The Challenge of Following Jesus in Today's World. Colorado Springs: NavPress, 1993.

Rainer, Thom S. and Eric Geiger. Simple Church: Returning to God's Process for Making Disciples. Nashville: B & H, 2006.

Reese, Randy D. and Keith R. Anderson. Spiritual Mentoring: A Guide for Seeking and Giving Direction. Downers Grove: InterVarsity, 1999.

Reid, Alvin,Introduction to Evangelism, Nashville, Tennessee, Broadman and Holman, 1998.

Russell, Bob. When God Builds a Church. West Monroe, Louisiana: Howard Publishing Company, 2003.

Simon, Caroline J., ed. Mentoring for Mission: Nurturing New Faculty at Church-Related Colleges. Grand Rapids: Eerdmans, 2003.

Smith, Fred. You and Your Network: Getting the Most Out of Life. Waco, TX: Word, 1984.

Stanley, Andy. The Next Generation Leader: Five Essentials for Those Who Will Shape the Future. Sister, OR: Multnomah, 2003.

Stanley, Paul D. and J. Robert Clinton. Connecting: The Mentoring Relationships You Need To Succeed In Life. Colorado Springs: NavPress, 1992.

Stoddard, David A. The Heart of Mentoring: Ten Proven Principles for Developing People to Their Fullest Potential. Colorado Springs: NavPress, 2003.

Stott, John R. W. Christian Basics: An Invitation to Discipleship. Grand Rapids: Baker, 2003.

Swindoll, Charles R. So You Want to Be Like Christ?: Eight Essentials to Get You There, Nashville, Tennessee: W. Publishing Group, 2005.

Thrall, Bill, Bruce McNicol, and Ken McElrath. The Ascent of a Leader: How Ordinary Relationships Develop Extraordinary Character and Influence. Nashville: Jossey-Bass, 1999.

Thomas, Gary. Sacred Marriage, Grand Rapids, Michigan: Zondervan, 2000.

Willard, Dallas. The Great Omission: Reclaiming Jesus' Essential Teachings on Discipleship. San Francisco: Harper San Francisco, 2006.

Whitney, Donald, Spiritual Disciplines for the Christian Life, Colorado Springs, Colorado, 1991.

CPSIA information can be obtained at www.ICGtesting.com
Printed in the USA
BVOW041507160912

300505BV00004B/5/P

9 781935 256137

10

ABSOLUTE
LIFE-CHANGERS
OF MEN;
GUARANTEED:

FROM THE BOOK WHICH CANNOT LIE

Mentoring Men for the Master Handbook /
10 Absolute Life-Changers of Men; Guaranteed:
From the Book Which Cannot Lie

Copyright © 2011

ISBN-13: 978-1-935256-13-7

Published by L'Edge Press
A ministry of Upside Down Ministries, Inc.
PO Box 2567
Boone, NC 28607

DEDICATION

For several years I have searched the Scriptures, researched the lives of godly men, and drawn from my own experience to find the 10 truths which transform men into the "image of Christ" (Romans 8:29). These 10 truths constitute the core of our curriculum in "Mentoring Men for the Master," and as men have obeyed these disciplines I have seen them become powerful "change agents" in their homes, churches, vocations, and world. It is to these men that I gratefully dedicate this book and to the growing number of men across the world who will yet be changed – all to the glory of God.

Deo Soli Gloria

ENDORSEMENT OF MY MENTORING

Dr. Adrian Rogers: "Being mentored by Bill Bennett would be a blessing that no seminary can give."

Dr. Daniel Akin, President of Southeastern Baptist Theological Seminary: "Bill Bennett's passion for mentoring young men to be leaders in the work of the Lord is well known...He recognizes that this was the model of Jesus and it should be our model as well. His approach is biblical, practical and devotional."

Dr. David Black, Professor of New Testament and Greek, Southeastern Baptist Theological Seminary: "Bill Bennett is one of my closest friends. Together for a year we met weekly for prayer and mutual encouragement. I know of few men I would rather be mentored by."

Dr. Jerry Falwell: "I have known Bill Bennett for nearly 35 years. The passion of his soul for many years has been to build up young men in their ministries. He has done this most effectively through mentoring them..."

Dr. Allen Moseley, Professor, Southeastern Baptist Theological Seminary: "Bill Bennett knows how to mentor men. He has done it effectively for decades. And the proof is in the pudding – many men who are walking with God and faithfully serving God proudly refer to Dr. Bennett as their mentor."

Dr. Jimmy Draper, Former President of Lifeway Christian Ministries: "Bill Bennett has spent his life in relationships and mentoring. No one does it better than he."

Dr. Jim Henry: "The word 'mentor' was not on my radar in early years of ministry. But it was in the heart of Bill Bennett when the Holy Spirit placed him in my life during seminary days. Forty years later I continue to learn from him."

Terry Fox, Pastor, Summit Church, Wichita, Kansas, Former Chairman of NAMB: "I had the privilege of training under Dr. Bennett's leadership. His mentoring changed my personal life and ministry and I am still using the tools for mentoring he taught me."

TABLE OF CONTENTS

CHAPTER 1

INTERNALIZING THE WORD

God clearly called me to preach in 1950, and this I did with a great joy and extraordinary results for 36 years. In 1986 God clearly called me to leave the pastorate and begin to mentor men as clearly as He called me to preach. However, He did not instruct me as to how I was to proceed in this task of mentoring, but simply said, "it would be the greatest ministry I had ever known."

I then began to search the Scriptures to discover what God had to say about mentoring. Then I discovered four fundamental facts relating to mentoring:

1. God's purpose for every child of His is for him to "be conformed to the image of Christ" (Romans 8:29) in order for him or her to become a true Christ-follower.

2. For one to be conformed to Christ's image he would need to discipline himself in specific activities. As the apostle Paul commanded, "Discipline yourself for the purpose of godliness" (1 Timothy 4:7b NASV).

3. Mentoring would include my "coming alongside" my students as well as teaching in class. My golden text is 1 Thess. 2:8 (NIV), "We loved you so much that we were delighted to share with you not only the gospel of God but our lives as well, because you had become so dear to us."

4. The specific disciplines required for "conforming to His Image" consisted of 10 imperatives clearly stated in the Scriptures. I spent considerable time in prayer and study before the Lord revealed these disciplines to me. I am not an incurable devotee to alliteration, but since I could clearly state each of these disciplines with a word beginning with the letter "I," I began to refer to them as "The 10 I's." Some clearer titles might be "The 10 Imperatives for Continuing

Spiritual Growth," "The 10 Life Changers," or "The 10 Steps to Becoming like Jesus," or "The Big 10 of the Kingdom." I finally settled on one title, which is "The 10 Absolute Life-Changers for Men – From the Book Which Cannot Lie:"

1. Internalizing the Word – Joshua 1:8; James 1:18-25

2. Infilling of the Holy Spirit – Ephesians 5:18

3. Intimacy with the Father – Psalm 27:4

4. Intentional Involvement in the World Mission of Christ – Matthew 28:18-20

5. Interrelating with others to share one's life – (Mentoring) – 1 Thess. 2:8

6. Investing your money redemptively with the Lord, beginning with the tithe to your local church – Matthew 6:19-20

7. Identification with, support of, and service in a local church – Hebrews 10:25

8. Intense devotion to one's family, especially his wife – Eph. 5:25; 1 Peter 3:7.

9. Intentional discipline of the physical body – 1 Cor. 9:27; Romans 12:1

10. Instant repentance and cleansing from all sin – Psalm 139:23-24.

We meet with our mentorees weekly to instruct them in the nature and practice of these 10 disciplines, and we also "come alongside" them during the week both to encourage them to obey these activities and to hold them accountable in so doing. As men have submitted themselves to these biblical teachings, we have witnessed phenomenal changes for the better in both their attitudes and actions. To be more specific, men who had been "wimps" have become godly husbands to their wives, wonderful fathers and examples to their children, faithful and effective church members, and outstanding Christian citizens. The wives of our mentorees are often saying to me, "Dr. Bennett, I don't know what you are doing in mentoring my husband; but whatever it is, please keep on doing it, for it has given me a new man."

With this background I will now list the 10 I's, define each one, and give supporting Scripture and collateral materials to further amplify their full meaning:

1. **The Internalization of the Word of God.** The Bible clearly commands us to take several actions concerning the Word of God:

    a. Read the Word (1 Timothy 4:13)

    b. Study the Word (2 Timothy 2:15)

    c. Search the Word (Acts 17:11)

    d. Desire the Word (1 Peter 2:2)

    e. Love the Word (Psalm 119:97)

    f. Treasure the Word (Job 23:12)

    g. Hide the Word (Psalm 119:11)

But the Bible commands far more than any of these things. The Bible commands us to "Internalize the Word," or to "eat" the Word (Jeremiah 15:16; Ezekiel 3:1; Revelation 10:9) until we "abide" in the Word or literally find nourishment for our souls and day-by-day guidance for our lives. In fact the very essence of our lives becomes the Word of God. As Jesus said, "Man shall not live by bread alone but by *every word* which is proceeding out of the mouth of God" (Matthew 4:4). Moreover, He asserted that the mark of the true disciple is abiding or internalizing the Word. "If you abide in my Word, you are my disciples indeed and you shall know the truth and the truth shall make you free" – John 8:31-32. Faithful believers read and even study the Word, and many hear the Word and even preach and teach it without ever "Internalizing" the Word.

Thus the Lord showed me that the "Internalization" of the Word consist of 4 steps. These steps are the heart of our "Mentoring curriculum," and so very important that we have incorporated them into our "Bible Pledge," which goes as follows: With everyone standing, holding his Bible in his right hand, we repeat together this pledge:

"This is my Bible. It is God's inerrant word. It is my most valuable earthly possession. I will, therefore, make it a lamp unto my feet and a

3

light unto my path and I will hide its words in my heart that I might not sin against God.

The Bible is God talking to me personally. I will, therefore, listen to it carefully and obey it fully. I will endeavor to internalize it in my life by doing 4 things:

1. I will *Know* it in my head by diligent *study*.
2. I will *Stow* it in my heart by *memorization and meditation*,
3. I will *Show* it in my life by *obeying* its teachings,
4. I will then *Sow* it into my world by witnessing.

Hereafter I will never be the same, never, never, never, in the name of Jesus and for His honor and glory both now and forever. Amen"

When we can truly offer the "Bible Pledge," we can joyfully repeat the "Victory Pledge," as follows:

"I am too anointed to be disappointed,
I am too blessed to be depressed,
I am too chosen to be frozen,
I am too elected to be rejected,
I am too inspired to be tired,
Have more to shout about
Than to pout about, And have more to sing about
Than complain about."

Our first lesson in Mentoring consists of "Internalizing" the 10 Commandments and the 8 Beatitudes. For example, take the 10 Commandments:

First, we ask our students to memorize each commandment (first step).

Secondly, we ask our students to "meditate" on the commandments until they understand their meaning and how each would apply to their individual lives (second step).

Thirdly, we ask our students to explain how they would keep this commandment in every day living (third step).

Fourthly, we ask our students to explain how they would use this truth in witnessing, teaching, preaching, telephoning (fourth step).

We go a step further and demonstrate by the acrostic FIRST what it means to "Internalize" the 1st commandment of the 10: First, we point out that the first commandment in plain language means "You shall put God first in every area of your life:"

F – in your **Finances** – Tithe to your local church, give offerings and use the rest for His glory.

I – in your **Interests** – show He is Lord over every aspect of your life.

R – in your **Relationships** – He is Lord over your relationships to everyone.

S – in your **Schedule** – put the Lord first.

T – in your **Time** – spend your time to do all He commands in His Word.

We continue to demonstrate how to internalize the remaining nine "I's" – these principles are applied to all the Scriptures.

The results: Most of our students have read the Bible, some have even memorized portions, before they come to our Mentoring School, but they had never gone on to "meditate" on it, understand its deep meaning, and how it applied to their everyday lives. One guy was brought up in an Independent Baptist Church where great emphasis was laid just upon memorizing the Bible, but nothing else. This brother began to follow our 4 steps in "Internalizing" the Word and exclaimed, "Up until now I thought there was something "magic" just in being able to quote the Word, but now I see that the real change comes when I "Internalize" the Word instead.

Conclusion: The Word of God will change any life but only if it gets on the "inside" of a person, and the word gets on the "inside" only when one internalizes it When it does, the Holy Spirit takes that Word and changes one's mind and behavior and he begins to conform into the image of Christ, making him a godly Christian, husband, father, church member – a true Christ-follower.

Permit me then to make it crystal clear that Bill Bennett nor has anyone else ever changed anyone, but the Holy Spirit, using the word on

the "inside," has and is changing hundreds of men across the earth and to Him be all the honor and glory. My guiding word is Isaiah 42:8, "I am the Lord; this is my name, and I will not share my glory with another..." God forbid that I do.

COLLATERAL MATERIAL ON THE FIRST "I"
DANGERS TO AVOID IN "INTERNALIZING THE WORD"

1. **Legalism** – Legalism would be seeking to Internalize the Word as a mere duty, void of love for Jesus and dependence upon the Holy Spirit.

2. **Ritualism** – Ritualism is a customarily repeated, often formal act or series of acts (Webster's) Thus ritualism is organized "legalism," requiring no heart or love but mere adherence to a prescribed procedure.

3. **Meritorious Righteousness** – Some may "Internalize the Word," believing the more they do so, the more righteous they become in the eyes of God and man. Such activity only builds our pride and rather than enhancing our relationship with God, it prevents it. Remember, "God resists the proud, but gives grace to the humble" – 1 Peter 5:6.

4. **Partial Internalization** – There are four steps in "Internalizing the Word." Satan would smile to see you memorize verses, but never really meditate on them, never applying them to one's life, and never sharing them. James warns "Be not hearers of the Word but doers, deceiving yourself" – James 1:22.

How do you know if you are falling into one of these dangers? Simply this way: If you are finding no joy, but only constant struggle, dread, and desire to stop, in all probability it is because you are approaching Internalizing as a legalistic duty, a ritualistic habit without heart, an act to make you more righteous, or you are only partially meeting the four requirements for internalization.

Interpret all Scriptures according to its contextual setting. Otherwise you stand in danger of completely falsifying the Scriptures and teaching plain error.

Example # 1 – "The Bible says that if you confess your sins you will be saved." False

"It really says, "If we confess our sins, He is faithful and just to forgive us our sins" (1 John 1:9). These familiar words are often quoted as a formula for salvation. But the presence of the word "we" in the immediate context makes it clear that John was not addressing the unsaved. Rather, he was talking to people who were already believers in Christ (vv. 6,7,9,10), and was showing them how to be restored to a right family relationship with the God who had saved them. If we don't consider the immediate context, we might conclude that we are saved by admitting our sins rather than by believing the gospel of Christ."[1]

Example # 2 – "The Bible says that it's wrong for a woman to wear jewelry?" False

"The actual quote is : 'Do not let your adornment be merely outward – arranging the hair, wearing gold, or putting on fine apparel' (1 Peter 3:3). Some have used these words to say that godly women should not style their hair, use cosmetics, or wear jewelry. But if we read on, we find these words, "rather let it be the hidden person of the heart" (v. 4). By these additional words we see that the apostle's main purpose was not to tell women that they either should or should not style their hair or wear jewelry. He was saying that they should focus on the beauty of a gentle and quiet spirit rather than relying on outward appearance."[2]

Example #3 – "The Bible says that studying for knowledge isn't necessary." False

"It actually says, 'If any of you lacks wisdom, let him ask of God, who gives to all liberally and without reproach, and it will be given to him (Jas. 1:5). These words of James have been seen by some as a promise that

---

[1] Martin De Hann II, *How Can I Understand the Bible*, Grand Rapids, Michigan: Discovery House Publishers, 2003, p. 9.
[2] Ibid. p. 9

we can receive unlearned skills and knowledge if we just pray. More than a few college students have claimed this promise before taking an exam for which they had not prepared.

The immediate context, however, is describing a reason for the joy we can have when difficult circumstances test our faith. James' promise is not that we can be successful without effort, but rather that God does not leave us alone when He allows trouble or temptation to come into our lives. James assured us that if we don't know how to let God do His work in us, we can have wisdom for the asking.

Later in the same letter, James told his readers how to recognize this wisdom when it comes. He said it is not marked by envy or selfish ambition, but is 'pure, then peaceable, gentle, willing to yield, full of mercy and good fruits, without partiality and without hypocrisy' (James 3:17). This is the kind of wisdom James had in mind."[3]

How may we avoid these errors? By loving the Lord Jesus Christ and thus His Word with all our hearts and desiring to please Him and bring glory to His Name. David internalized the Word of God because he had such a heart, as shown in his testimony thereunto, "O how I love your law; it is my meditation day and night" – Psalm 119-97. "How sweet are thy words unto my taste! Yea, sweeter than honey to my mouth!"- Psalm 119-103. Jesus plainly said, "If you love me, you will obey my commandments" – John 14:15. The apostle John wrote, "The proof that you love is that you keep His commandments, and His commandments are not burdensome" – 1 John 5:3.

Thus the answer to Legalism, Ritualism, Meritorious Righteousness, and Partial Internalization is to obey our Lord Jesus Christ out of sheer love. If your motivation is anything else, you cannot succeed in internalizing the Word in a way that will bring glory to Jesus Christ and "joy and rejoicing" to your own soul – Jeremiah 15:16. The church at Ephesus performed many outward acts of righteousness, but having lost their "first love" for Jesus, they lost the reality of Jesus and He threatened to remove His light and mission from them – Revelation 2:1-4. Be a true "Internalizer of the Word," and you will discover "life and discover it more abundantly"– John 10:10b.

---

[3] Ibid. pp. 9-10.

UNDERSTANDING MEDITATION

1. **Meditation** – Biblical meditation involves emptying the mind and filling it with God's Word. It is tuning out the world and tuning into a specific Scripture or attribute of God. Choose to block out everything else for a specific period of time. Focus upon Jesus and the words of the Bible.

   "This book of the law shall not depart from your mouth, but you shall meditate on it day and night, so that you may be careful to do according to all that is written in it; for then you will make your way prosperous, and then you will have 'good success' " – Joshua 1:8.

2. **Disconnection** – A time comes each day when we need to disconnect from the computer, the telephone, cell phones, pagers, VCRs, DVDs, TVs, and radios. In other words, disengaging from anything that beeps, blows, goes off, rings, honks, or says, "You've got mail." In sports it would be called a "time-out."

3. **Concentration** – "We need times of being still and simply listening to God. Too often we are moving targets, moving too quickly to hear what God has to say to us. Concentration is a way to practice silence before God. We deliberately think about God."[4]

"Blessed be the Lord who daily loads us with benefits." – Psalm 68:19

---

[4] Jay Dennis, *The Jesus Habits*, Nashville, Tennessee: B & H Publishing Group, 2005, p. 13.

30 WONDERFUL BENEFITS OF INTERNALIZING THE WORD

1. ITW Keeps you in close relationship and intimacy with Jesus.

2. ITW Empowers you to overcome sinful lusts.

3. ITW Keeps your mind focused on Jesus.

4. ITW Enables you to take every thought captive to Christ.

5. ITW Deepens your understanding of God's Word dramatically.

6. ITW Increases your love for the living and written Word.

7. ITW Grows your faith dramatically.

8. ITW Enables you to answer accusations of Satan.

9. ITW Cleanses you of your sinful ways.

10. ITW Is a powerful deterrent to sin.

11. ITW Enables you to mediate on the Word day and night.

12. ITW Keeps you constantly refreshed and fruitful.

13. ITW Prevents you from backsliding.

14. ITW Makes your personal witness powerful, believable, and winning.

15. ITW Greatly strengthens your devotional life: worship and prayer.

16. ITW Makes your teaching and preaching authoritative, believable, and effective.

17. ITW Increases the confidence and response of your audience when speaking.

18. ITW Makes you an effective and courageous communicator.

19. ITW Equips you to be a Christian apologist (defender of the faith).

20. ITW Is a huge time saver.

21. ITW Assures you of excitement and vitality and joy.

22. ITW Cures boredom and prevents burnouts.

23. ITW Enables you to speak off the cuff.

24. ITW Makes you a constant discoverer of exciting truth.

25. ITW Qualifies you to be filled with the Holy Spirit.

26. ITW Assures you of real success and prosperity God's way.

27. ITW Enables you to be a Christ honoring conversationalist.

28. ITW Makes you especially useful in small group discussions.

29. ITW Enables you to mentor your family.

30. ITW Enables you to be a godly husband, father, Christian, church member, etc. having the character and conduct of Jesus or conforming into "Christ's image."

14 SIMPLE STEPS IN STUDYING AND GRASPING THE BIBLE

1. The Bible is one complete book. Those who skip the first 39 books will never understand the correct meaning of the rest. The Bible Jesus used was the 39 books of the Old Testament (Deut. 8:3; Luke 24:44ff) and also Paul and Timothy (2 Timothy 3:17-17).

2. You must know ALL the Scriptures on one subject to know what the Bible teaches. Example: Prayer – John 14:14 says you will get your prayers answered; but Isaiah 59:1-3 and James 4:2-3 says there are prayers God does not answer.

3. The Bible interprets the Bible. Example – The Book of Revelation is full of symbols, which are explained in Genesis, Daniel, etc, without which Revelation cannot be understood.

4. Be very careful to interpret every verse of Scripture according to its contextual setting. Example – Romans 10:13 says, "Whosoever shall call upon the Name of the Lord will be saved." Many take this verse to mean that all a person has to do to be saved is to get on his knees and ask the Lord to save him. But the verses following Romans 10:13 goes on to say that a person cannot call on One in whom he does not believe and he cannot believe on Him of whom he has not heard and to hear he must have a witness (Romans 10:14-15).

5. All the Bible is relevant and useful. "All Scripture is God-breathed and useful…" (2 Timothy 3:16). "Man shall not live by bread alone, but by every Word that proceeds out of the mouth of God." (Jesus, Matthew 4:4, quoting Deut. 8:3).

6. Do not expect to grasp the full meaning of all the Bible when you first study it. The great Bible expositor, Campbell Morgan wrote, "Often I do not understand what God is saying in a given Scripture. When I have this experience I am more convinced than ever that the Bible is God's Word, and the fact I don't understand it all confirms my conviction that it is the Word of God, not the Word of man. Then I bow my head and worship God."

7. The Word of God is inexhaustible in its treasures of truth and will continually reveal deeper truths as we meditate upon it and the Holy Spirit opens its true meaning. Example – Many times in my life I have carried a text in my heart and meditation for months and years before its full truth sprang forth to capture my heart and mind and give me the most powerful sermons I ever preached.

8. The Bible is open to the contrite and fearful heart (Psalm 25:14; Isaiah 66:2) and is closed to the prideful and self-sufficient. "…Jesus answered and said, "I thank you Father, Lord of heaven and earth, that you have hidden these things from the wise and prideful and revealed them to babes." (Matthew 11:25). Illus. Scholars from across the world assembled on the campus of Duke University to discuss the meaning of grace. While these intellectuals were wrangling over the subject, an uneducated, simple janitor in the hall was humming, "Amazing Grace, How Sweet the Sound…" A fellow student of mine passed by and said, "This simple man sweeping the floors knows more about grace than all these PhD's from around the world."

9. Pray without ceasing that God will reveal the truth of the Bible to your heart. (Psalm 25:4-5).

10. Prove the Bible by obeying it. God commands that we "prove all things" (1 Thess. 5:21). Illus. A noted scholar asked me this question one day, "Bill, how would you prove the existence of God?" I immediately replied, "Tithe." He laughed at me until I quoted Mal. 3:10 which invites the tither to tithe and he will see for himself how God will keep His promise to bless those who do.

11. You can prove almost anything from the Bible, but only if you interpret verses out of context. Example – Recently I heard a widely known TV evangelist teach that God promises His people 120 years, not 70. In fact he boasted that he would live 120 years himself. He did so by taking Genesis 6:3 out of context. In this verse the Lord warned that His Spirit would not strive with man forever, but that there would be a delay of 120 years before the judgment of the flood would occur.

12. The Bible sheds a lot of light on the commentaries. Great errors have been passed down through generations because some commentator was believed rather than the Bible. Example – the famous Scofield Bible divides Christians into two classes:

   a. Spiritual, and

   b. Carnal, but the Apostle Paul makes it crystal clear that the "carnal mind is enmity against God and is not subject to the law of God, nor indeed can be" (Romans 8:7) and that Christians are "not in the flesh (not carnal) but in the Spirit...(Romans 9:9). Yet, vast numbers of evangelicals, following Scofield's Bible, teach and preach the two kinds of believers, leaving multitudes in my opinion in their sins and lost who believe they are saved.

13. No translation of the Bible is perfect. I love the language of the original or the New King James version and have memorized from them, but there are deficiencies in them- Transliterated words:

   a. "Baptize" which if translated would have read "immersed" and would have avoided much confusion through the centuries.

   b. "Deacon" which means servant, not a church boss. Many deacons think the term "deacon" is an honorary title which bestows upon them the right to run the church and dictate to the pastor. This false impression has resulted in serious troubles in many local churches through the years.

   c. Acts 19:2 – The word "after" should be "when." "After" leaves the impression that you receive the Holy Spirit after you're saved when in reality you receive the Holy Spirit the moment you're saved (Romans 8:9b).

14. The best translation of the Bible is "The gospel according to Tom, Dick and Harry." Dr. Donald Barnhouse said the world may never read the Bible in leather or morocco, but it will never fail to read the Bible in shoe leather." What do people see when they read the gospel according to your life?

SCRIPTURE TO INTERNALIZE FOR THIS CHAPTER:

Joshua 1:8 – This Book of the Law shall not depart from your mouth, but you shall meditate in it day and night, that you may observe to do according to all that is written in it. For then you will make your way prosperous, and then you will have good success.

Psalm 119:11 – Your word I have hidden in my heart, That I might not sin against You.

CHAPTER 2

INFILLING OF THE HOLY SPIRIT

The ministry of the Holy Spirit is absolutely indispensable in the life of any person who would be "conformed to the image of Christ" and serve Him effectively; for it is the work of the Holy Spirit to make real in our lives what Christ has provided for us in His death, burial and resurrection. God the Father *thought* our salvation; God the Son *bought* our salvation, and the Holy Spirit *brought* us salvation (Ephesians 1:3-13).

When I began to preach I knew the Holy Spirit was of utmost importance in the Christian life, but I knew very little of how He works in human experience. But I was hungry to know, and He taught me seven monumental truths:

1. The Holy Spirit is a Person.

2. He comes into our lives when we repent, trust Christ, and are born again.

3. He baptizes us into the body of Christ simultaneously with our new birth.

4. He indwells us and our bodies become His temple.

5. He fills and refills with the Holy Spirit which is followed by His anointing.

6. He never glorifies Himself but Jesus only.

7. He reproduces in us the blessings Jesus has provided for us in His death, burial, and resurrection.

The *new birth* and consequent indwelling represent our salvation; the *baptism* represents our spiritual position in Christ, the *infilling* represents our spiritual condition, and the *anointing* represents our vocation, that is, our empowerment to exercise our spiritual gifts – the "special touch for the special task." To be anointed one must:

(1) Live a life of holiness,

(2) Live a life of yieldedness, and

(3) Live a life of prayerfulness. [5]

I was saved at the age of nine. Thus I was born of the Holy Spirit, indwelt by His presence, baptized into the body of Christ, but not filled until I was 34 years old. It happened on the streets of Greensboro and at a time of desperate need. My experience was not an emotional one. I saw no angels. I did not go into a trance. I did not speak in tongues. I did not swoon, nor was I "slain in the Spirit." I was overwhelmingly conscious in my spirit that the Holy Spirit was with me and beside me and walking with me. I saw no physical person. But I was as conscious of the presence of the Holy Spirit as I would have been if my wife in her physical body had been walking beside me. In a word, the Holy Spirit revealed Himself to me in the way Jesus had promised He would: The PARAKLETOS (John 14:16), ONE like Himself Who would be called beside His children forever. I cannot describe the assurance that came over my soul. I knew without a doubt that I was not alone in living a godly life and experiencing a powerful ministry, but that I dared not speak of it publicly for a long time and now only cautiously and reverently. However, one can't hide anything from his wife though he tries. Thus within an hour or less when I joined my wife, she turned to me and asked, "Bill, what has happened to you?" I replied, "Has something happened that is unusual?" She replied, "Yes." Then I asked, "Is it something good or bad?" She replied, "Good." At that point I shared of my encounter with the Holy Spirit on Davie Street in downtown Greensboro. Since then I have heard my wife say time and time again, "I received a new husband that day and our marriage became a joy." As for myself I do not mean to imply that my encounter with the Holy Spirit that day exempted me from some struggles, disappointments, hardships, even some "Dark Gethsemane" nights. But I do say that though I have found myself at times in the valley, I have never doubted that the wonderful *Parakletos* was with me and would sustain me in the darkest hour. In those moments I have experienced many "infillings." My encounter occurred some fifty years ago, however, and I continue to draw immeasurable strength from it. At the present, I sense in my life His overflowing love, joy, hope and power

---

5 Stephen Olford

as I pour my life into hundreds of men who seek to become true Christ followers.

COLLATERAL MATERIAL ON THE SECOND "I"

UNDERSTANDING THE INDISPENSABLE ROLE OF THE HOLY SPIRIT IN THE CHRISTIAN LIFE.

If one would know Jesus Christ and keep growing in His grace, he must understand and appropriate the work of the Holy Spirit in his life.

A Mini Course on the Person and Work of the Holy Spirit:

1. *Attitudes* Toward the Holy Spirit:
   a. Ignorance – Acts 19:2
   b. Indifference
   c. Ignition
2. *Attributes* of the Holy Spirit:
   a. Person
   b. God
   c. Jesus' Personal Representative in the world today
3. *Advantages* of the Coming of the Holy Spirit – John 16:7-11 (See page 22)
4. *Accomplishments* of the Holy Spirit:
   a. The Virgin Birth – Matthew 1:20; Luke 1:35
   b. The New Birth – the key to his baptism, indwelling, infilling, and out-going.
5. *Acceptance:*
   a. Repent and trust Jesus as Lord and Savior – Acts 2:38

D. L. Moody, "You can eat without a tongue, breath without lungs, see without eyes, sooner than you can live the Christian life without the Holy Spirit."

AMAZING "ADVANTAGES" OF THE ADVENT OF THE HOLY SPIRIT

When Jesus announced to His disciples that He would soon be departing from them, great sorrow filled their hearts, for they assumed they would be left in this world without a Teacher, Guide, Power, or Comforter (John 16:1-5). But Jesus assured His followers that they would be better off after His departure than they were with His presence (John 6:7-11). How could this possibly be? Jesus sets forth the specific advantages that would occur:

1. **Jesus would prepare a place in heaven for His followers after His departure.** "I go to prepare a place for you" (John 14:2). Many have thought Jesus went to heaven to build the place called heaven, using His great carpentry skills. Primarily what Jesus meant was that He was going to Calvary (the Cross) to die for sinners that they might be forgiven and saved and made ready for the home in heaven. As the hymn says, "The Way of the Cross Leads Home," and Jesus had to die before that home was ready.

2. **The Holy Spirit has come to be our Great Comforter by coming "alongside" of us under all circumstances.** Jesus said "And I will pray to the Father that He send you another Comforter that He may abide with you forever" (John 14:16). The Greek word translated Comforter is *Parakletos* which means "called alongside to assist." True comfort strengthens us to face life bravely and keep on going. The Holy Spirit does not rob us of our responsibility but enables us to stay in the race and not give up. Some translators call the Holy Spirit "the Encourager," and I would call Him the "Great Encourager." Also the "Great Remembrancer" (John 14:26).

3. **The disciples would experience Jesus in a more personal way after the coming of the Holy Spirit than they did before.** "I will not leave you spiritual orphans: I am coming to you" (John 14:18). What Jesus meant was "My departure will not be like that of a Father whose children are left orphans when he dies. In the Spirit I am coming back to you." The Holy Spirit reveals Jesus, glorifies Him, applies His blood and merits to the hearts of believers, makes His teachings effective in their lives. Hence, when the Spirit was poured out, Christ truly returned. Liberals, desiring to deny the Second Coming, have said the

coming of the Holy Spirit is the Second Coming, but not true.

4. **The disciples would be enabled to "do greater works" than they had ever witnessed Jesus Himself doing in the days of His flesh.** "Verily, verily, I say unto you, He that believeth on me, the works that I do shall he do also; and greater works than these shall he do; because I go unto my Father" (John 14:12). This would be possible, for after the coming of the Holy Spirit at Pentecost every believer would have the presence and power of Jesus in them through the Person of the Holy Spirit. Prior to the coming of the Holy Spirit, Jesus was limited to one locale at a given time. After Pentecost He is present in every believer and every believer is to witness of His saving grace, resulting in multitudes being saved (Acts 2:41).

5. **Jesus went to heaven and sent the Holy Spirit to live in the heart of all believers, so that they might be powerful witnesses of His saving grace.** "When the Spirit is come (to the church) He (the Holy Spirit) will convict the world of *Sin*, of *Righteousness*, and of *Judgment*. Of sin, because they believe not on me; of righteousness, because I go to my Father and you will see me no more, of judgment because the prince of this world (Satan) is judged" (John 16:8-11). "But you shall receive power when the Holy Spirit has come upon you; and you shall be witnesses to Me both in Jerusalem, and in all Judea and Samaria, and to the end of the earth" (Acts 1:8).

It is important that we note that the Holy Spirit comes to believers (the church) and not to the world. This means He works in and through you and me if we are born again. The Holy Spirit does not minister in a vacuum. Just as Jesus had a body in order to do His work on earth, so the Holy Spirit needs a body to accomplish His ministries and that body is His redeemed church. Our bodies are His temples and tools, and He wants to use us for His glory. Illus: Often we hear people pray, "Lord, send your Holy Spirit to speak to the lost." Such praying sounds good, but is it biblical? Many think the Holy Spirit "floats" up and down the pews in a ghostly manner. No, the Holy Spirit works through His people in whom He lives. This does not mean the Sovereign Holy Spirit could never speak directly to someone, but it does mean that He speaks primarily through believers who are surrendered to Him. I sense very little of the Holy Spirit's convictions in churches today. This means one tragic thing: Members of the church are not instruments through which

the Holy Spirit can convict the lost because they are grieving (Ephesians 4:30 and quenching (1 Thess. 5;19) the Holy Spirit.

What does the Holy Spirit do through believers? Jesus said "He convicts or reproves the world of three things" (John 16:8). The word "convict" means "to convict and convince," or simply to pronounce the verdict. Believers are the witnesses, the Holy Spirit is the prosecuting attorney, and the unsaved are the guilty prisoners:

1. **The Holy Spirit convicts the world of one particular sin: The Sin of Unbelief.** The conscience will convict men of their sins, but only the Holy Spirit can convict the lost of unbelief. After all, it is unbelief that condemns the sinner and sends him to hell (John 3:18-21), not the committing of individual sins. A person could "clean up his life" and quit his bad habits and still be lost and go to hell. Many seek to win the lost by seeking to persuade them to quit drinking, etc., never showing them that their damning sin is the rejection of Jesus as Savior and Lord.

2. **The Holy Spirit convicts the world of Righteousness, not unrighteousness.** Whose righteousness? The Righteousness of Jesus, who returned and was received by His Father in heaven to show He was righteous. Men must see their righteousnesses as "filthy rags" (Isaiah 64:6) and know that the only righteousness that will save is that of Jesus Himself.

3. **The Holy Spirit convicts the world of judgment.** "Of judgment because the prince of this world (Satan) is judged." Jesus is saying that just as Satan has already been judged and sentenced, so will the sinner who persist in unbelief and rejection of the true righteousness of Jesus.

In a word, there can be no true conversion without conviction of sin, righteousness, and judgment, and there can be no conversion apart from the Spirit of God using the Word of God generally through the witness of the child of God. Do you not see how Christians desperately need to understand and surrender to the Holy Spirit? Yet the fact is that most believers believe only that they need to accept Jesus as their Savior and are either totally ignorant or indifferent to the wonderful work of the Holy Spirit. But as D. L. Moody said, "You can eat without a tongue, breath without lungs, see without eyes, sooner than you can live the Christian life without the Holy Spirit."

Illus.: As a young pastor I knew from reading the New Testament that the Holy Spirit was crucial in the Christian life, so I approached an "elder" statesman expressing my concern that we honor the Holy Spirit, and he replied, "Bill, don't bother with the Holy Spirit; just preach Jesus," not realizing that we experience the life of Jesus only through the Holy Spirit.

Illus.: When I was discouraged, tired, defeated, depressed, and ready to give up, the Holy Spirit joined me on the streets of Greensboro, assuring me of His glorious presence and Helper for every need I had. That was the beginning of a new day in my personal life, my marriage, and my ministry.

THE HOLY SPIRIT PASSIONATELY YEARNS FOR YOU – JAMES 4:5

One of the most amazing truths concerning the love of the Holy Spirit for every single child of God is hid away in the little book of James, chapter four, verse 5. "Do ye think that the Scripture saith in vain, The spirit that dwelleth in us lusteth to envy?" The key word in the verse is *Lust*, which is the Greek word, *epipotheo*, meaning an intense desire, a craving, hunger, a yearning, longing or pining for something. What does the Holy Spirit yearn for so passionately that the Bible would picture Him that way? He yearns that each believer give his time, devotion and total surrender to Him so that He may produce the life of Christ in Him. That should not surprise us. He is our life through the new birth, our Indweller, our Controller (filler), Sealer, Sanctifier, and Source of power. The word *epipotheo* (lust) means that the Holy Spirit wants all of us, or as one commentator observed, "The Holy Spirit can never get enough of us." In Romans 12:1 God through the Apostle Paul is begging us to "present our bodies as a living sacrifice." This verse does not say to whom we should present our bodies. However, we know it is not to God the Father who is heaven and needs no body; it is not God the Son, for He already has a body. So that leaves it to be the "Holy Spirit," who has no body, except the bodies of born again individuals. Just think – you are the dwelling place, the residence, the home of the living God through

21

the Holy Spirit. Thus the Holy Spirit is jealous to claim all of you for the glory of Christ, for whom He has come to glorify. Will you permit Him to do so NOW?

I. Understanding the Work of the Father, the Son and the Holy Spirit in Redemption

The Father, Son and Holy Spirit are active in every step of redemption. However, there is a difference in the function of each. It is necessary to recognize the differences in operation in order to cooperate in the fulfillment of God's purpose for our lives.

To make the difference simple, we could say that the Father *prescribes* redemption, the Son *provides* redemption, and the Holy Spirit *applies* redemption. Or the Father *thought* redemption, the Son *bought* redemption, and the Holy Spirit *brought* redemption. Or as one theologian put it, "God is the originating cause; God the Son is the mediating cause, and God the Holy Spirit is the effecting cause (Dr. James McKee Adams). These three roles are set forth in chapter one of Ephesians.

A practical illustration of the teamwork of the Trinity in redemption:

A striking analogy is afforded in the realm of medicine. "There are three professions involved in the treatment of disease: the physician who diagnoses the case and prescribes the treatment; the pharmacist who compounds the remedy; and the nurse who faithfully waits at the patient's bedside and administers that which the doctor has prescribed and the druggist prepared. In the analogy, of course, the physician represents the Father, who has diagnosed the need of the sinner and prescribed the remedy. The druggist represents the Son, who by achieving a perfect human life, provides through His shed blood the only specific cure of sin. The nurse represents the Holy Spirit, who applies the remedy by quickening the Word to challenge the faith of the sinner.[6]

I love this analogy because it pictures the loving and practical nature of the part of the Holy Spirit in recovery from the disease of sin. Anyone who has ever been seriously sick knows what it means to have a compassionate and loving nurse at his or her bedside, administering every aid and literally pulling him through his illness. Such is the wonderful ministry of the Holy Spirit.

---

[6] Ralph Herring, God Being My Helper, Nashville, Tennessee: Broadman Press, 1955, pp. 10-11.

II. The Crucifixion of King Self

The greatest problem by far, that anyone of us faces, is the problem of Self. King Self is the chief hindrance to being filled with the Holy Spirit. What is Self? It is the rebellious, even incorrigible, nature of every human, passed down from Adam, which seeks its own way, pleasure, comfort, viewpoint, etc. with little or no regard for the rights of others. Paul's word for this attitude is flesh.

The big question is, how we can gain victory over this ungodly disposition? To make this victory ours is the first work of the Holy Spirit after that of regeneration (the new birth). The way the Holy Spirit gives this victory is by the "crucifixion (or death) of the flesh" (Romans 8:13).

Now positionally , every true believer is already dead to sin through the cross (including self) and alive to God through the resurrection (Romans 6:4). In accepting Christ, he accepts Christ's death to sin (Gal. 2:20). Having been crucified with Him, it is only natural that he would be buried with Him also, for after death comes burial. Hence in God's sight the rebel self, the big "I" is dead and buried. However, the young believer does not journey far before he discovers through painful experience that if self is dead, it is the livest dead thing he has ever encountered. Paul testifies to this dilemma and cries out "O wretched man I am. Who shall deliver me from the body of death?" (Roman. 7:24).

The question is: how can the flesh be put to death in our experience?

1. Certainly not by the energy of the flesh. Some pray, "Lord, help me crucify myself?" Multitudes rededicate their lives, seeking to overcome the flesh, but such is only the rededication of the flesh.

2. The flesh must be crucified. But how? No man can crucify himself. It is a physical impossibility. One may commit suicide in many different ways, but if he ever dies by crucifixion, someone else will put him on the cross.

3. The Holy Spirit is God's agent to bring crucifixion to pass. As Romans 8:13 specifically states, "If you by the Spirit do put to death the deeds of the body, you shall life." However, to understand how the Spirit works with us to put the death sentence into effect, we must understand the words, "put to death." These three words are one word in Greek, *thanatoute*, which literally means "to cause to be

23

put to death" the "deeds of the body." Note: the "deeds of the body," (or doing's of the body) meaning acts of evil which come through the body, not the body itself.

4. We cannot crucify ourselves. We are only to give the Holy Spirit the permission to get it done. We must say the word, because God does nothing in us without our own active cooperation.

Illustration of Crucifixion: The best way I know to explain crucifixion is to quote the words of a brother who impacted my life as no other person I ever knew in understanding the mysterious work of the Holy Spirit. So here goes:

"An experience some years ago brought home to me this aspect of the Holy Spirit's ministry. We had at that time a pet dog named Skipper which had won his way into our affections – especially those of our children. One day Skipper was struck by a passing automobile. Though he recovered in a measure from his injury, Skipper was never himself again. His disposition was ruined and he became a problem in the neighborhood. One day after he had snapped at my little daughter I sent him to the veterinarian for observation. The doctor explained that sometimes a dog's disposition was permanently altered by an injury of that nature. He stated that Skipper would probably be a dangerous pet to have with the little children in the home and frankly advised me to put him out of the way.

The veterinarian had made his recommendation. He stood ready to carry out the course that he had advised. But the problem was mine – the dog was mine, and the children were mine. It was my responsibility to say the word, and I said it. I have always felt that I said the right word, and ever since I have held in grateful appreciation the friend who counseled me so wisely and who then so faithfully did the "dirty work" for me. So far as I know that is the only sentence of execution I have pronounced – except that which time and time again I pronounce when the Holy Spirit reveals to me the working of a vicious nature within and waits my word to carry out the death sentence which he so strongly recommends.

My relation to Skipper in the incident referred to above designates the position which the believer must take in regard to the problem of self. But the act of pronouncing God's sentence must be cultivated until it becomes a habit of mind. That attitude is described in Romans 6:11 where Paul say, "Even so reckon ye also yourselves to be dead unto sin,

but alive unto God in Christ Jesus." The tense of the verb is present, indicating a continuing process of reckoning. The figure is that of a bookkeeper making his entries, or of a navigator setting his course in a given direction. Appearances to the contrary, our old man has been crucified, as God's Word plainly states. "Ye died, and your life is hid with Christ in God" (Col. 3:3). "They that are of Christ Jesus have crucified the flesh with the passions and the lusts thereof" (Gal. 5:24). The inference is unavoidable. The thing is done. The crucifixion has already taken place. By faith we must accept the bearings God has given us and hold to the course in a steady reckoning."[7]

A final caution: This business of being "dead to sin" (crucified) does not necessarily take away its appeal, nor does it render us incapable of responding. We are free to do as we choose. But God's perfect will is that we "play" by His rules, and the Holy Spirit is yearning for us to do so (James 4:5). His rule is this: Quietly reckon ourselves to be dead unto sin and alive unto God as He has said (Romans 6:11). And the wonderful thing is that when we make His reckoning a "lifestyle" and take the position that we are dead to sin (including self) and do not have to commit it and are alive to God, the victory is ours, as we find ourselves being filled moment by moment by the Holy Spirit and walking in His power.

WHAT'S THE BIG DEAL ABOUT FRUIT?

Jesus said, "By their fruits you shall know them" (Matthew 5:20).

1. **Your fruit reveals your identity.** Illus.: In nature you know a tree is a peach tree if it bears peaches. In the kingdom you know a person possesses the Holy Spirit, if he bears the fruit of the Holy Spirit (Gal. 5:22). If not, you know he does not have the Holy Spirit.

2. **Your fruit reveals your spiritual health.** True naturally, also true spiritually. Illus.: I noted recently a very sick tree in my back yard. How did I know it was sick? It had no life nor leaves. Illus.: I observe people all the time, some of them at close sight. On some I find great fruit; others I find no fruit. If a natural tree has no fruit, you know it is

---

[7] Ibid. pp. 25-25.

dead; if a professing Christian has no fruit, you can know He is dead (James 2:26).

3. **Your fruit reveals God's purpose for your life, which should also be your purpose. A natural tree does not produce fruit for itself but for others. Likewise, the spiritual fruit is for others to eat and nourish their souls.** Illus.: The Spirit-filled life is described as a flowing river going out of one's innermost being into the lives of others. "He who believes on me as the Scriptures say, out of his inner being shall flow rivers of living waters" (John 7:37). I believe there are nine of these rivers flowing from any Spirit-filled person (Gal. 5:22-23):

   a. A river of love

   b. Joy

   c. Peace

   d. Patience

   e. Gentleness (kindness)

   f. Goodness

   g. Faithfulness

   h. Meekness

   i. Self-control

Thus the ultimate purpose of the Spirit-filled life is not primarily to make us happy, or emotional or flashy, but to make us winning witnesses for Jesus Christ, soul-winners if you like. "When the Holy Spirit is come upon you, you shall receive power and you shall be witnesses unto me in Jerusalem, Judea, Samaria, and to the uttermost parts of the earth." (Acts 1:8).

The fruit of a Spirit-filled Christian is another Christian. Only 5 percent of professing believers ever witness and of those who witness, very, very, very few bring the lost to a saving knowledge and confession of Jesus Christ as Lord and Savior. What does this tell us about the need for God's people to be Spirit-filled?

Illus.: A faithful member of our Mentoring School mailed me the following powerful illustration, showing how we can be continually filled with the Holy Spirit.

An illustration of being filled by the Holy Spirit by Rick Simpson

"Picture a powerful rushing river, this living water represents the Holy Spirit. Picture us as empty vessels, a cylinder open on both ends like a paper towel roll. We are submersed, baptized, engulfed by the living water. We are completely filled from top to bottom and the river's current rushes past us. The empty vessel, now totally filled, becomes stagnant until the cylinder, our life, is turned sideways in the direction the river is flowing. Still totally filled, same water, but now it rushes thru the vessel with the power of the river, unrestricted, freely flowing through and being constantly renewed simply by changing the orientation of the cylinder.

When my mind wrapped around this picture it helped me with the questions; Am I not filled up all the way? Am I saved, then "zapped" by the Holy Spirit later? How can I be filled and have no power? Is the Holy Spirit leaking out of my vessel & what happens when I'm empty? The Scripture says be continually filled but I thought I was filled?

The answer: I'm filled with the Holy Spirit but my life is somewhere between 0 & 90 degrees. Standing straight up I'm filled and on my own but when I offer to lay down my life in alignment with the direction of the Holy Spirit – power flows through me. Not for me, not because of me and not even controlled by me…it just does."

Understanding The Infilling Of The Holy Spirit – Ephesians 5:17-18

Next to the new birth there is nothing more important for a Christian to understand and to experience than that of the infilling of the Holy Spirit. In order to understand this glorious truth, we must raise and answer some crucial questions.

I.   **What Is The New Birth of The Holy Spirit?** The new birth of the Holy Spirit is the entrance of the Holy Spirit into our lives when we truly repent of our sins and surrender our lives to Jesus. When this occurs the Holy Spirit regenerates us or gives us a new birth. This marks one's entrance into the kingdom of God and assures one of his salvation (John 3:3,5).

II. **What Is The Baptism of The Holy Spirit?** The baptism of the Holy Spirit is the gracious act by which the Holy Spirit baptizes or incorporates each believer into the body of the living Christ (1 Cor. 12:13). This baptism is a once-for-all unrepeatable act of God. The baptism occurs at the time of the new birth. Thus the Bible never commands us to be baptized by the Holy Spirit, since that act occurred the moment one trusts Jesus as Lord and Savior.

III. **What Is The Indwelling of The Holy Spirit?** The indwelling is the presence of the Holy Spirit (the same as the Spirit of Christ) which begins the moment one is born again of the Holy Spirit and will continue until the day of redemption (resurrection of the body) (Ephesians 4:30). The Holy Spirit indwells the body of every believer, making our bodies the "temples of the Holy Spirit" (1 Cor. 6:19-0). This permanent indwelling began on the Day of Pentecost when the Holy Spirit transferred His place of abode from the throne in heaven into the bodies of all believers, and "if any person has not the Spirit of Christ, he does not belong to Christ" (Romans 8:9b; Acts 19:2).

IV. **What Is The Sealing of The Holy Spirit?** This means that every true believer receives the Spirit of God as a sign that he belongs to God and that he will be kept safe by God until the time he receives his glorified body. Just as in legal matters, a seal indicates ownership and security, so it does in divine affairs. The indwelling brands us as God's property (1 Cor. 6:19-20) and guarantees our preservation until the day of redemption (Ephesians 4:30).

V. **What Is The Infilling of The Holy Spirit?** The infilling of the Holy Spirit is the control of the Holy Spirit over the believer's life and occurs when one surrenders his life completely to the control of the Holy Spirit. Luke 5:26 states that the disciples were "filled" with fear, meaning they were controlled or dominated by the emotion of fear. The word "filled" in Luke 5:26 is the same word found in Ephesians 5:18, "Be ye filled with the Holy Spirit." While the baptism of the Holy Spirit occurs only once, the infilling may occur at a crisis moment, but it continually occurs as one surrenders to the Holy Spirit. Examples: Stephen Olford, Billy Graham, and myself.

VI. What Are The Great Hindrances To Being Filled And Continually Filled?

1. The grieving of the Holy Spirit (Ephesians 4:30).

2. The quenching of the Holy Spirit (1 Thess. 5:19).

3. Ignorance of the truth and necessity for the infilling (Ephesians 5:17).

VII. Can One Lose The Infilling? Indeed he can and often does.

VIII. Why Do We Need To Be Filled When We Already Have The Holy Spirit Through The New Birth?
Through the new birth, the Holy Spirit indwells us. He is present and resident within us. But He can be present and resident without being president. Unfortunately when the Holy Spirit comes to live within us, we often push Him off into a closet or some dark wing of our soul. Then He has no access to the TV room, the master bedroom, the kitchen, the refrigerator, etc. – that is, He is resident but He isn't president.

IX. What Is The Relationship Of The Average Church Member To The Holy Spirit?
It is my experience that the average church is filled with three different kinds of people:

1. Those who come to church but don't know the Lord at all. The Holy Spirit doesn't live within them, so they can't be filled with Him.

2. Those who come to church who are Christians and the Holy Spirit lives within them, but they never give Him control of their lives.

3. Those who have consciously and knowingly given over their lives to the Spirit's control.

X. Why Do We Need To Be Filled With The Holy Spirit?

1. You must be filled to be obedient to God's commands (Ephesians 5:18).

2. You must be filled to fulfill the requirements of the Christian life. Example: "Jesus commands,...Thou shalt love the Lord thy God with all thy heart, and with all thy soul, and with all thy mind. This is the first and great commandment. And the second is like unto it, Thou shalt love thy neighbour as thyself. (Matthew 22:37-39). How can I attain that?

Scripture says, 'Rejoice always, pray without ceasing, in everything give thanks' (1 Thessalonians 5:16-18). Who can live like that?

Scripture says, 'Take captive every thought to make it obedient to Christ.' (2 Cor. 10:5, NIV). Every thought? How in the world could I do that?

Scripture says, 'Do good to those who hate you, and pray for those who spitefully use you and persecute you' (Matthew 5:44). Even on the freeway, Lord?

These standards, and many more I could mention, are just...well, impossible. If we don't have a power that is beyond us as human beings, we can't live the Christian life."[8]

3. You must be filled in order to exercise your spiritual gifts (1 Cor. 12:7).

4. You must be filled to receive the anointing (1 Cor. 1:21).

5. You must be filled to walk in victory (Romans 15:13).

6. You must be filled to overcome the flesh (Romans 8:13).

XI. Who Is Commanded To Be Filled? Ephesians 5:18 answers this question.

1. This command is in the *imperative* mood. It isn't optional. Every believer is commanded to be filled and controlled by the Spirit.

2. The command is *plural* which means that the command is given to all of us – not just to "super saints" or "spiritual giants."

3. The command is in the passive voice. This means we don't fill ourselves. The filling comes from an outside source – the Holy Spirit.

---

[8] David Jeremiah, *God in You*, Sisters, Oregon: Multonomah Publishers, 1998, pp. 76-77.

4. The command is in the present tense. This means the filling is a repeated event.

XII. **What Are The Requirements To Be Filled?** Assuming you already have the Holy Spirit through the new birth, you must meet the following conditions.

1. **Desire to be filled.** Being filled begins with desire. As a good football coach tells his embattled troops at half-time, "Guys, you gotta want to." Jesus said "If anyone thirst or hunger, he shall be filled." (Matthew 5:6; John 7:37). Does this describe you? Are you thirsty – maybe a little desperate – for a closer walk with God? Do you ever find yourself crying out with the psalmist, 'My soul thirsts for God, for the living God. When shall I come and appear before God?' (Psalm 42:2).

    Jesus said that when the Holy Spirit controls you, you will have a hunger and a thirst to know God and grow in Him. Out of this acute, life-defining thirst comes the Spirit-controlled life."[9]

2. **Denounce all the known sin in your life.** "Confession of sin is critical, but denunciation is a step beyond confession. I might confess to a problem with impure thoughts, but what good does that do if I go out and buy a Playboy magazine this afternoon? Paul explained it like this:

    'Since we have these promises, dear friends, let us purify ourselves from everything that contaminates the body and spirit, perfecting holiness out of reverence for God' (2 Cor. 7:1, NIV).

    When we come to be filled with the Spirit, we have to cleanse our hearts through the shed blood of the Lord Jesus Christ. We have to say, 'God, if there is any sin in my life, if there's something I'm doing that isn't pleasing to You, put Your finger on it. Show me what it is, and Lord, I will denounce it. I will confess it, and I will turn from it.

    You can't be filled with the Holy Spirit while you're harboring your own little pet sins. Maybe it's a place to which you go, a relationship in which you're involved, the types of entertainment you indulge

---

⁹ Ibid, Jeremiah, p. 81.

in, or a habit you've clung to for years—something that you know violates God's standards. You will never be filled with the Spirit of God until you denounce it, confess it, and forsake it. The Holy Spirit isn't just a title, that's who He is, and He doesn't enjoy living in an unclean environment. If there is known, unconfessed sin in your life, the Holy Spirit will not take control. The very fact of your sin is evidence that He isn't in control."[10]

3. **Die to self** (2 Cor. 4:10). To be filled with the Spirit is to yield to His control. It is to take self off the throne of your heart and enthrone Jesus. Romans 12:1-2 are absolute keys to the Spirit-controlled life.

4. **Depend fully upon the Holy Spirit.** A better word is surrender. Surrender is just the opposite of rededication of life or what we call commitment. When we commit to the Lord, we name the terms of our commitment. When we surrender, we let Him set the terms. Illus.: Just suppose Jesus was standing before you and asked you to demonstrate your commitment on a blank sheet of paper He would hand to you. He would not ask you to list on the paper the things you would commit and then sign your name at the bottom. He would just ask you to sign your name at the bottom, and He would fill in over your signature what He would expect and require.

In summary, the requirements are:

(1) I want to be filled – *desire*

(2) I want to get rid of the sin in my life – *denounce*

(3) I want to give control of myself to God – *die*

(4) I am depending absolutely on the Holy Spirit – *dependence* or surrender.

XIII. What Are The Consequences Of Being Filled?

1. When you are filled you reflect the character of Jesus (Galatians 5:22-23).

2. When you are filled, you have victory over indwelling sin (Galatians 5:16).

3. When you are filled, the Bible comes alive (1 Cor. 2:14).

---

[10] Ibid., Jeremiah, pp. 81-82

4. When you are filled, prayer is urgent and compelling (Romans 8:26).

5. When you are filled, you have constant fellowship with the living Christ (John 14:21).

6. When you are filled, you have boldness to witness (Acts 1:8; Acts 4:31).

7. When you are filled, you have great joy (Acts 13:51).

8. When you are filled you are empowered to keep the moral law of God (Romans 8:2-4).

9. When filled, Jesus lives his life through you. Paul testifies to this experience in Gal. 2:20. Illus.: Only if Christ is living in you can you live the Christian life. Suppose I went to play basketball and tried to take the place of Michael Jordan. Could I? Absolutely not. But suppose I showed up and played as well or better than Jordan. How could that be? If Michael Jordan took up his residence within, then he could play the game for me. So it is with the infilling. (Gal. 2:20).

The one indisputable proof of being filled with the Holy Spirit – the fruit of the Holy Spirit

The beautiful fruit of the Holy Spirit is understood best when viewed in the light of the ugly works of the flesh. Thus in the Bible, Paul first identifies the "works of the flesh" (Galatians 5:19-21) and then follows with the "fruit of the Holy Spirit."

1. **The flesh produces works.** The word "work" in Greek is *Ergos*, meaning hard work or labor. A life dominated by the flesh, which is the life style of any unsaved person, is filled with bitterness, excesses, imbalance, self-abuse, laziness, strife, irresponsibility, depression, emptiness, and finally death. It is the hardest route for any individual to take. Yet the flesh cries out to be in charge, screaming to have its own way, demanding to be the boss, all the time promising to bring happiness and fulfillment, when in reality it brings emptiness, frustration, horror, and death – in a word ungodliness. Illus: Like drinking salt water, the more you drink, the thirstier you become.

2. **The Holy Spirit produces fruit,** and the life filled with the Holy Spirit brings forth godliness, the very character of Jesus (God) into

33

our hearts and actions. What produces the fruit? All fruit is produced by some kind of seed. The moment you were born again God sowed His Spirit and Word into your heart like a seed, and you were made spiritually alive by "the incorruptible seed of the Word of God" (1 Peter 1:23). Just like apples produce apples, oranges produce oranges, God's seed in you immediately begins to produce God-like fruits.

Paul lists nine expressions of the "fruit of the Holy Spirit" in Galatians 5:22-23. The great expositor, G. Campbell Morgan, believed that all 8 pieces of the fruit of the Spirit is contained in the authentic love of God (agape). So Galatians 5:22-23 could well be translated like this, "The fruit of the Spirit is love, that is, joy, love, peace, long suffering, gentleness, goodness, faith, meekness and temperance." The Apostle John seems to imply the same truth in 1 John 4:7-8, "Love is of God and everyone who loves is born of God and knowth God." And Paul writes, "The love of God is poured out in our hearts by the Holy Spirit which is given unto us." (Romans 5:5).

Since love capsulates all the fruit of the Holy Spirit, we must ask, "What kind of love?" There are four primary Greek words to describe the various expressions of love:

1. **Eros love** – a term for sexual love, where we get the word erotic. It is significant that this word never appears in the New Testament, not even in the context of sex in marriage.

2. **Stergo love** – the love that exists between parents and children.

3. **Phileo love** – the love between two persons who feel compatible and well matched.

4. **Agape love** – a love that has no strings attached, divine love not looking for what it can get from another but what it can give to that person for his very highest welfare, spiritually, physically, emotionally, psychologically.

Thus you can see the limitations of human love compared to Agape:

1. **Eros** – is self-seeking

2. **Stergo** – is limited only to your family

3. **Phileo** – is based on mutual satisfaction

34

4. **Agape** – is totally unselfish, not limited to one's family, not dependant on mutual benefits, but totally self-giving, absolutely sacrificial, never conditioned by circumstances. The best example of Agape love is found in the best known verse in the entire Bible, John 3:16, "For God so loved (Agapao) the world…"

Now let us observe how Agape sharply contrast with the other expressions of love and what Agape love looks like in the common relationships of life:

1. If Eros is the basis of your sexual relationship with your spouse instead of Agape, you will be self-centered and focused only on your needs, which does not long satisfy and accounts for many divorces. But if your relationship is based on Agape, you will seek to serve and please your spouse and your marriage will improve rather than deteriorate.

2. If Phileo is the basis of your friendship, you will be a "come and go" friend and faithful only as long as you get what you want out of the relationship. If Agape is the basis, you will be a faithful, immovable friend for life.

3. If Stergo is the basis of your love for your family, you will live in disappointments all your life, but if based on Agape, you will always be devoted to your family no matter the disappointments.

4. If Agape is the driving motivation of your life and the force behind all your relationships, you will be the best, reliable, faithful, helpful, understanding individual anyone has ever known. In a word you will be conformed to the image of Christ. To put it another way:

a. Your relationship with God will be marked by love, joy and peace

b. Your relationship with *others* will be marked by long-suffering (patience), gentleness (kindness), goodness

c. Your relationship with *yourself* will be marked by meekness, self-control and faithfulness.

"Love in a Word is the gift of yourself to God and man." No person can naturally give this gift. Only as he surrenders to the Holy Spirit can he give this gift. And this is what it means to be filled or controlled by the Holy Spirit.

THE SPIRIT-FILLED LIFE IS A LIFE OF LOVE

If a person is truly filled with the Holy Spirit, he will make love as a way of life. My favorite marriage counselor is Dr. Gary Chapman, whom I have known some 20 years. His book, *The Five Love Languages* is a classic on the subject of relationships in marriage. *The Five Love Languages* has sold more than four million copies in the USA and been translated into thirty-five languages around the world.

In his latest book, *Love as a way of Life,* Gary has shown how love is the key to the transformation of every aspect of life. He names seven characteristics of a loving person:

1. Kindness – Discovering the joy of helping others.

2. Patience – Accepting the imperfections of others.

3. Forgiveness – Finding freedom from the grip of anger.

4. Courtesy – Treating others as friends.

5. Humility – Stepping down so someone else can step up.

6. Generosity – Giving yourself to others.

7. Honesty – Revealing really who you are.

Gary concludes his book by showing how these seven characteristics transform:

a. Marriages

b. Parenting

c. The Workplace

When you ponder these seven characteristics of love, you immediately see that they cannot flow from our fleshly nature, which is self-serving. These traits can only come from the person who is born of the Holy Spirit "for everyone who loves (agape) is born of God and knoweth God" (1 John 4:7).

It is easy to say you are Spirit-filled. Many do who live totally self-centered lives. If you would know whether or not you are filled with the Holy Spirit, do this: On a scale of one to ten, with ten being the highest, rank yourself on how well you've shown the following characteristics:

I. To Your Spouse: (1-10)

1. Kindness ____
2. Patience ____
3. Forgiveness ____
4. Courtesy ____
5. Humility ____
6. Generosity ____
7. Honesty ____

II. To Your Children (1 -10)

1. Kindness ____
2. Patience ____
3. Forgiveness ____
4. Courtesy ____
5. Humility ____
6. Generosity ____
7. Honesty ____

III. To Your Co-workers (1-10)

1. Kindness ____
2. Patience ____
3. Forgiveness ____
4. Courtesy ____
5. Humility ____
6. Generosity ____
7. Honesty ____

Now ask yourself this question: am I Spirit-filled?

Dangerous and often damnable errors concerning the Holy Spirit

1. A Ghost – In 1611 ghost meant spirit, but a ghost today is a very bad critter hovering over a grave yard or haunted house.

2. A good feeling – emotionally

3. A good feeling – Physically – Ex. Tingle up the spine

4. Loud and noisy – Sometimes He is. Illustration: Fire fell at 16th Baptist Church, Greensboro, North Carolina in 1955. But more often the Holy Spirit manifests Himself by a "still small voice." Illustration: I was in a prayer meeting in Trinity Methodist church, Greensboro, North Carolina, 1958, when a "holy hush" came over us until I could not speak for a time, and turning to my dear friend Roy Putnam and said, "Please pray for me," and he replied, "I can't afford to, I must pray for myself."

5. Speaking through vocal chords – Never has He spoken to me through the English language. However, I was called to my largest and longest pastorate when the Holy Spirit spoke to a brother who had just heard me preach on the Holy Spirit, saying in the English language, "The man you just heard preach should pastor the First Baptist Church, Fort Smith, Arkansas." Whereupon, he notified the Search Committee of that church and the church called me as pastor where I served as pastor for almost twenty years. Never before or after have I known of the Holy Spirit speaking in vocal chords to any person but only in the "still small voice."

6. That He can be used and manipulated – The only predictable thing that the Holy Spirit is that He is unpredictable, except He always glorifies Jesus, not Himself, and speaks in accord with the Bible.

7. That you "get the Holy Spirit." For example, I have heard some say, "I was saved years ago but just 'got the Holy Ghost.'" Wrong. Acts 19:2; Romans 8:9b.

8. That you can be saved without the Holy Spirit. Wrong. John 3:5; Romans 8:9b; 1 Cor. 6:19-20.

9. That you can live the Christian life without the Holy Spirit. Illus: Galatians made this mistake (Gal. 3:1).

10. Separating the Holy Spirit from Jesus (John 14:18).

11. That you can do anything spiritually without the Holy Spirit. Illustration: During the days of His flesh, Jesus said to His followers "Without me you all can do nothing." (John 15:5). But when Jesus ascended to heaven, He commissioned the Holy Spirit to carry on His work in His place. So today we can truthfully say "Without the Holy Spirit, we can do nothing."

12. 12 things you cannot do without the Holy Spirit:

    (1) Be saved – John 3:5

    (2) Know you are saved – Romans 8:16

    (3) Understand the Bible – 1 Cor. 2:14

    (4) Pray – Romans 8:26

    (5) Worship – John 4:24

    (6) Witness – Acts 1:8

    (7) Bear godly fruit – Gal. 5:22-23

    (8) Have hope and joy – Romans 15:13

    (9) Overcome sin and the flesh – Romans 8:13

    (10) Have boldness – Acts 4:31

    (11) Preach or teach – 1 Cor. 2:3-4

    (12) Possess real joy – Acts 2:47

Five Positions On The Miraculous Gifts Of The Holy Spirit

The evangelical world is divided into five camps regarding their views of the operation of miraculous gifts of the Holy Spirit in the church today. Dr. Wayne Grudem, professor of theology at Trinity Evangelical Seminary, Deerfield, Illinois, summarizes the five views as follows, concluding with this statement, "I THINK WHAT PEOPLE REALLY WANT IS TO BE IN THE PRESENCE OF GOD." (Are Miraculous Gifts for Today, p. 347)

1. The CESSATIONIST Position:

The cessationist position argues that there are no miraculous gifts of the Holy Spirit today. Gifts such as prophecy, tongues, and healing

were confined to the first century, and were used at the time the apostles were establishing the churches and the New Testament was not yet complete. This is a well-defined and often-defended position within evangelical scholarship.

There are cessationists within both the Reformed and the dispensational segments of evangelicalism. Reformed cessationism is represented by many of the faculty at Westminster Seminary, especially Richard Gaffin. Dispensational cessationists hold similar positions on this question but are in different institutions; they are represented by institutions such as Dallas Seminary and The Master's Seminary. Within the Lutheran tradition, conservative groups such as the Missouri Synod also hold mostly to a cessationist position.

Standing in clear opposition to the cessationist position are three groups that encourage the use of all spiritual gifts today: Pentecostals, charismatics, and the Third Wave. Although sometimes people have used the terms "Pentecostal" and "charismatic" indiscriminately to refer to all of there groups, the terms are more accurately understood in the following way:

2. **The PENTECOSTAL Position:**

Pentecostal refers to any denomination or group that traces its historical origin back to the Pentecostal revival that began in the United States in 1901, and that holds the following doctrines: (1) All the gifts of the Holy Spirit mentioned in the New Testament are intended for today; (2) baptism in the Holy Spirit is an empowering experience subsequent to conversion and should be sought by Christians today; and (3) when baptism in the Holy Spirit occurs, people will speak in tongues as a "sign" that they have received this experience. Pentecostal groups usually have their own distinct denominational structures, among which are the Assemblies of God, the Church of God in Christ, and many others.

3. **The CHARISMATIC Position:**

Charismatic, on the other hand, refers to any groups (or people) that trace their historical origin to the charismatic renewal movement of the 1960s and 1970s and that seek to practice all the spiritual

gifts mentioned in the New Testament (including prophecy, healing, miracles, tongues, interpretation, and distinguishing between spirits). Among charismatics there are differing viewpoints on whether baptism in the Holy Spirit is subsequent to conversion and whether speaking in tongues is a sign of baptism in the Spirit. Charismatics by and large have refrained from forming their own denominations, but view themselves as a force for renewal within existing Protestant and Roman Catholic churches. There is no representative charismatic denomination in the United States today, but the most prominent charismatic spokesman is probably Pat Robertson with his Christian Broadcasting Network, the television program "The 700 Club," and Regent University (formerly CBN University).

4. **The THIRD WAVE Position:**

In the 1980's a third renewal movement arose, a movement called *The Third Wave* by missions professor C. Peter Wagner at Fuller Seminary (he referred to the Pentecostal renewal as the first wave of the Holy Spirit's renewing work in the modern church, and the charismatic movement as the second wave). Third Wave people encourage the equipping of all believers to use New Testament spiritual gifts today and say that the proclamation of the gospel should ordinarily be accompanied by "signs, wonders, and miracles," according to the New Testament pattern. They teach, however, that baptism in the Holy Spirit happens to all Christians at conversion and that subsequent experiences are better called "fillings" or "empowerings" with the Holy Spirit. Though they believe the gift of tongues exists today, they do not emphasize it to the extent that Pentecostals and charismatics do. The most prominent representative of the "Third Wave" is John Wimber, the late pastor of the Vineyard Christian Fellowship in Anaheim, California, and leader of the Association of Vineyard Churches.

5. **The OPEN BUT CAUTIOUS Position:**

There is yet another position, held by a vast number of evangelicals who think of themselves as belonging to none of these groups. These people have not been convinced by the cessationist arguments that

relegate certain gifts to the first century, but they are not really convinced by the doctrine or practice of those who emphasize such gifts today either. They are open to the possibility of miraculous gifts today, but they are concerned about the possibility of abuses that they have seen in groups that practice these gifts. They do not think speaking in tongues is ruled out by Scripture, but they see many modern examples as not conforming to scriptural guidelines; some also are concerned that it often leads to divisiveness and negative results in churches today. They think churches should emphasize evangelism, Bible study, and faithful obedience as keys to personal and church growth, rather than miraculous gifts. Yet they appreciate some of the benefits that Pentecostal, charismatic, and Third Wave churches have brought to the evangelical world, especially a refreshing contemporary tone in worship and a challenge to renewal in faith and prayer. The "Open but Cautious Position" is the one held by the majority of evangelicals today.

The renewal of interest in the gifts of the Holy Spirit is perhaps the most encouraging development of our time. Why? Because it says that God's people are tired of religion without reality and hunger for the reality of the living God in their lives. I agree with Dr. Grudem, "What people really want is to be in the presence of God." Brother Pastors, you and I must see to it that this hunger of our people is met through our ministry to them. If we do so, the church faces its most glorious future. If not, churches by the thousand face their demise. You and I hold the answer.

HOW DOES ALL THIS AFFECT OUR PERSONAL MINISTRIES?

1. The Local Church – Each pastor should search the New Testament and decide his position on the miraculous gifts. Then he should fully explain his position to his people and specify in writing the policy he would follow in the church. For instance – how he would handle speaking in tongues, words of prophecy, etc.

2. Inter-denominational (ecumenical) meetings – In such meetings essentials which unify must be stressed, not the matters about which

42

there are disagreements. All evangelicals agree on the authority of the Word, the deity of Jesus, salvation by grace, etc., but not on such matters as tongues, words of prophecy, the ordinances of baptism and the Lord's supper, church government, details of the second coming, etc. The rule has long been stated "In essentials, unity; in non-essentials, liberty, and in all things charity."

I preside over a city wide inter-denominational prayer group which meets every Tuesday, 6 AM-7 AM. This prayer group began meeting in April 1999 and has continued to the present time. I suspect that all five views have been represented in our meetings – the Cessationists, Pentecostals, Charismatics, Third Wave and Open-but-Cautious. Great unity has marked our fellowship because we have stressed our likenesses, not our differences.

SCRIPTURE TO INTERNALIZE FOR THIS CHAPTER:

Ephesians 5:18 – And do not be drunk with wine, in which is dissipation; but be filled with the Spirit.

Galatians 5:16 – I say then: Walk in the Spirit, and you shall not fulfill the lust of the flesh.

CHAPTER 3

INTIMACY WITH THE FATHER THROUGH PRAYER

No person will ever conform to the "image of Christ" apart from having a meaningful time with God daily in prayer. It may be trite but it is tritely true that "You can do more than pray after you have prayed, but you can never do more than pray until you have first prayed." Thus prayer should be the top priority in every believer's life, for it is out of one's personal relationship with the Father that one finds strength to live a victorious life and to minister effectively. Jesus Himself said that men "should always pray and not give up," (Luke 18:1), meaning that if one does not constantly pray he will lose heart and live a defeated life out of his flesh. Therefore, I believe that the "one thing" every child of God should do is the very same "one thing" David said he was seeking. "One thing I have desired of the Lord, that will I seek after, that I may dwell in the house of the Lord all the days of my life, to behold His beauty and inquire in His tabernacle" (Psalm 27:4). Robert Murray McCheyne lived only 29 years, but impacted the world as few men have. His "Memoirs" is one of the most valuable books in my library of 12,000 volumes. Of prayer he wrote, "A calm hour with God is worth a lifetime with man."

I have struggled all my life to learn more about prayer, and the greatest single truth I ever learned is this: "When we work, we work, but when we pray, God works." Years ago a whole book was written on the subject, *They Found the Secret*. This book simply recounts the experiences of 20 ordinary guys who discovered life's greatest secret in my judgment, namely, that prayer brings into our lives all "the good things" God has for us (Matthew 7:11), the best being the fullness of the Holy Spirit, which Jesus promised comes through prayer (Luke 11:13).

Charles Steinmetz, a great discoverer and a greater Christian, was asked the question, "Mr. Steinmetz, what is the next great discovery man needs to make?" And he replied, "The thing we need to discover above all is "Prayer." Since prayer is absolutely indispensable for those who would be conformed to the image of Christ and who would serve him effectively, it must not be left to our convenience, moods or feelings.

HOW TO HAVE A MEANINGFUL TIME WITH THE LORD

We have got to understand that the best way to experience spiritual power, direction, and purpose is to have a meaningful time with God daily.

The number one priority in the life of a true disciple should be having a meaningful time with God daily. If nothing else gets done in your day, this must get done.

Seven guidelines for having this meaningful time:

1. A Special Time – "The first guideline to having a meaningful time with God daily is to have a special time that you meet with Him. It is your most important appointment, and you need to make and keep it daily. Ask yourself right now, 'What time am I going to meet with God every single day for the rest of my life?' Since this is the number one priority in the life of a true disciple, I believe that your appointment with God should take place before anything else in your life.

Your time with God should take place before you read the newspaper each day. It should take place before you turn on the television to watch your favorite newscast. Since a meaningful time with God is imperative for you to have a vital relationship with God, then the priorities of your day should reflect this truth. The moment you wander around the house or leave for work or school in the morning without having a meaningful time with God, you make yourself vulnerable to attacks from the enemy."[11]

"Some of you may protest, 'I am not a morning person.' Even if you are not a morning person by nature, it is still important for you to make your time with God the first thing every day. When you meet with God, it shows you depend upon Him. When you do not, it shows you depend upon yourself. If you are going to be involved in effective praying – talking to God and listening to what He is saying

---

[11] Dr. Ronnie Floyd, How To Pray, (Nashville: Word Publishing, 1999). p. 33.

– then you must set aside a time for this to happen, or else it will probably not happen."[12]

I have a time set aside for God. I meet God for a private devotion at 3:00 a.m. or 3:30 a.m. every morning. Yes, the Holy Spirit is awake at this time.

2. Sufficient Time – There is a place for short, even an "arrow" prayer. Jesus often prayed one sentence. But if you have a meaningful time with God, you must take some time. Jesus chided His disciples for not praying one hour. I recommend that you begin with thirty minutes, move to one hour, and often you will need to tarry longer. Jesus commanded persistence in prayer if we expect to get answers (Matt. 7:7; Luke. 11:8). Persistence means time. How do you think God feels when we give Him no more than 2, 3, 4, 5 or 10 minutes in prayer? How much time are you praying daily?

3. A Special Place – "Places are important to God. All through Scripture, we read various accounts of God's activity, and often the place of the activity receives special attention. If you are going to have a meaningful time with God every day, then set aside a special place to meet with Him. This special place needs to be somewhere you enjoy. It needs to be somewhere private. The fewer interruptions you have, the easier it is for you to have a meaningful time with God.

I meet with God every morning in my study at home. This is my special place to be with Him. He has been so real to me in this place. He has spoken to me through His Word. He has built me back up when I have been discouraged. He has put me back together when I am broken. Yes, it is a special place—not because of the color of the room, the beauty of the desk, or the books on the shelves. The thing that makes it really special is that is where God and I hang out together."[13]

4. A Special Plan – "If you do not have a plan to meet with God and pray, then you probably will not do either one. If you are going to have a meaningful time with God daily, you need to develop a game plan. Every day is game day for the Christian. There are no off days or off seasons. In order to be ready for your game day every day, you need to follow a plan when you meet with God."[14]

---

[12] Ibid. p. 34
[13] Ibid. pp. 34-35
[14] Ibid. p. 35

I have used several prayer plans. I began with the Lord's Prayer, then the One Year Bible,[15] the ACTS (Adoration, Confession, Thanksgiving, Suffocation), then one chapter each day, Monday through Friday. Sometimes I combine plans. "Just remember this, if you do not plan to pray, you will not pray. In order to be an effective prayer warrior, you need to plan to meet with God daily."[16]

5. A Special Book – "The special book that you need to read is a compilation of sixty-six smaller books…This book is called the Bible. The Bible is essential for your life. It needs to be studied. It needs to be memorized. It needs to be read daily.

   There is no way that you can have a meaningful time with God without reading the Bible daily. The Bible is the main way God speaks to you. The Bible is His love letter to you. God's Word is intended to be a lamp for our feet and a light for our path. This kind of guidance is possible when you read it and study it during a daily time with Him."[17] It is by hearing the Bible that faith arises in our hearts (Rom. 10:17).

6. A Special Spirit – A special time, a sufficient time, a special place, a special plan, a special book—none of these will result in a meaningful time with the Lord unless you possess a special spirit. What is that spirit? A broken spirit and a contrite heart. This is the sacrifice God requires. This is the sacrifice He honors (Ps. 51:16-17). God dwells in only two places: in heaven and in a humble heart (Is. 57:15). He dwells through the Holy Spirit, the mediator of Jesus, in the humble spirit. But He mediates only with the humble spirit. "God resists the proud but gives grace to the humble" (1 Pt. 5:5 and James 4:6).

   You must have His effectual indwelling to have a meaningful time with the Lord, and you have it only if you approach Him with a repentant and broken heart.

7. A Special Hunger for God – We know it is God's will for us to have a hunger for Him (Matt.5:6 and John 7:37). If you don't have a hunger, you can pray and He will give it to you according to 1 John 5:14. What sends you to the refrigerator day and night? Hunger for food. Hunger for God will also send you to Him to pray daily.

---

[15] For example, *see One Year Bible: The New International Version* (Wheaton, IL: Tyndale, 1986).
[16] Dr. Ronnie Floyd, p. 36
[17] Ibid. p. 36

TEN REQUIREMENTS FOR ANSWERED PRAYER

1. To Get Your Prayers Answered, You Must Pray in Jesus Name (John 14:14).

   When you pray in the name of Jesus, you are praying to the God who manifest Himself in Jesus. You are not praying to Allah or Buddha or some pantheistic force. Pastor Bob Russell was asked not to pray in Jesus name at a civic event. He ended his prayer "in the name of the Lion of Judah." After praying he thought to himself, "I am so clever, how smart I am." Then the Lord convicted him that he was shrewd but was a coward. "Jesus said, if you are ashamed of me and my words, I will be ashamed of you."[18]

   When you pray in Jesus name you are praying to the only way to God. This is clearly stated in 1 Timothy 2:5, "For there is one God and one Mediator between God and men, the Man Christ Jesus,"

2. To Get Your Prayers Answered, You Must Pray According to God's Will.

   When you pray in the name of the Lord, you are submitting your will to His will. You are acknowledging that if both parties don't agree, you want God's will to prevail. Bob Russell states, "We don't dictate to God what He is supposed to do. As Jesus Himself prayed in Gethsemane, so we should pray, 'Not my will, but Yours be done.'"[19]

3. To Get Your Prayers Answered, you must pray with dependence upon the Holy Spirit.

   Romans 8:26 is a special promise. "Likewise the Spirit also helps in our weaknesses. For we do not know what we should pray for as we ought, but the Spirit Himself makes intercession for us with groanings which cannot be uttered." Often we really don't know what to pray for, but when you sincerely pray in Jesus name, the Holy Spirit intercedes for you. He knows you better than you know yourself. He brings your heart and God's heart together to make something happen that is agreeable to both parties.

---

[18] Adapted from Bob Russell, *When God Answers Prayer* (West Monroe, LA: Howard, 2003), 45-46.
[19] Bob Russell, *When God Answers Prayer* (West Monroe, LA: Howard, 2003), p. 48.

4. To Get Your Prayers Answered, You Must Pray in Faith.

Mark 11:24, James 5:15 and Hebrews 11:6 all speak of the importance of faith. The Apostle James says that when we pray, we must believe and not doubt (James 1:6-8). Does that mean that if you have any doubts, your prayers will not be answered? No. In Mark 9:20-24 a father requested of Jesus that He heal his son and Jesus replied, "If you can believe, all things are possible to him who believes, but Lord help my unbelief." (said the man). Jesus did not refuse to help the man because he had doubts. He proceeded to heal the man. God does not require perfect faith, but sincere faith.

5. To Get Your Prayers Answered, You Must Be Righteous in Your Lifestyle.

James 5:16 says, "Confess your trespasses to one another, and pray for one another, that you may be healed. The effective, fervent prayer of a righteous man avails much," now consider the following.

You must have right relations with God – "Behold, the LORD's hand is not shortened, That it cannot save; Nor His ear heavy, That it cannot hear. But your iniquities have separated you from your God; And your sins have hidden His face from you, So that He will not hear" (Is. 59:1-2).

You must have right relations with your fellow man – "If someone says, I love God, and hates his brother, he is a liar; for he who does not love his brother whom he has seen, how can he love God whom he has not seen? And this commandment we have from Him: that he who loves God must love his brother also" (1 John 4:20-21).

"Therefore if you bring your gift to the altar, and there remember that your brother has something against you, leave your gift there before the altar, and go your way. First be reconciled to your brother, and then come and offer your gift" (Matt. 5:23-24).

If you are at odds with another Christian, if you are at odds with God, you are not ready to pray. Go and make things right with your brother and then pray. Confessing your sins does not mean spilling your guts to everyone or airing your dirty laundry in public. Warren Wiersbe offered words of wisdom: "We must never confess sin beyond the circle of that sin's influence. Private sin requires private confession; public sin requires public confession. It is wrong for

Christians to hang dirty wash in public, for such confessing might do more harm than the original sin."[20]

6. To Get Your Prayers Answered, You Must Pray Fervently.

"Confess your trespasses to one another, and pray for one another, that you may be healed. The effective, fervent prayer of a righteous man avails much" (James 5:16)

"Therefore I say to you, whatever things you desire when you pray, believe that you receive them, and you will have them" (Mark 11:24).

Just mumbling some words with no passion and sometimes half asleep will not be honored by God.

Permit me to give you three practical suggestions for praying with greater fervency.

* Kneeling. It is nearly impossible to sleep when on your knees and harder for your mind to wander.

* Pray aloud. When you pray aloud, you impress your spirit and keep your focus.

* Fast. Fasting demonstrates your seriousness. Fasting reminds you that spiritual things are more important than physical things.

7. To Get Your Prayers Answered, You Must Persist in Prayer.

Luke 11:5-8 and Matthew 7:7: "And He said to them, "Which of you shall have a friend, and go to him at midnight and say to him, 'Friend, lend me three loaves; for a friend of mine has come to me on his journey, and I have nothing to set before him'; and he will answer from within and say, 'Do not trouble me; the door is now shut, and my children are with me in bed; I cannot rise and give to you'? I say to you, though he will not rise and give to him because he is his friend, yet because of his persistence he will rise and give him as many as *he needs.*" "Ask, and it will be given to you; seek, and you will find; knock, and it will be opened to you." The words *ask, seek* and *knock* are in the present tense which means keep on asking, seeking and knocking. Russell states, "Don't quit praying just because your prayers aren't answered on the first request."[21] Jesus said, "Men ought always to pray and not give up" (Luke 18:1).

---

[20] Quoted in Russell, pp. 51-52.
[21] Ibid. 63.

51

Remember that God's delays are not His denials but a display of His grace. Isaiah 30:18 says "Therefore the LORD will wait, that He may be gracious to you; And therefore He will be exalted, that He may have mercy on you. For the LORD is a God of justice; Blessed are all those who wait for Him."

8. To Get Your Prayers Answered, You Must Pray With Boldness.

You are invited to pray boldly in Hebrews 4:16. Russell says he memorized the words of John Newton regarding asking largely of God, "Thou art coming to a King, large petitions with thee bring, for His grace and power are such, none can ever ask too much."[22] It is alleged that D. L. Moody prayed for $50,000 when the pastor suggested $5, and received $50,000.

9. To Get Your Prayers Answered, You Must

Incorporate Thanksgiving into Your Petitions "Be anxious for nothing, but in everything by prayer and supplication, with thanksgiving, let your requests be made known to God; and the peace of God, which surpasses all understanding, will guard your hearts and minds through Christ Jesus" (Phil. 4:6-7). With all your groaning, shove in a few Hallelujahs and Thanksgivings.

10. To Get Your Prayers Answered, You Must Abide in God's Word

"If you abide in Me, and My words abide in you, you will ask what you desire, and it shall be done for you" (John. 15:7)

"One who turns away his ear from hearing the law, Even his prayer is an abomination" (Proverbs28:9).

A PERSONAL PRAYER PLAN

Prayer must not be left to convenience, our feelings or our moods. The command of our Lord is to pray continually (Luke 18:1) and persistently (Luke 18:5-12). He, Himself, prayed several hours per day before the light of day (Mark 1:35). I believe every believer should also pray continually, persistently, and prior to daybreak if possible.

One fact is well attested: No one will ever have a powerful prayer life unless he plans it. Left to convenience and feelings, you would do well to pray two hours per week.

---

[22] Ibid., 67.

Consider the following "Personal Prayer Plan."

1. **Step One: Read The Bible.**

   - Before you begin to read, bow your head, be quiet for a moment and clear your mind.

   - Then pray this prayer, "Dear Father, speak to me through your Word today."

   - Use the One Year Bible or some systematic plan.

   - Now take your time.

   - You may want to write meaningful verses in your notebook.

2. **Step Two: The Four "Talking Principles" Begin With The Letters – ACTS:**[23]

   Adore or praise the Lord. Praise is your adoration for Him who loves you so much.

   Confess. Sin clogs the lines of communication between you and God. Claim the promise of 1 John 1:9 which says, "If we confess our sins, He is faithful and just to forgive us our sins and to cleanse us from all unrighteousness." Also Proverbs 28:13, "He who covers his sins will not prosper, But whoever confesses and forsakes them will have mercy."

   Thanksgiving. Thanksgiving is a verbal expression to God for all He has done for you. Be specific. "In everything give thanks; for this is the will of God in Christ Jesus for you" (1 Thess. 5:18).

   Supplication. This is petition and intercession.

   - Focus your prayer on personal needs (petition).

   - Stand in the gap between God and the person for whom you pray (intercession).

   - One may also use the Lord's Prayer.

3. **Step Three: Weekly Prayer Calendar.**

   In order not to miss important objects of prayer, you will need to

---

[23] Bill Bright, *The Coming Revival*,(Orlando, Florida: Newlife Publications, 1995) p. 188.

organize your prayer according to the days of the week. The following is an example:

Sunday – World Missions, Evangelism, Missionaries. Your praying is part of your vital involvement in world evangelization And Jesus came and spoke to them, saying, "All authority has been given to Me in heaven and on earth. Go therefore and make disciples of all the nations, baptizing them in the name of the Father and of the Son and of the Holy Spirit, teaching them to observe all things that I have commanded you; and lo, I am with you always, even to the end of the age." Amen (Matt. 28:18-20).

Monday – United States of America, The President, your Congressman, Senators, Mayor, Governor, etc. You are to "pray for all men in authority" (1 Tim. 2:1-2), regardless of whether you agree with them or not. "Therefore I exhort first of all that supplications, prayers, intercessions, and giving of thanks be made for all men, for kings and all who are in authority, that we may lead a quiet and peaceable life in all godliness and reverence."

Tuesday – The lost, unchurched, lost people in China, India, the Middle East, Europe, the USA and around the world (Rom. 10:1). "Brethren, my heart's desire and prayer to God for Israel is that they may be saved."

Wednesday – Friends.

Thursday – Christian Leaders of the nations and world.

Friday – Relatives.

Saturday – Local churches and pastors.[24]

There are two Urgent Categories of Prayer: 1) Urgent Current Needs – There are always immediate critical needs that require daily prayer; and 2) Continuing Needs – There are always critical needs which never cease to be needs, such as prayer for your children by name, for the Holy Spirit's infilling, for the boldness to witness daily.

---

[24] Quoted in Ronnie Floyd, *How to Pray* (Nashville, Tennessee: Word Publishers, 1955), pp. 217-219.

4. Step Four: Journal.

I say to my students "Anything worth speaking is worth writing down." Also, anything worth praying is worth writing down. I regret that I have not done this through the years.

My nervousness, mobility, and unending labors have prevented this. Also, I have depended on my God-blessed memory, but no mind can recall everything. I have a friend, Ronnie Floyd, who closes his prayer time by writing a one-page letter to God. This letter records his main burdens of that day and also the joy of answered prayer.

5. Step Five: Pray it through.

Some years ago the word circulated that if one asked God more than once he was showing his lack of faith. This teaching is totally contrary to the teaching of Jesus. Jesus commands us "To ask and keep on asking." "Seek and keep on seeking." "Knock and keep on knocking" (Luke 11:9 and Matt. 7:7). Jesus illustrates this truth by telling of an unwilling neighbor who gave his friend bread simply because he kept on asking, seeking and knocking. Woodrow Kroll goes to the heart of the matter when he states, "If persistence was the key to the unwilling heart of a neighbor, how much more effective will persistence be to the willing heart of God."[25]

How long should you pray through? Ronnie Floyd says to pray until one of the following three things occur, and I agree: 1) Until you know it is not God's will; 2) until God answers your prayer; or 3) until God releases you.[26] I say, "Pray when you feel like it, pray when you don't feel like it and pray until you do feel like it." (Stephen Olford)

---

[25] Quoted in Ronnie Floyd, *How to Pray*, (Nashville, Tennessee: Word Publishers, 1955), p. 106.
[26] Ibid. pp. 106-109

PRAYER BUSTERS AND HOW TO BUST THEM

If you are not getting your prayers answered, you should ask three questions:

1. Are my prayers right?

2. Is the timing right?

3. Am I right?

If constantly your prayers are not answered, it is unlikely that your prayers are wrong or that the timing is wrong. The major problem is probably you. So let's look at twelve prayer busters and how to bust the prayer busters:

The first prayer buster is *lostness.* Without a personal relationship with the Father, you cannot pray. Romans 10:13 says,…"whoever calls on the name of the LORD shall be saved." and in John 14:6, "Jesus said to him, "I am the way, the truth, and the life. No one comes to the Father except through Me." So it's clear that no man or woman comes to the Father except through Jesus. The answer is to get truly saved.

The second prayer buster is *prayerlessness.* Jesus said, "Ask and it shall be given" (Matt. 7:7). James spells it out further, "You have not because you ask not" (James 4:2). The answer is to begin praying and keep on praying no matter your discouragements.

The third prayer buster is *partial-praying.* Jesus said not only to "ask" but to "seek" and to "knock." Sometimes you can receive an answer by merely asking, but in most cases you must also "seek" and then "knock." I arise early to first ask; then I seek; and then I go to my office to knock. The answer is more time in prayer each day.

The fourth prayer buster is *heartless praying.* Just saying words is not praying. Prayer is passion, conviction, urgency and feeling (James 5:17-18 and Mark 11:24). The answer is to surrender to the Holy Spirit.

The fifth prayer buster is *unconfessed sin.* (Is. 59:1-2 and Ps. 66:18). The answer is true confession, not just naming your sins, but naming them personally and specifically and turning from them in the power of God (Prov. 28:13). "Lord, forgive me of my many sins" is a cop out. You

must name your sins one by one and specifically, "Lord, I backbited Hazel Snodgrass today. I repent and ask your forgiveness and cleansing."

Broken Relationships "Therefore if you bring your gift to the altar, and there remember that your brother has something against you, leave your gift there before the altar, and go your way. First be reconciled to your brother, and then come and offer your gift" (Matt. 5:23-24). John states, "If you say you walk in light and hate your brother you are still in darkness" (1 John 2:9). The answer is to seek reconciliation. It may not be possible but we must try. "If it is possible, as much as depends on you, live peaceably with all men" (Romans 12:18).

Mistreating your spouse (1 Pet. 3:7). The answer is to obey Eph. 5:25 which says, "Husbands, love your wives, just as Christ also loved the church and gave Himself for her,"

Uncaring Attitude toward the oppressed (Prov. 21:13). "Whoever shuts his ears to the cry of the poor will also cry himself and not be heard." The answer is to ask forgiveness and repent and start helping the oppressed.

Stingy heart (Luke 16:11). "Therefore if you have not been faithful in the unrighteous mammon, who will commit to your trust the true riches?" The answer is to start tithing and giving as a way of life. Claim the promise of Luke 6:38. "Give, and it will be given to you: good measure, pressed down, shaken together, and running over will be put into your bosom. For with the same measure that you use, it will be measured back to you."

Bad Motives (James 4:3). "You ask and do not receive, because you ask amiss, that you may spend it on your pleasures." Many good prayers go unanswered because of their selfish motives. The answer is to check your prayers by four questions:

- Does this prayer glorify Jesus Christ?
- Does this prayer help carry out the Great Commission?
- Does this prayer build the local church?
- And does this prayer build the kingdom and help me spiritually?

Hostility toward the Word of God (Prov. 28:9). "One who turns away his ear from hearing the law, Even his prayer is an abomination." The answer is to search your soul to see if you are saved. Repent. Get back under the Word. Read it. Hear it on every occasion possible, internalize it and obey it.

Unbelief. (Heb. 11:6). "But without faith it is impossible to please Him, for he who comes to God must believe that He is, and that He is a rewarder of those who diligently seek Him." The answer is a steady dose of the Word, answered prayer, and close contact with those walking in victory.

Do you have to be sinlessly perfect or possessing flawless faith? No, but Psalms 66:18 must be taken seriously, "If I regard iniquity in my heart, The Lord will not hear." In 1981 Doris and I were asked by the International Mission Board of the SBC to go to Thailand to minister to our missionaries. Upon arriving we learned that the President of the Thai Convention, Brother Bonkramp, had terminal cancer. After two days of praying we felt led, at his invitation, to pray for his healing. We did so in faith and, believing God had directed us to do so, but at the same time doubting that he would live at that point. About a year later, we were surprised when he appeared at our church to attend our annual clinic on evangelism. When asked how he was doing, he exclaimed victoriously, "After you prayed for me, I was healed." So God honored our prayer, not because our faith was perfect, but it was earnest, sincere and obedient.

COLLATERAL MATERIAL FOR THE THIRD "I"
WHAT MOVES US TO MAKE PRAYER THE PRIORITY OF OUR LIVES

Prayer should be the #1 priority of every Christian, but it is not with most Christians. What, then, moves a Christian to make prayer the priority of his or her life? I believe there are seven paramount and compelling movers to pray:

I. **A Realization of The Greatness of God** – His total sufficiency to meet every human need. A. W. Tozer said, "What we believe about God is the most important thing about us." Certainly when it comes to prayer, the concept we have of God determines our praying. Our belief or lack of it translates into our attitudes and actions concerning prayer. Corrie Ten Boom said, "The size of our prayers is determined

by the size of our God." If our God is big, our prayers will be big, but if our God is little, our prayers will be little and anemic. Illus: Rabbi Kushner wrote a best seller, *Why Bad Things Happen to Good People*, in which he says God wants to answer all our prayers and meet every need, but He is not able to do so under many circumstances. How much praying do you think people will do who believe in such a limited God?

- Illus: Many times as I have struggled in prayer I have found it very helpful to review in my mind the greatness of God (His total sufficiency under all circumstances) by recalling His Names in the Old Testament:

1. **Jehovah Raah** – "The God who sees" (Gen 16:13)

2. **Jehovah Ropha** – "The God who heals" (Exodus 15:26)

3. **El Elyon** – "God the Most High" (Gen. 14:22). Notice its use in connection with Lucifer's desire to be like the Most High (Is. 14:14)

4. **El Olam** – "The everlasting God" (Gen. 21:33). Notice this use in connection with God's inexhaustible strength (Is. 40:28).

5. **El Shaddai** – "The Almighty God" (Gen 17:1). This probably derives from a related word which means "mountain" and pictures God as the overpowering Almighty One standing on a mountain. The name is often used in connection with the chastening of God's people, as in Ruth 1:20-21 and the thirty-one times it is used in the book of Job.

6. **Jehovah Jireh** – The Lord provides (Gen 22:14). This is the only occurrence in the Bible. After the angel of the Lord pointed to a ram as a substitute for Isaac, Abraham named the place, "the Lord provides."

7. **Jehovah Nissi** – The Lord is my Banner (Ex. 17:15). Similarly, after the defeat of the Amalekites, Moses erected an altar and called it "Yahweh Nissi." Actually this and the other compounds are not really names of God, but designations that grew out of commemorative events.

8. **Jehovah Shalom** – The Lord is peace (Judges 6:24).

9. **Jehovah Sabbaoth** – "The Lord of hosts" (1 Sam 1:3) The hosts are the angels of heaven which are ready to obey the Lord's commands. This title was often used by the prophets (Isaiah and Jeremiah) during times of national distress to remind the people that Yahweh was still their Protector.

10. **Jehovah Maccaddeshcem** – The Lord thy Sanctifier (Ex. 31:13).

11. **Jehovah Roi** – "The Lord...my shepherd" (Psalm 23:1).

12. **Jehovah Tsidkenu** – The Lord our Righteousness (Jer. 23:6). This title was a direct thrust against King Zedekiah (which means Yahweh is righteousness) who was a completely unrighteous king (2 Ch. 36:12-13).

13. **Jehovah Shammah** – "The Lord is there" (Eze. 48:35).

14. **Jehovah Elohim Israel** – "The Lord God of Israel" (Judges 5:3). This is a designation frequently used by the prophets (Is. 17:6), similar to the God of Abraham, Isaac and Jacob.

15. **Qadosh Israel** - "The Holy One of Israel" (Is. 1:4).

- **The "Great I Am's" Concerning Jesus in the Gospel of John:**

1. John 6:35 – I am the bread of life.

2. John 8:12 – I am the light of the world.

3. John 10:9 – I am the door.

4. John 10:11 – I am the good shepherd.

5. John 11:25 – I am the resurrection and the life

6. John 14:6 – I am the way, the truth, and the life

7. John 15:1 – I am the vine

Prayer hinges on the confidence we have to whom we are praying, and that confidence is directly proportional to the greatness of God spelled out in His name.

II. **The Recognition of The Greatness of Our Needs** – Our total insufficiency in meeting them. Most people recognize at least some of their needs, and they think they have the ability to meet them, or some other human being can meet them. This explains why very few people, including most professing Christians, make prayer the number 1 priority in their lives. Thus the problem is pride (*hubris*), which St. Augustine called "the mother of all sins." The constitution of the Kingdom of God is the beatitudes, and the first beatitude states that entrance into the Kingdom of God is only for "the poor in spirit" (Matthew 5:3). The Greek had two words for "poor." One

was *penes*, which means "needy." The other was *ptochos*, which meant "total bankruptcy." Such poverty is the door way into the Kingdom or salvation, and it is also the key to effective prayer. That is why "humility" must precede prayer if we expect our prayers to be effective. "If my people…will humble themselves first and then pray…then will I hear from heaven…" (2 Chron. 7:14).

III. **The Experience of Answered Prayer.** If one has experienced answered prayer, he will be moved to keep on praying because he knows prayer works. Statistics reveal that many people who once prayed quit because they said their prayers were not answered. Most of the latter were unbelievers, prayed unanswerable prayers, the timing was wrong, or they just quit praying before God chose to answer. The word of Jesus to Jarius and others was "Keep on Believing." I prayed for 33 years before my father-in-law was saved. Don't quit praying if your prayers have not been answered. Find out why, make corrections, and see your prayers answered. Answered prayers of the past will move your heart to pray in the present.

IV. **The Sheer Joy of Communicating With The Heavenly Father or Coming into His Presence.** "The joy of the Lord is our strength" (Neh. 8:10). There is no greater joy than being in the presence of God through prayer. "In thy presence is fullness of joy and at thy right hand there are pleasures forevermore" (Psalm 16:11). Those who experience this joy, even once, will be moved to experience it often. Such was David's highest desire. "One thing have I desired of the LORD, that will I seek after; that I may dwell in the house of the LORD all the days of my life, to behold the beauty of the LORD, and to enquire in his temple" Psalm 27:4).

V. **The Compelling Example of God's Love Demonstrated at Calvary.** "What shall we then say to these things. He who spared not His Son but delivered Him up for us all, how shall He not by Him give us all things" (Romans 8:31-32). The logic of those verses is irresistible: An all loving God, who has already given His very best, will not refuse to give us lesser things, provided we ask in prayer.

VI. The Intercession of The Holy Spirit to make up for our ignorance of God's perfect will when we pray (Romans 8:26). This shows how very important it is for us to be surrendered (filled or controlled) to the Holy Spirit. Thus God commands every believer not to grieve the Holy Spirit by sinning (Ephesians 4:30) nor quench (1 Thess. 5:19) Him (refuse to obey His leading), lest He become somewhat "dysfunctional" and cease His intercession for us.

One could meet all six requirements discussed above, but to make prayer a priority he would need one more thing:

VII. Faith Strong Enough to Trust God to Meet Our Needs. How do we get such faith? The Bible says real faith comes from hearing the Word of God. What does it mean to hear? To hear not just with our ears but to hear in our heart and souls with a desire to obey what we hear. Samuel cried out to God, "Speak Lord, for thy servant heareth." Samuel was not just pledging to God that he would hear sounds and words, but that he would hear God's message so he would know and obey that message. Millions sit in churches every Sunday and hear good messages and are never changed. Some hear and are radically changed. PTL.

But how can we hear the Word so that it will produce a trusting or surrendering faith? By just reading the Word? No. By just studying the Word? No. By hearing the Word taught or preached? No. By teaching and preaching ourselves? No.

1. We must *know* the Word in our head by diligent study.

2. We must *stow* the Word in our heart by memorization and meditation.

3. We must *show* the Word of God by obeying its teaching.

4. We must *sow* the Word of God by our witnesses.

   This is what we call "Internalizing the Word of God."

   So let us now "Internalize" some key verses on prayer:

1. Hebrews 11:6

2. Mark 11:24

3. Jeremiah 33:3

4. Matthew 21:22

WHY GOD DESIRES THAT PRAYER BE OUR # 1 PRIORITY

The Bible makes it clear that prayer should be the priority in the lives of His followers. Jesus prayed without ceasing (Mark 1:35) and commands the same for His children (Luke 18:1). Paul prayed without ceasing (Phil. 1:3-4) and commanded the same for us (1 Thess. 5:17). The early church was birthed through a ten-day prayer meeting (Acts 1:14) and in the Book of Acts we see believers always doing three things: *praying, praising,* and *witnessing* (Acts 8:4). When we read church history, we note that every effective servant of Jesus Christ made prayer the #1 priority in his life or her life. But why?

1. When Prayer is your priority, God is your priority and Jesus is Lord.

2. When Prayer is your priority, you show you are dependant upon God, not self.

3. When Prayer is your priority, you show that you are thinking of heavenly things, rather than materialistic and sensual matters (Col. 3:1-2).

4. When Prayer is your priority, you show you desire fellowship with God more than any other thing in your life (Psalm 27:4).

5. When Prayer is your priority, obedience to His Word is a priority. Example: the first Commandment and the Great Commandment.

6. When Prayer is your priority, you are protecting yourself from evil which may assault or tempt you (Matt. 6:9-13; Ephesians 6:18-19).

7. When Prayer is your priority, you are enabling yourself to do all the other things God requires of you (Romans 15:30).

8. When Prayer is your priority, you show that you have a living and genuine faith in God (Hebrews 11:6).

9. When Prayer is your priority, you become the recipient of all the marvelous benefits God promises but only through prayer. Jesus says, "Ask and it shall be given" (Matt. 7:7) but "You have not because you ask not" (James 4:2).

10. When Prayer is your priority, you demonstrate that you love Jesus with all your heart and hunger to be with Him above all. "A calm hour with God is worth a life time with man." (Robert McCheyne).

11. When Prayer is your priority, you have impossible and unthinkable and inexplicable blessings (Jer. 33:3; Ephesians 3:20).

12. When Prayer is your priority, it shows you have a personal, saving relationship with Jesus Christ (Psalm 27:4).

BENEFITS WHICH COME WHEN PRAYER IS A PRIORITY:

1. Spiritual healing (salvation) – Rom. 10:13

2. Physical healing – James 5:14-16

3. Strength for daily living – Luke 18:1

4. Peace rather than worry – Phil. 4:6-7

5. Daily needs – food, clothing, shelter – Matthew 6:9-13; 6:33.

6. Freedom from fear – Psalm 34:4

7. Power for witnessing – Acts 4:31

8. The continual infilling of the Holy Spirit – Luke 11:13

9. Nearness to God – James 4:8

10. Protection from evil – Matthew 6:9-13

11. Prevention from burn-out – Luke 18:1

Illus: It is alleged that a certain man went to heaven. St. Peter escorted him into a large warehouse where he noted many unwrapped gifts lying on shelves. When he asked Peter what these gifts were for, he replied, "These were the many wonderful gifts God had for His children, but they never asked Him for them." How about you?

"What a man is: He is on his knees before God – nothing more and nothing less." (Robert Murray McCheyne).

THE THREE STAGES OF PRAYER

Charles Steinmetz, a great Christian Scientist and discoverer, was asked, "Mr. Steinmetz, what should be our next discovery?" To which he replied, "We need to discover prayer." How profound and spiritually instructing and how it resonates with my own experience. From my own experience I would say that the greatest growth I have undergone has been in the area of prayer. I like to think of this as my "progressive maturity" in my relationship and partnership with God.[27] Since I moved to Wilmington in 1993, I have experienced a dimension in prayer I never knew previously in fifty years of ministry. There are three stages of prayer through which I have passed: Biblical praying consists of more than three elements, but the three below describe my progress in discovering the growing depths of prayer.

1. **Prayer Stage # 1 – A simple childlike request for something.** This is a very vital part of prayer and a point where any born again person can begin. Why? Because prayer is a child talking to His father. One of the best books I ever read on prayer is titled, *"Prayer: Asking and Receiving,* by John R. Rice. In this book, the author likens prayer to your backing up a pick-up truck to a large warehouse and saying, "fill it up" with whatever you desire. Another way to put it is this: Prayer is a young guy going to a Burger King and ordering "A Whopper well-done, but hold the pickles and lettuce – with extra ketchup."

   I became strongly conscious of this kind of praying when I was 26 years old and joined a classmate of mine in Duke University in praying this prayer, "Lord, please have someone send me $100 so I can attend Campus in the Woods in Canada." To my amazement my friend, Ed Hackney, received exactly $100 within a few days. To make simple requests to God is a necessary part of prayer. Jesus used this method. He commands direct petition in the Lord's prayer (Matthew 6:9ff). Paul commands this – "Let your request be made known unto God" (Phil. 4:6). However, if one never moves beyond simple petition, he runs into grave danger of missing other dynamics in prayer (such as meditation

27 Philip Yancy, *Prayer, Does it Make a Difference*, p. 106

and practicing the presence of the Lord) and looking upon prayer as a very selfish and self-serving act. Illus: Lord, bless me, my wife, my son Bill and his wife, us 4 and no more." So let's move on to another stage in prayer.

2. **Prayer Stage #2 – Meditation, or what some call "Keeping Company with God."**[28] We should move beyond mere request and make meditation our experience in prayer. Meditation is a vital and necessary part of prayer. Why? Because meditation can refine or even change our requests as we talk to God and seek His direction. Ultimately you want to pray for what God wants, and He may show you during meditation, that what you requested was not what He wanted at all. There is certainly no doubt that meditation adds a sweet dimension to prayer and gives you a great desire to meet with the Lord every day. However, meditation moves prayer from beyond requesting to a relationship which makes prayer enjoyable and exciting. A pastor friend of mine wrote a classic on prayer, in which he says, "Nothing lies beyond the reach of prayer, except that which lies outside the will of God." (Jack Taylor). It is often as we wait in meditation that we come to see God's will and see our prayers answered.

3. **Prayer Stage #3 – Submission to God's Will.** This stage of prayer has become very important to me in recent years. Jesus Himself makes simple requests to His Father in prayer and commands us to do the same (Mk. 11:24). Jesus also no doubt meditated as He prayed. But the climax of His praying was in the Garden of Gethsemane when He in agony said to His Father, "If possible, remove this cup from me; Nevertheless, not my will but yours be done" (Matthew 26:39). Strange as it may seem the Father did not answer that prayer of His Son, and there are times when He cannot answer our prayers which are contrary to His holy purposes and our personal good.

I think the highest experience in prayer comes when we learn that God has ordained prayer as a means of getting God's will done on earth, not ours. As one great scholar wrote, "Prayer is not overcoming God's reluctance but laying hold of God's highest willingness."

---

[28] Ibid. p. 107

Conclusion: Why not use the three stages of prayer in one prayer experience: For instance:

1. Make your request known to God.

2. Meditate on it and dialogue with God for fuller understanding and finally be willing to say to the Father,

3. Father, not my will, but yours be done.

Example: Last Monday, on Laborless Day, as I prayed, my heart being filled with my message to you today, I felt impressed to go through the three stages. First, I prayed that the Lord provide us a lot and building for MMM (Stage 1). Then I began to think and talk to God, asking if we really needed the building now and could we maintain it with our resources or should we wait on the Lord for this (Stage 2). Finally, I said to the Lord, "Not my will, but yours be done." (Stage 3). Will the Lord provide us a place? I cannot say so with eternal certainty, but I am absolutely convinced that He will, in His timing, for His ultimate glory, and the maximum benefit for MMM. *Soli Deo Gloria.*

SCRIPTURE TO INTERNALIZE FOR THIS CHAPTER:

Psalm 27:4 – One thing I have desired of the LORD,

That will I seek:

That I may dwell in the house of the LORD

All the days of my life,

To behold the beauty of the LORD,

And to inquire in His temple.

Matthew 7:11 – If you then, being evil, know how to give good gifts to your children, how much more will your Father who is in heaven give good things to those who ask Him!

CHAPTER 4

INTENTIONAL INVOLVEMENT IN THE WORLD MISSION OF CHRIST

The World Mission of Christ dictates that every follower of Christ would "go into all the world" and "make disciples of all nations" (Matthew 28:18-20; Mark 16:15; Luke 24:47-49; John 20:21b and Acts 1:8) Obedience to this commandment is not optional. Every born again individual is under orders of the risen Christ to carry out this Commission. His Commission is His final word to His people after His ascension – what I like to call "Our Orders from Headquarters."

Two questions arise relating to Christ's Great Commission?

1. **How can the individual carry out the Great Commission?** Someone has observed that there are four requirements for carrying out the Great Commission in the local church. (1) Genuine Care, (2) Intercessory Prayer, (3) Personal Affair, (4) Financial Share. Let us focus on the fourth requirement – Financial Share. While care, prayer, and personnel are absolutely required for the fulfillment of the Great Commission, finances are also indispensable. As Louis Evans said, "The water of life is free, but it takes money to buy pails to carry this water across the earth." Since finances are essential, the Lottie Moon Christmas Offering is crucial for our Foreign Mission enterprise in the Southern Baptist Convention. (Also Annie Armstrong offering for Home Missions). In fact we might say, as the Lottie Moon Christmas offering goes, so goes Foreign Missions in the Southern Baptist Convention. (I am not discounting the critical role of the Cooperative Program). I am advised that the Lottie Moon Christmas offering provides one-half of the budget of our International Mission Board. Therefore, if we can find a way to substantially increase the giving of our people to the Lottie Moon Christmas offering, we will enter into an exciting new day in our missionary outreach. I desire to share with you two things which I have done which dramatically increased the giving to the Lottie Moon Christmas offering in the churches I served:

ANNUAL WHITE CHRISTMAS SERVICE

1. Held the first Sunday in December – before the people spend all their money for Santa.

2. Church decorated in white. Beautiful Christmas tree erected at front of sanctuary decorated with chrismons.

3. Each member of Sunday School instructed one month in advance to bring *two gifts: A gift for local missions* wrapped in white, and labeled appropriately (ex. Socks for 5 year old girl) to be put under the Christmas tree. Also a *monetary gift* for Lottie Moon offering in Lottie Moon envelopes.

4. Each person sits with his or her Sunday School class in the worship service.

5. *Great Mission March* – Pastor preaches 12 minute sermon on The Great Commission. Then he calls the names of each class and leaders, beginning with the youngest. The people march down to deposit two gifts and return to their seats. The choir and congregation joyfully sing Christmas carols while the people come down. (Teachers provide gifts for anyone present who may not bring or cannot afford a gift).

The Mission Savings Club This idea jumped out at me one day as I read 1 Cor. 16:2 in the NIV. It reads like this, "On the first day of each week, each one of you should set aside a sum of money in keeping with his income..." When I saw the words, "set aside a sum of money each week," I thought of the "Christmas Savings Clubs" by which people set aside money for Christmas throughout the year. I then asked myself, "Why couldn't we have Mission Savings Clubs to set aside money for missions throughout the year?" I decided we should and could. In fact, I was compellingly convinced that the Holy Spirit was leading me to do so. I obeyed Him. Here's the way the Mission Savings Club works:

- Print on all offering envelopes the words, "Mission Savings Club," alongside General Fund, Building Fund, etc. Persons electing to give would mark the slot, "Mission Savings Club."

- Encourage your people to give a small offering through the church each week to the Lottie Moon Christmas offering above the tithe. Sometimes the gifts are no more than 50 cents or $1.00.

- Inform the people regularly what has been given toward the Lottie Moon goal. The annual goal is set and announced at the beginning of the budget year. I first used the Mission Savings Club in the First Baptist Church, Fort Smith, Arkansas. Our goal was $100,000 and by the time of White Christmas the church had given about half of this goal through the Mission Savings Club.

RESULTS OF WHITE CHRISTMAS AND MISSION SAVINGS CLUB:

1. First Baptist Church, Fort Smith (8000 members). The Lottie Moon Christmas offering increased from $3,300.00 to $100,000.

2. Clifton Baptist (85 members) – Lottie Moon Christmas offering increased from $140.00 to $540.00 the first year.

3. Houston Northwest Baptist, Houston, Texas (3000 members) – Lottie Moon Christmas offering increased from $2,700.00 to $41,000 in three years.

4. First Baptist, Leland, NC (300 members) – Lottie Moon Christmas offering increased the first year from $1,800 to $10,200.

5. Calvary Baptist Church, Wilmington, NC (1700 members) – Lottie Moon Christmas offering increased the first year from $11,000 to $30,000.

If our churches would use the two above ideas, I am convinced that our mission offerings would quadruple or more within three years. If any church is afraid that Home Missions would be slighted by this arrangement, I would suggest that the offering in December include all missions. In Fort Smith I used the two ideas just for Foreign Missions and took special offerings for Home Missions. Home Missions was not hurt at all. However, in Houston, I included all missions in the special December emphasis. The WMU has historically promoted the Lottie Moon offering. They could still do this with my suggestions, with the added plus of having the pastors promoting missions throughout the church.

How does obedience to this Commission help to "conform us to the image of Christ," which is the sole purpose of Mentoring Men

for the Master? The answer to this question is obvious. How could anyone expect to be "conformed to the image of Christ" or to be a true Christ-follower and not seek to win the lost for whom He died and for which He so clearly commands that we do the same.

Moreover, the sharing of our faith is a major factor in our spiritual growth. The Apostle Paul is bold to pray this prayer for every believer, "I pray that you may be active in sharing your faith that you may have a full understanding of all the good things he has in Christ." (Philemon 1:6 NIV). The Scripture promises that God gives the fullness of the Holy Spirit to those who obey Him (Acts 5:32b). This promise is for those who already have the Holy Spirit in them, thus meaning that there will be an overflow of the Holy Spirit in all who "make disciples" in the Name of Jesus; and the greatest gift of all is the Holy Spirit in all His fullness (Luke 11:13) Why? Because the Holy Spirit is the bringer of "all the spiritual blessings in the heavenly places in Christ." (Ephesians 1:3). The words translated, "spiritual blessings" *pneumatike*, mean all the things bestowed by the Holy Spirit, chief of which would be: the fruit of the Holy Spirit (Galatians 5:22-23), which is the character of Jesus Himself; the power of God to witness (Acts 1:8); the overflowing "joy and hope" of the Holy Spirit (Romans 15:13) victory over all indwelling sin (Romans 8:13); victory over the self life (Romans 8:13) and constant fellowship with the living Christ.

The truth of what I am saying is witnessed when anyone wins a soul to Christ. When he does, he is filled with joy, those around him rejoice, and when the saved person professes his salvation before the church, a spirit of revival sweeps the church. What a thrill to see a local church bubbling with the joy of the Holy Spirit because souls are being won by the members, and what a pitiable, even depressing experience to see a church as dead as a corpse when no soul winning is going on.

COLLATERAL MATERIAL FOR THE FOURTH "I"

26 VITAL QUESTIONS TO CLARIFY THE WORLD MISSION OF CHRIST AND OUR PERSONAL RESPONSIBILITY IN THIS MISSION

1. **What is the "World Mission of Christ"?** The Father sent Jesus into the world "to seek and save that which is lost," (Luke 19:10) and after His resurrection from the dead Jesus commanded His followers to carry out the same mission. "As the Father has sent me into the world, so do I send you" (John 20:21b).

2. **Is the "World Mission of Christ" spelled out by Jesus in the New Testament?** Absolutely in 5 places in the New Testament: Matt. 28:18-20; Mark 16:15; Luke 24:47-49; John 20:21b; Acts 1:8.

3. **What are three imperatives in the Great Commission?**
   a. Make Disciples
   b. Mark Disciples
   c. Mature Disciples

4. **Who is responsible for carrying out the "World Mission of Christ"?** Every truly saved or born again individual. The Great Commission plainly commands, "Go ye or all of you go…"

5. **What is the geographical extent of our going?** Into all the world.

6. **Where should we start in carrying out the mission?** Acts 1:8 says the believer is to witness <u>Both</u> in Jerusalem, Judea, Samaria and to the ends of the earth, but to begin in Jerusalem.

7. **How can one living in Wilmington, N.C. carry out the Great Commission at the same time into all the world?**
   a. Pray urgently for missionaries around the world
   b. Tithe through your church.
   c. Be involved in a witnessing program in your church.
   d. Give to special mission offerings like Lottie Moon and Annie Armstrong.
   e. Make periodic trips to the mission field.
   f. Teach your children to be missionaries
   g. Become a career missionary if God leads.

8. **What is the purpose of the "World Mission of Christ"?** To win lost persons to a saving knowledge of Christ until they will openly confess their salvation before men and become a member of the "University of Christ," the local church.

9. **What is the ultimate purpose of the mission?** That those who are won may become soul-winners themselves. Notice these final words of the Great Commission, "Teaching them to obey all things I have commanded them" (Matt. 28:20).

10. **What are the things He has commanded us to do?** To share the gospel and win the lost, and this privilege and responsibility we are to teach new converts to do. "The task of evangelism is not finished until the evangelized (the saved) becomes an evangelist" (a soul winner himself).

11. **The word "go" is a simple word which all should understand, but most professing believers have misspelled it like this:** attend, give, pray, teach, sing, visit, preach, write, read, seminars, Bible studies, CD's, travel, etc.

12. **Will God hold us accountable for obeying the Great Commission?** Absolutely – Ezek. 33:7-8

13. **Suppose you faithfully share the gospel with the lost and they refuse to receive Christ, will God "free you from their blood" in the judgment?** Yes – Ezek. 33:8.

14. **What person in the New Testament testified that he was "innocent from the blood of all men?** Paul See Acts 20:26.

15. **Why has Jesus delayed His coming?** To give us more time to win the lost. (2 Peter 3:9-11)

16. **Does one need to be highly educated to be a soul-winner?** Absolutely not – There was only one college graduate among the Disciples, Judas Iscariot.

17. **Who was perhaps the greatest soul-winner in the Bible?** Andrew

18. **What was perhaps the most significant conversion in history next to that of Paul?** D. L. Moody

19. **List the basic qualifications of an effective soul-winner:**
    a. He must be saved himself – Luke 6:39.
    b. He must love Jesus above everything else – John 21:15-17.

c. He must be empowered with the Holy Spirit – Acts 1:8.

d. He must pray for lost souls. Thus he needs a "soul" book.

e. He must internalize the Word.

f. He must focus on specific lost individuals.

g. He must be willing to take time to show the lost from the Bible three truths:

(1) His predicament – lostness and separation from a Holy God.

(2) God's provision in Christ

(3) How the lost must respond

23. **How is MMM carrying out the "World Mission of Christ"?**

(1) Stressing the 4th "I".

(2) Participation in Mission efforts abroad in Ecuador, Africa, E-3 led by Tom Jaski, Russia, India and others.

(3) Linkage with Alpha International Ministries of India of which the President of MMM is Chairman of the Board of Trustees.

(4) Making Disciples in the manner of Jesus

(5) The School of Evangelism as a part of MMM.

HOW TO KEEP THE GREAT COMMISSION FROM BECOMING YOUR GREAT OMISSION

Some years ago an avid believer in missions wrote a strong article, encouraging Christians to obey the Great Commission. Then he turned it over to the printers, and to his outrage when he read the printed article, he noted that the printer had left the letter "C" off the word "Commission," making it read "Great Omission." So rather than promoting obedience to the Great Commission, the article recommended that Christians "Omit" the Great Commission.

When I read this article, I said to myself, "Modern Day Christians have done just that – they have 'Omitted the Great Commission.' " Statistics show that only 5% of Baptists ever seek to win the lost to Christ and only 1% succeed. Last year, about 10,000 or more of our 43,000 SBC churches did not baptize one person – almost one out of four churches. What a tragedy and yet how easy it is for the "Great Commission" to become your "Great Omission." How can you and I prevent this? If we would avoid this terrible sin, we must take four positive actions:

1. **PRAY – You and I must pray regularly for the world mission of Christ.**

   (1) We should pray that we ourselves would have a heart for the lost. Naturally we are turned inwardly and focused on self, family, close friends. Only the Holy Spirit can change your heart from this selfish state.

   (2) Pray that the Holy Spirit will fill and refresh your life. Jesus told His first disciples not to leave Jerusalem until they were endued with the power of the Holy Spirit, and then He later said, "When the Holy Spirit is come upon you...you shall receive power" (Acts 1:8). In the book of Acts we see the early Christians witnessing across the earth boldly and successfully. The disciples were waiting for the Holy Spirit, for Pentecost had not come; today Pentecost waits for us. You, if you are a Christian, you have the Holy Spirit, but does the Holy Spirit have you?

   (3) Pray for the missionaries already on the fields of the world. Paul prayed for many he did not know, so can we.

   (4) Pray that the Lord of the harvest will send out others – Matt. 9:37-38. When you do, you may be the answer to your own prayers.

   (5) Pray that missions will be a vital part of the DNA of your local church.

2. **PARTICIPATE – Personally in Sharing the Gospel** according to your opportunities. Assuming you are saved and have prayed and depending on the Holy Spirit, take these practical steps:

   (1) Entertain the idea that God may be calling you to serve on some mission field. "No one has the right to hear the gospel twice until everyone has heard it once." Jesus commanded that we pray that the Lord of the harvest would send out laborers – Matt. 9:38. If anyone prays this prayer sincerely, many will find themselves being thrust out.

   (2) If your children or grandchildren feel a call to the mission field, please encourage them to do so.

   (3) Become a member of a Bible class where you can cultivate lost persons.

(4) Select a visiting partner

(5) Sanctify time each week to witness.

(6) Visit the mission field to see a lost world with your own eyes.

(7) Train your heart to be soul minded.

(8) Buy up your opportunities to witness (Ephes 4:15).

(9) SLAY your excuses for not witnessing:

(a) "I don't have time" – You make time for the important things.

(b) "I don't know how" – Train and visit with experienced partner.

(c) "Witnessing is the job of the pastor" – See Acts 8:4.

(d) "Already busy in the church" – Be sure you're doing 'the work of the Lord' – 1 Cor. 15:58.

(e) "Let the dead bury the dead."

3. **PAY** – God gives us our directions in 1 Cor. 16:2. Paul is taking a missionary offering, and he gives specific words:

(1) Give on the first day of the week (Sunday) – give as an act of worship and give regularly.

(2) Everyone – every believer is to give "According as God has prospered."

4. **PROMISE – God's Promise**

(a) To the Church – Be assured I am with you.

(b) To the Individual – Phil. 4:19 – to individuals who support those who go and give their lives.

SCRIPTURE TO INTERNALIZE FOR THIS CHAPTER:

Matthew 28:18-20 – And Jesus came and spoke to them, saying, "All authority has been given to Me in heaven and on earth. Go therefore and make disciples of all the nations, baptizing them in the name of the Father and of the Son and of the Holy Spirit, teaching them to observe all things that I have commanded you; and lo, I am with you always, even to the end of the age." Amen.

Acts 1:8 – But you shall receive power when the Holy Spirit has come upon you; and you shall be witnesses to Me in Jerusalem, and in all Judea and Samaria, and to the end of the earth."

CHAPTER 5

INTERRELATING WITH OTHERS TO SHARE YOUR LIFE

Christ must be received individually, but He must be shared corporately with our brothers if we would grow into the likeness of Christ. In fact, we never find the word "saint" in the New Testament, but only the word "saints." As John Wesley said, "There is no such thing as a solitary Christian in the New Testament."

But how does our relationship to other Christians contribute to our own spiritual life and being conformed to the image of Christ? Simply because God Himself has created us as inter-dependent or "members one of another." (Ephesians 4:25; Romans 14:7). How do we show this inter-dependence or how can one believer contribute to the life of another brother or sister?

1. By meeting together for mutual encouragement. Thus God commands in Hebrews 10:25. The word "encouraging" is the Greek word *Parakaleo*, meaning "come alongside" to help another. Jesus Himself calls the Holy Spirit, the *Parakeletos*, the One who comes alongside of each believer to be his Comforter, Teacher, Helper, etc. However, the way the Holy Spirit accomplishes this wonderful ministry is often by sending believers through whom He works.

2. By ministering to others by the use of our spiritual gifts. Thus the Apostle Peter writes, "As every one has received a gift (the charisma), even so minister the same one to another, as good stewards of the manifold grace of God." (1 Peter 4:10). What an amazing statement – that God gives each individual gifts, not for him to use for himself but for fellow Christians by which he ministers all kinds of graces to them. Example: I think God has given me the gift of preaching and teaching. But these gifts are not for me, but for my brothers and sisters. When I share them with others, they are greatly blessed, and not only so, but I myself feel greatly fulfilled and made more and more like Christ. Suppose I fail to share my gifts: I lose them. One wise writer wrote, "When you fail to share Christ with others, you lose Him in your own heart."

3. By mentoring others through spiritual partnerships. Every Christian needs a person who will meet with him regularly and hold him accountable for the way he is living. Such a mentor should love his partner so much that he will not just enjoy a "coffee-drinking" relationship, but will ask the tough questions:

   a. Are you having a meaningful time with the Lord each day?

   b. Are you Internalizing the Word of God constantly?

   c. How are you loving your wife as Christ loved the church?

   d. Are you guilty of internet adultery?

   Illus.: A young college student confided in me that he was being tempted to sin sexually, whereupon he shared his problem with his godly roommate, whose counsel kept him from doing so.

4. By intercessory prayer. There is nothing one Christian can do for another brother as important as intercessory prayer. Intercessory prayer was not a vital part of my praying in my earlier years, but today it has become the heart of all my praying. What a joy and what a privilege. In fact when I find it hard to pray, I begin to intercede and the Holy Spirit comes upon me in a wonderful way.

I have often said, "When we work, we work; but when we pray, God works." I witness this truth frequently in the lives of those for whom I intercede. Example: I have one grandson, who at the age of 12 was very rebellious and was almost becoming incorrigible. I talked to him often, sent him emails, showed my love in a hundred ways, but I saw no change in his life. Then suddenly God told me to stop talking and working, to lay him upon the altar, and begin interceding for him. I did precisely that and within a few months God began to work in him, turned him around completely and today he is an exemplary young man.

So in conclusion I am confident in saying that "You can do more than pray after you have prayed, but you can never do more than pray until after you have prayed." How true, how true, and in no area is it more true than when we pray for one another. And at the same time we are praying for others, we are becoming more and more like Christ, conforming to His image, and developing into a true Christ follower.

COLLATERAL MATERIAL FOR THE FIFTH "I"
WHEN THE BIBLE DOES NOT SPEAK – WHAT THEN?
ROMANS 14 AND 15

God commands that Christians relate to fellow believers so they can minister to their needs. But how can this be when there is serious disagreement over certain practices and especially when the Bible does not specifically permit or forbid certain activities. As someone observed, "where you find two church members, you have three votes."

The problem of disagreement among believers is not new. In fact, it raised its ugly head in the great church at Rome. The Holy Spirit had brought together a remarkably heterogeneous group of Jewish and Gentile Christians. Paul divided the church into two parties, calling the law-observing Jews "the weak," and the liberated Gentiles "the strong." The "weak party" would not eat meat which had been offered to idols, and the "strong party" saw no evil. The solution to this problem could have been to form two churches, "The Church of the Carnivores," or meat eaters, and "The First Church of the Vegetarians." But Paul did not do this, because he knew the church should be one in the midst of their differences over matters which were neither moral nor immoral but amoral. At this point we must realize that there are some things which are always right and always wrong and thus non-negotiable. Such things are summarized in the 10 Commandments. Having stated this let us now note how Paul tells us to deal with "the negotiables." So Paul tells the Romans how to handle their troubling difficulties in Romans 14 and 15:

I.   First, the members of the Church must *Respect* the differences of their fellow members. "Receive one who is weak in the faith, but not to disputes over doubtful things. For one believes he may eat all things, but he who is weak eats only vegetables. Let not him who eats despise him who does not eat, and let not him who does not eat judge him who eats; for God has received him" (Romans 14:1-3). The one who is weak is not weak in his Christian faith, but he is

weak in believing he can not eat meat offered to idols. The "strong" are not stronger Christians, but they have a strong faith to believe they can eat meat. So Paul calls on each group to accept one another, for all had been accepted by God. Now Christians aren't divided today over eating meat and vegetables, but I know of several issues which divide Christians today:

a. Going to the theater

b. Wearing make-up

c. Tobacco

d. Card playing

e. Dancing

f. Wearing shorts

g. Music

h. Bible translations

i. Sports

j. Television

k. Alcohol

Leslie Flynn wrote a whole book on *Great Church Fights* in which he says, "Wide disagreements exist today in our churches over certain practices. A Christian from the South may be repelled by a swimming party for both men and women, then offend his Northern brother by lightning up a cigarette. At an international conclave for missionaries, a woman from the Orient could not wear sandals with a clear conscience. A Christian from western Canada thought it worldly for a Christian acquaintance to wear a wedding ring, and a woman from Europe thought it almost immoral for a wife not to wear a ring that signaled her status. A man from Denmark was pained to even watch British Bible school students play football, while the British students shrank from his pipe smoking."[29]

---

[29] Leslie Flynn, Quoted in R. Kent Hughes, *Romans*, Wheaton, Illinois, Crossway Books, 1991, p. 259.

II. Members must *Realize* that members with opposing views on non-essentials can both be perfectly right with God. "One person esteems one day above another; another esteems every day alike. Let each be fully convinced in his own mind. He who observes the day, observes it to the Lord; and he who does not observe the day, to the Lord he does not observe it. He who eats, eats to the Lord, for he gives God thanks; and he who does not eat, to the Lord he does not eat, and gives God thanks" (Romans 14:5-6).

"This controversy over days probably involved Sabbath observance. The Christian Jews' conscience demanded that they observe it. The Christian Gentiles' conscience argued that every day is equally devoted to the service of God. Paul's advice to both is simply, 'Each one should be fully convinced in his own mind.' Each believer is to use his or her powers of reasoning which have at least begun to be renewed by the gospel under the authority of God's Word and act accordingly. The same is to be true of eating and abstaining from meat. The evidence that both the "weak" and the "strong" have right hearts is that they both give "thanks" to God. That is, both do what they do with the intention of serving the Lord."[30]

Illus.: Two of the mightiest preachers of England in the 19th century were Charles Spurgeon and Joseph Parker. Early in their ministries they were close friends and even changed pulpits. Then they had a disagreement. Spurgeon accused Parker of being unspiritual because he attended the theater, and Parker condemned Spurgeon because he smoked cigars. Spurgeon argued that he did not smoke to excess, but when asked what he meant, he said, "No more than two at a time." Who was right? Perhaps neither. Certainly these preachers were not justified in condemning each other. However, if the Holy Spirit convicts you that something is wrong in your life, you had better not do it, even if other Christians are doing it. In my humble (but accurate) opinion, I believe attending most movies and smoking are sins, and I cannot participate in either. But I must not condemn my brother who may disagree.

III. Each member of the church should *Recognize* that one day he will give an account of himself to the Lord Jesus Christ. "But why do

---

[30] R. Kent Hughes, Ibid. pp. 262-163,

you judge your brother? Or why do you show contempt for your brother? For we shall all stand before the judgment seat of Christ. For it is written:

"As I live, says the LORD,
Every knee shall bow to Me,
And every tongue shall confess to God."
So then each of us shall give account of himself to God" (Romans 14:10-12).

The apostle Paul is simply saying this: "Stop trying to be God to one another." You "weak," why do you pass judgment on your brother? You "strong" why do you look down with contempt on your brother? Remember each of us will stand before the judgment seat of Christ (the Bema). Your works will be judged there, especially your motives. Paul graphically describes the scene in 1 Cor. 3:13-15, "Each one's work will become clear; for the Day will declare it, because it will be revealed by fire; and the fire will test each one's work, of what sort it is. If anyone's work which he has built on it endures, he will receive a reward. If anyone's work is burned, he will suffer loss; but he himself will be saved, yet so as through fire."

Realizing the differences that believers were bound to have on matters not clearly forbidden in the Bible, St. Augustine coined a helpful motto which I have endeavored to follow in my churches: "In essentials, unity; in non-essentials, liberty; in all things, charity."

There is room in Christ's church whether you use my translation or not, whether you attend the movies or not, whether you walk to church or ride in your Mercedes, whether you wear wingtips or sandals, whether you sing hymns or choruses, whether you powder your nose or not, whether you watch television or abstain.

The hardest church fight I ever heard about was a conflict over which side of the church the piano should be stationed.

I read of a father and son who parted forever over the color of a boat. Here goes the story. The two were discussing great events of the past – about the years in Little League, hunting expeditions, swimming together, etc. The son said to his dad, "Dad, do you remember the time we were on the lake in that green boat?" His father said, "You are mistaken. The boat was blue, son." The son said, "No, it was green." Again the father

said "You are mistaken, it was blue." "Green." "Blue." "Green." "Blue." And his son departed, and never returned.

Some things just don't matter. May we have the patience and humility to allow the Holy Spirit to give the wisdom to see what is essential and what is not.

Lest some one take my above observations to think that there are no fixed standards in the Christian life, I want to make it crystal clear that I am not promoting a damnable heresy. Some have thought Paul was infinitely flexible when he says, "I have become all things to all men that if by any means I may win some." (1 Cor. 9:22). Wrong, wrong. Paul would never say, "I am free to do anything I want." Paul is under "Christ's law." To say "to the thief I became a thief to win the thief; to the drunkard, "I became a drunkard to win the drunkard" is nonsense and a total misrepresentation of what Paul is saying. One person said to me, "I love our pastor because he just lets down his hair, gets on the floor and acts like the rest of us, including drinking a bottle of beer." Pastors or anyone who lives just "to fit in" cannot win anyone. As D. A. Carson says, "They hold to nothing stable or solid enough to win others to it." (The Cross and Christian Ministry, pp. 120-121).

TAKING CARE OF "ONE ANOTHER" – ACCORDING TO GOD'S WORD

1. Love one another. John 13:34-45

2. Be devoted to one another. Romans 12:10

3. Give preference to one another. Romans 12:10

4. Don't judge one another. Romans 14:13

5. Build up one another. Romans 14:19

6. Accept one another. Romans 15:7

7. Serve one another. Galatians 5: 13

8. Carry each other's burdens. Galatians 6:2

9. Forgive each other. Ephesians 4:32

10. Encourage one another. Hebrews 3:13

11. Pray for one another. James 5:16

12. Offer hospitality to one another. 1 Peter 4:9

13. Be kind to one another. 1 Thessalonians 5:15

"Kindness makes a person attractive. If you would win the world, melt it, do not hammer it." Alexander Maclaren.

SCRIPTURE TO INTERNALIZE FOR THIS CHAPTER:

1 Thessalonians 2:8 – Because we loved you so much, we were delighted to share with you not only the gospel of God but our lives as well.

Hebrews 10:24 – And let us consider one another in order to stir up love and good works.

CHAPTER 6

INVESTING ONE'S MONEY REDEMPTIVELY, BEGINNING WITH THE TITHE TO ONE'S LOCAL CHURCH – MALACHI 3:8-10 AND 2 CORINTHIANS 9:6-11

Someone said, "The universal passport to happiness on this earth is money." This statement is true up to a point, but not unless one invest his money in redemptive purposes. If one should do so, he must view and use money according to the ten principles laid down in God's Word:

1. God is the Owner of all material things, including money – Haggai 2:8; Psalm 24:1.

2. God has given us all the money and material things that we possess – 1 Cor. 4:7b.

3. We own nothing – Acts 4:32.

4. We are stewards of all God has given us, not owners.

5. We must give an account one day to God as to how we have used our material gifts.

6. If we give as God has commanded, beginning with the tithe to our local church, God will bless us above measure – Mal. 3:10; Luke 6:38 – meaning that we will have what we need when we need (our need, not our greed) – Phil. 4:19.

7. Our giving must be from our hearts, prompted by the grace of God, not because of "compulsion or of necessity" – 2 Cor. 9:7.

8. Because of our grace living, God's grace will enrich us morally and spiritually on this earth so that we grow in Christian character – 2 Cor. 9:7; Luke 16:12.

9. We will experience financial freedom which is essential for abundant living in this life – Mal. 3:10; 2 Cor. 9:7,11.

10. When we get to heaven we will be welcomed by those who were won to Christ because of our giving – Luke 16:9.

Now the question arises, how can we apply the above principles in a practical way? The answer is: By earning and managing our money for the redemption of human kind and the glory of God.

The Bible teaches that God has five fundamental laws on how to make and use our money. Before naming these laws, permit me to summarize the viewpoint of Jesus Christ on money.

Did you know Jesus said more about money than on any other subject? In fact one third of His teaching concerned material matters. Why? Jesus' answer is the most enlightening word in the Bible about money when He stated, "He that is faithful in that which is least is faithful in that which is much" (Luke16:10). Jesus makes the point that that which is least is money and that which is much is spiritual things.

In simple English, Jesus is saying "Money is very important because it is a test—God's test of a person's spiritual relationship to God." In fact, Jesus declares that if a person is faithful in managing his money he will be faithful in spiritual things and if unfaithful in money, he is unfaithful in spiritual things. Furthermore, He asserts that if one is unfaithful in the use of mammon (money) God cannot trust him with spiritual riches. The result of course, is spiritual disaster. Therefore, I appeal to you, "Manage your money God's way or money will murder you spiritually." But how should we manage money?

The Bible teaches that God has five laws for successful money management:

LAW # I – Secure your money righteously. Money is "filthy lucre." No, money is neither moral nor immoral. But it becomes tainted if earned immorally.

- Money should not be earned in violation of your character.
- Money should not be earned when it injures other persons. For example, cheating, selling drugs, alcohol, or the lottery.
- Money should not be earned to the neglect of family, church, and devotion.
- Money should not be earned to fulfill your greed, but your need.
- Money should not be earned by crooked investments.
- Money should not be earned by the desecration of the Lord's Day.

LAW # 2 – Save your money *realistically*.

- Don't spend all you make. Save some for the inevitable uncertainties of the future. The wisdom of Solomon says, "Go to the ant, you sluggard! Consider her ways and be wise, which, having no captain, overseer or ruler, provides her supplies in the summer, and gathers her food in the harvest" (Prov. 6:6-8}.

- Save 10% of what you make for unexpected and emergency needs.

But do not hoard your money. Invest your money in souls for heavenly reward or in the judgment your money will "eat your flesh like fire" (James 5:3). This means that your failure to use your riches for God and others will cause you the keenest remorse. When your eyes see the cruelty of your selfishness and greed (costly jewelry, elegant clothing, extravagant homes, high-priced cars, and huge bank accounts) it will be a hellish experience. James 5:1-5 says, "Come now, you rich, weep and howl for your miseries that are coming upon you! Your riches are corrupted, and your garments are moth-eaten. Your gold and silver are corroded, and their corrosion will be a witness against you and will eat your flesh like fire. You have heaped up treasure in the last days. Indeed the wages of the laborers who mowed your fields, which you kept back by fraud, cry out; and the cries of the reapers have reached the ears of the Lord of Sabbath. You have lived on the earth in pleasure and luxury; you have fattened your hearts as in a day of slaughter."

LAW # 3 – Spend your money *responsibly*. You are as responsible for the 90 % as the 10 %.

- Stay out of debt.
- Do not engage in credit buying.
- Do plastic surgery, "cut up your credit cards."
- Avoid impulse buying.
- Avoid ego spending.
- Live within your income.
- Remember, you can buy all kinds of things on credit, but none of it is yours until you pay for it. Purchasing something, when you know you can't pay for it, is stealing.

- Be guided by this economic principle: "If your outgo exceeds your income, your upkeep will be your downfall."

LAW # 4 – Share your money *redemptively.* Jesus said, "Do not lay up for yourselves treasures on earth, where moth and rust destroy and where thieves break in and steal, but lay up for yourselves treasures in heaven, where neither moth nor rust destroys and where thieves do not break in and steal." (Matthew 6:19- 20). How can you lay up treasures on earth? We do this by spending our money on things which are going to heaven. Stocks, bonds, and money are not going to heaven—only redeemed souls. How can we get souls into heaven?

- Start with the tithe. The tithe is 10% off the top given to God weekly through the storehouse, that is, the local church to pay the expenses of the churches incurred in winning the lost (Malachi 3:10; 1 Corinthians 16:2; and Leviticus 27:30).

- Give "as God has prospered you" (1Corinthians 16:2). Everyone is commanded to tithe (Malachi 3:10, Matthew 23:23), but many should give more. You rob God in offerings as well as tithes (Malachi 3:8) if you do not give "as God has prospered."

- Especially invest in areas of direct missions. For example, Mentoring Men for the Master has a goal to train 10,000 pastors and laymen in America. Alpha Ministries, Int'l., has a goal to train 100,000 pastors in India. Ministries which are making an impact for the kingdom of God are worthy of your support.

- Pay your way to the mission field.

LAW # 5 – Send your money *before you.* You can't take it with you, but you can send it on before you. How? You can send it before you by using your money to get people into heaven. This is precisely what Jesus commands us to do and promises an incredible reward in heaven for those who do. Jesus said, "I say unto you, make friends for yourself by the use of your unrighteous mammon so that when you check out, they will welcome you into everlasting habitations." (Luke. 16:9). This is the teaching of our Lord. By the wise investment of material possessions, we can have part in the eternal blessing of men and women. We can make sure that when we arrive at the gates of heaven, there will be a

"welcoming committee" of those who were saved through our sacrificial giving and prayers. These people will thank us, saying, "It was you who made it possible for me to be here."

Conclusion

I can say all that I have said above in one statement: God is measuring you and me by the way we *secure* our money, the way we *save* our money, the way we *spend* our money, the way we *share* our money, and the way we are *sending* our money ahead.

- Are you securing your money *righteously?*
- Are you saving your money *realistically?*
- Are you spending your money *responsibly?*
- Are you sharing your money *redemptively?*
- Are you sending your money *before you?*

COLLATERAL MATERIAL FOR THE 6TH "I"
GIVE UNTIL YOU GIGGLE
2 COR. 9:6-8, 11

Our motive in giving is vitally important. Our motive in giving should come from the heart, and the motive in the heart must please God. The finest passage on right giving in the Bible is found in 2 Cor. 9:6-11. In this section, Paul describes 4 kinds of givers – *Bad* Givers, *Sad* Givers, *Mad* Givers, and *Glad* Givers.

1. **Bad** givers give sparingly or nothing. Such givers give out of selfishness if they give at all. Such giving is not acceptable to God – 2 Cor. 9:6.

2. **Sad** givers give grudgingly. Such giving is done "grudgingly," not freely, and is also not acceptable to God – 2 Cor. 9:7a.

3. **Mad** givers give "of necessity." Such giving is not acceptable with God, for the giver does not give because he desires to give but he gives only because he feels he has to give – 2 Cor. 9:7b.

4. **Glad** givers. Such giving is highly acceptable and praised of the Lord, because such givers give from their heart – a heart freed from sin and selfishness and a heart in love with Jesus Christ and the gospel. Jokingly I have often said "God loves a cheerful or hilarious giver, but He will take from a "tight wad." Not really. No gift is acceptable to God unless the giver is motivated by love for God and man, and he is able freely to give with great joy and thanksgiving, all the time praying that he can give more and more.

Illustration: Adrian Rogers used to say, "In the event you can give freely and joyously at church, you ought to go home and "giggle" all night long." Often we hear the words, "give until it hurts." Wrong. God's way of giving is to give until it does not hurt but brings great joy to the heart and positive glory to the God who gives to us that we might give to Him and others.

What blessings flow into the lives of the "Glad or Hilarious Givers?" Paul answers in 2 Cor. 9:8, "God is able to make all grace abound to you that you having all sufficiency in all things may abound unto every good work." Then Paul spells out the blessing in even greater detail in 2 Cor. 9:11, "You will be made rich in every way so that you can be generous on every occasion, and through us your generosity will result in thanksgiving to God."

Caution: God does not promise to make us rich materially if we are a glad giver, but He does promise to give us what we need when we need it. Such is the promise of Phil. 4:19, "My God shall supply all your need according to His riches in glory by Christ Jesus." This promise is only for glad givers, as were the Philippian Christians.

Concrete ways to invest your money redemptively:

- Tithe through a Great Commission local church. "That there may be meat in mine house" (Mal. 3:10).

- Give generous offerings to support foreign and home missions.

  a. Lottie Moon at Christmas (IMB)

  b. Annie Armstrong (NAMB).

- Pay expenses on short term missions – (STM)

- Give to special ministries which are training people to win the lost – For example, AIM (Alpha International Ministries) has a goal of training 100,000 church planters by 2020.

- Help missionaries get their education.

- Provide home for missionaries on furlough.

- Purchase equipment for missionaries.

THE CHRISTIAN'S RESPONSE TO OUR ECONOMIC CRISIS
HABAKKUK 3:17-19

The floundering economy has caused many Americans to be concerned about the future. The economists are convinced that some form of economic Armageddon looms just over the horizon. But what should be the response of the people of God? A question every Christian should be asking is: could God be using these uncertain times as a wake-up call to see where our trust really lies? Dr. Paul Brewster, whom I have mentored for years, writes that "many American Christians are far more concerned about the collapse of their investment portfolios than about the spiritual collapse of the nation, and that while secular economists see certain doom just around the corner, God's people should view our economic distress as a *blessing in disguise*."

Let us, therefore, consider some biblical principles which should guide Christians during these uncertain days:

1. **Recognize** that God is sovereign over the economic situation – Psalm 103:19 "The LORD has established His throne in heaven. And His kingdom rules over all."

2. **Realize** that God has a redemptive purpose in allowing the economic crisis:

    (a) to expose corruption not just of Fannie and Freddie but of Tom, Dick and Harry.

    (b) to wake up a sleeping and Laodicean church – Revelation 3:16-17, "So then, because you are lukewarm, and neither cold nor

hot, I will vomit you out of My mouth. Because you say, 'I am rich, have become wealthy, and have need of nothing'—and do not know that you are wretched, miserable, poor, blind, and naked."

(c) to show a nation that you cannot serve God and mammon – Matthew 6:24 "No one can serve two masters; for either he will hate the one and love the other, or else he will be loyal to the one and despise the other. You cannot serve God and mammon."

(d) to get the attention of the lost.

3. **Repent** of our personal greed (coveting) which has become the American idol – Col. 3:5, "Therefore put to death your members which are on the earth: fornication, uncleanness, passion, evil desire, and covetousness, which is idolatry."

4. **Relieve** our suffering brothers and ministries if possible – 1 John 3:17, "But whoever has this world's goods, and sees his brother in need, and shuts up his heart from him, how does the love of God abide in him?."

5. **Rejoice** in the God of our salvation when the economic situation is bleak. "Although the fig tree shall not blossom, neither shall fruit be in the vines; the labour of the olive shall fail, and the fields shall yield no meat; the flock shall be cut off from the fold, and there shall be no herd in the stalls: Yet I will rejoice in the LORD, I will joy in the God of my salvation. The LORD God is my strength, and he will make my feet like hinds' feet, and he will make me to walk upon mine high places" (Habbakuh 3:17-21).

6. **Resort** to practical steps to address your economic problems:

    a. Learn to be content – Heb. 13:5; Phil. 4:11.

    b. Pay your bills faithfully.

    c. Prioritize your debt, making sure you don't compromise your home or transportation.

    d. Negotiate with your creditors as needed. Make payment arrangements with your creditors rather than waiting until you miss payments and they come flocking for you.

    e. Downsize if it puts you in a better cash position.

f. Pay extra whenever you can to accelerate your payoff dates.

g. Have a garage sale to generate extra cash to pay down debt or to increase savings.

h. Capitalize on your most valuable assets, your family.

i. Learn to garden, use fresh vegetables and fruit when in season, try a new recipe."[31]

j. If guilty, quit robbing God. Tithe – Mal. 3:10; 2 Cor. 9:6-11.

k. Revisit your spending habits and cut out the ridiculous and unnecessary. Examples:

- Americans spent $21.3 billion on pets in 2002 (twice the amount given to foreign missions}

- $224 billion on eating out

- $67 billion on frozen dinners

- $15 billion on junk food snacks

- $25 billion on gardening

- $22.1 billion on hunting

- $191 billion on personal watercraft

"Where your treasure is, there your heart will be also" – Matthew 6:21.

a. Invest all you can in ministries which change lives and save souls – Luke 16:9

b. Undergo plastic surgery and live within your means, for if your outgo exceeds your income, your upkeep will be your downfall. (The average American has 9 credit cards).

c. Be generous in giving and leave the consequences with God. I have followed this rule in the worse of economic times and have experienced miracle, after miracle, after miracle. Praise the Lord!

[31] Crown Finance.com

SCRIPTURE TO INTERNALIZE FOR THIS CHAPTER:

Matthew 6:19-20 – Do not lay up for yourselves treasures on earth, where moth and rust destroy and where thieves break in and steal; but lay up for yourselves treasures in heaven, where neither moth nor rust destroys and where thieves do not break in and steal.

2 Corinthians 9:6-8 – But this I say: He who sows sparingly will also reap sparingly, and he who sows bountifully will also reap bountifully. So let each one give as he purposes in his heart, not grudgingly or of necessity; for God loves a cheerful giver. And God is able to make all grace abound toward you, that you, always having all sufficiency in all things, may have an abundance for every good work.

CHAPTER 7

THE 7ʰ "I"

IDENTIFICATION WITH, SUPPORT OF AND SERVICE IN A LOCAL CHURCH

Just as the family is indispensable in God's plan for the human race, so is the church for God's people. In our day the church has fallen on evil days, and even some sincere people have said, "Jesus, Yes, but the church, No." But those who would make such a statement do not know or understand what God says about the church and its necessary place in His plan to redeem the world. Of course, many local churches and some pastors have failed miserably and become the "laughing stock" of the media and the world. But this must not be the opinion of those of us who know our Bible and would follow its instruction regarding the church. So let us take note of the biblical description of the church.

1. The church is the "body of Christ." The church is a "body of baptized believers," but it is far more. The church is the creation of God through the new birth, the baptism of the Holy Spirit, and the bestowal of spiritual gifts.

2. The church belongs to Jesus. Jesus categorically defined the church as, "My church." "Upon this rock, I will build my church" – Matthew 16:18. We know that often people think of the church they attend as "my church," and it is good to have devotion to our church, but let us never forget that the church belongs to none other than Jesus Christ.

3. Jesus and the church are not exactly the same, but they are inseparable. Proof of this statement is this fact: Paul persecuted the church severely, and when Jesus encountered Paul on the road to Damascus, Jesus asked him the question, "Saul, Saul, why do you persecute me?"(Acts 9:5), when in fact from Jesus' standpoint, to attack His church was the same as attacking Him.

4. The church is the only institution on earth that will exist forever. Even the family and government shall cease in eternity. But Jesus said, "The gates of Hades (death) shall not prevail against the church" – Matthew 16:18.

5. So precious is the church in the sight of God that for one to "defile" it would be to bring destruction upon his soul. "If any man destroys the temple of God (the local church in this context), God will destroy him, for the temple of God is holy, and that is what you are" – 1 Cor. 3:17.

6. The church is not our Savior, only Jesus is, but the church is the University of Christ, designed by God to "make disciples" of all nations and then to teach them how to be true Christ-followers – Matthew 28:19-20.

7. The church is the only institution on this earth to whom He entrusted the Great Commission of our Lord Jesus Christ. Many Para-church organizations perform valuable ministries in the world, such as the Billy Graham Evangelism Association, Mentoring Men for the Master, Int'l., Campus Crusade for Christ, etc, but none of these can take the place of the church. In fact I have never known a Para-church group to be blessed by God who did not honor the local church. Billy Graham has always stressed the indispensable place of the local churches in his evangelistic ministry, and I make it very clear that MMM is not a church and is devoted to strengthening the local church and helping the pastors who shepherd the flocks of churches.

Of course, there are many more details we need to know about the church than we have covered above. I hope all your questions concerning the church are answered in my treatment to follow:

CHURCH MEMBERSHIP

Salvation is the most important gift you will ever receive. In it, you find new life. Baptism is an important step of obedience because through it you openly, publicly, and unashamedly identify yourself with the new life. Yet, after salvation and baptism, there is still much more that God wants you to have. He wants you to incorporate your new life into His church, the collective body of believers. This is accomplished by uniting with the fellowship and work of a local church.

What is the church?

The Greek word for church, used in the New Testament, is *ekklesia,* which means "the called out ones" or "the assembly." The word is used in the New Testament in two ways. First, it is used to speak of individual local congregations (1 Cor. 1:2). Second, it is used to speak of all Christians in the world who form the church universal (Matthew 16:18).

The universal church, or the whole of all saved people, is the body which you joined automatically when you got saved. You became a member of God's family. You were baptized into this body by the Holy Spirit (1 Cor. 12:13). All Christians everywhere instantly became your brothers and sisters in Christ Jesus. Isn't that great? Welcome to the family!

Now, you need to join a local church family. Of course, this is a decision which you must make as it pertains to which church and which denomination. If you are to grow as a Christian, you must involve yourself in a local church. For your growth as a Christian, church membership is not an option.

Why Join a Church?

As a Christian – especially if you are a new Christian – you have many needs. God established the church to meet the basic needs you have. This section will tell you some of the reasons why you need the church.

First, you need fellowship with other Christians (1 John 1:3). A saved person needs the encouragement and companionship of others who are also Christians. To deny yourself of Christian fellowship is to suffer spiritually. It is hard to grow in the world unless you have a church where you can have a positive Christian fellowship and influence.

Second, you need to identify publicly with the family of God (Acts 2:41-42). By joining and attending a church, you are telling those around you that you are a Christian and a disciple of the Lord Jesus. It serves as a witness and an example to others. It allows them to see who you are and what Christ has done for you.

Third, you need the worship experiences that the church provides. One of the purposes of the church is to worship God through music, praise, petition, and preaching. The church is unique in that it offers this unique opportunity in one setting.

Fourth, you need the church because of its education ministry. The church offers many opportunities to learn the Bible, how to grow as Christians, and many other things which pertain to the Christian life. You can learn from the wealth of knowledge possessed by many mature and wise Christian people.

Fifth, you need the opportunities of services that the church provides. As a Christian, you will never be totally satisfied until you are serving God to your fullest potential. In the church, you can serve by being a soul winner, choir member, teacher, usher, prayer partner, deacon or a host of other things.

Sixth, you need the ministry that a church provides. In your life, you will face many times of crises. You need a group of people who will support you, pray for you, and encourage you. Also, you need the constant ministry of being loved and genuinely cared for. The church provides these things as does no other institution.

Seventh, you need the spiritual direction that the pastor provides. The pastor is a man who is called by God to lead a church and its people. He will help bring spiritual direction to your life and instruct you through his ministry of teaching and preaching the Word of God. He will serve as a counselor and as a special friend.

Eighth, you need the special place for your family that the church provides. The church is a place where you can bring your entire family and find special ministries for each member. The church is capable of ministering to infants, toddlers, children, youth, singles, and adults of all ages. It provides a place where you can be together, grow together, and worship God together.

Ninth, you need the recreation a church provides. Your church will offer activities such as sports leagues, picnics, banquets, special trips, and many others. It is a place where you can enjoy quality recreation with fine Christian friends.

Tenth, the church provides you with the necessary resources to share your faith. It gives you a place to bring your lost friends to hear the

wonderful gospel. The church can train you to witness to others through special outreach programs.

Eleventh, and finally, the church gives you a place to give your tithes and offerings which will be used to spread the gospel in your city and across the world.

How do you join a church?

There are a number of ways to join a local church. Most denominations use the following ways of accepting new members. However, these may not be true for every church. After finding a church you want to join, you will want to ask one of its ministers how it receives new members.

First, you may become a part of a local church by professing your faith in Jesus and being baptized (Acts 2:41, 47).

Second, you may join by statement of faith. This means you have already made a profession of faith and have been baptized in another church of like faith and order.

Third, you may join by transferring your letter from another church. This simply means the church which you are presently a member will remove you from its rolls and recommend you to be enrolled into the membership of the other church.

How to find the right church.

This is a very important decision. Finding the right church isn't always easy and may take some searching; but pay the price. It will take time and prayer, but the right church is out there for you. Most of them may not be quite right, but certainly there is one that will meet your needs. You should use the following criteria in finding a new church.

First, does the church believe and preach the Bible? You may be surprised to hear that many do not. They may use the Bible and yet deny its significance. Many churches place tradition and experience above the Bible or equal to it. Beware, because this is not a good practice. The Bible is the authoritative word about God, the Christian life, and other things which pertain to the spiritual and the eternal. The Bible was inspired by God for our instruction and must be preached and taught in the church (2 Peter 1:20-21; 2 Timothy 3:16).

Secondly, does the pastor of the church fulfill his role adequately? The pastor should genuinely love the people and seek to be the shepherd of that local flock. He must place himself under the direct authority of God and lead the church as God instructs him. He should practice what he preaches and be a man who is above reproach. He should be a godly man who is able to lead you to Christian maturity. But, there is one word of warning. Do not look for a perfect man. There is no perfect pastor, and to search for one is as hopeless as the search for a perfect church. Yet, there is a pastor who is just right for you.

Third, does the church have a vision to grow and reach lost souls for Christ? Our Lord gave us the Great Commission (Matthew 28:18-20), but unfortunately, many churches are failing to obey Him. You need to find an evangelistic church which is ever seeking to find the lost and win them to a saving knowledge of Jesus Christ.

Fourth, does the church have a good program for educating you and your family in the faith? A church is a place to grow as a Christian. You should be part of a church which can instruct you and mature you in your Christian walk. The church should have a good Sunday School or small groups with classes for everyone in your family, as well as other educational ministries.

Fifth, does the church have special ministries for you? A church should be able to provide evangelism training, prayer meetings, special programs on the home and finances, social occasions and other ministries for your enjoyment and enrichment.

Sixth, does the church provide you with opportunities to serve? You need a church in which you are not only receiving ministry, but also doing ministry. A church that is doing much of anything will have a job for you. Make sure you can become actively involved in the ministry of the church.

Seventh, does the church have a "Vision" – a Divine Blueprint – under which it is marching. Remember Proverbs 29:18 says, "Where there is no vision, the people perish."

These guidelines will help you, but they are in no way exhaustive. You may have some expectations and qualification of your own. Make sure you take a good look at the church and pray for God's wisdom and leadership. Don't seek a church to satisfy your selfishness. Find a church,

first of all, where you can serve the Lord, and you will find a church that will serve you. Be assured that the right church is God's provision for your spiritual growth.

By all means, join a church.

COLLATERIAL MATERIAL FOR THE 7ᵀᴴ "I"

EVERY MEMBER A MINISTER
1 COR. 12:7; 1 PETER 4:10

I read that Napoleon looking at a map of China said, "There lies a sleeping giant. If China ever wakes up, it will be unstoppable."

I submit to you that the Church today is a sleeping giant, for the pews of the average church are filled with people who are doing nothing with their faith except "keeping it." Do you know what we consider an active church member to be?

1. One who attends some.

2. One who gives some money.

But the Bible says a member is active when he is performing a place of service in the church. Illus.: Mr. Gallup took a recent poll which revealed only 10% of church members serve in their church, and 50% said they don't want to serve. "I don't feel led. They have another kind of led – LEAD. They have LEAD in their pants, says Rick Warren.

On the other hand Mr. Gallup took a poll which revealed that 40% of church members say they want to serve if they knew where and how.

I say to you: The church will never be stronger than the core of its lay members and the church is built on *The Nine Pillars Of Lay Ministry:*

1. PILLAR #1 – Every Believer is a Minister.

   (a) Ephesians 2:10 says we were CREATED anew to serve.

   (b) 2 Timothy 1:9 says we are saved to serve

   (c) Matthew 28:18 says we are empowered to serve.

   (d) Acts 1:8 says we are empowered to serve

2. **PILLAR #2 – Every Member is Indispensable to the Body.** No "little people" or insignificant ministry. Some ministries are more visible and some are behind the scenes, but all are indispensable to the body. Example: A 79 year old member climbed up many stairs to visit with me in my study. I was thrilled to see this wonderful man. I said, "I've been missing you." He replied, "Pastor, I haven't missed. I have been serving in the nursery." I thanked him most sincerely and profusely. Example: A member with bad health said to me, "Pastor, I'm not able to attend church and help you. All I can do is pray." I replied, "That's the greatest service anyone can render."

"The most important light in the house is not the chandelier in the dining room, but the little night light in my bedroom which keeps me from stubbing my toe when I get up at night. **It's More Valuable Than The "Show Off" Lights.**" (Rick Warren)

3. **PILLAR # 3 – Every Believer is Gifted for Some Place of Service.** 1 Peter 4:10; 1 Cor.12:7 – Everyone is given a gift for the common good. Illus.: "I don't have a gift, I was behind the door when the gifts were passed out." No, to be a child of God is to be a gifted child of God. The absence of natural abilities does not disqualify you from serving God acceptably, and the abundance of ability does not qualify you to serve.

4. **PILLAR # 4 – No One on This Earth Can Take Your Place.** You have a place in your church and no one else can do it for you. Illus.: I cannot be a W.A. Criswell or Billy Graham, but I am the best and only specimen of Bill Bennett this world has ever seen. God made me to serve in my place. He made me and redeemed me to make a difference, and I intend to do this until God retires me which will be when I expire. Illus.: In 1 Cor 12, Paul say just as every part of your physical body is required to make your body function, it takes every member of the church body to make it function. Humor: R. G. Lee said if the average car had as many missing parts as the average church, it wouldn't go down hill.

5. **PILLAR # 5 – The Way to Find Your Place Is Not Primarily to Know Your Gift, but to Start Serving Somewhere.** Experiment with the different ministries, and God will soon show you where you should be permanently. Illus.: Make yourself useable and the Lord will wear you out.

6. **PILLAR # 6 – You Are Never More Like Jesus Than When You Serve –** Matthew 20:28; Phil. 2:5-9.

7. **PILLAR # 7 – Every Believer Will Give an Account of His Service at The Judgment Seat of Christ –** 2 Cor. 5:10; 1 Cor. 3:11-15; Rev. 22:12.

8. **PILLAR # 8 – Each Believer Will Be Held Accountable Not Only For What He Did But What He Could Have Done –** Luke 12:48.

9. **PILLAR # 9 – The Reward for the Faithful Will Be Absolutely Glorious** because Jesus will say to them, "Well done thy good and faithful servant. You have been faithful over a few things, I will make you ruler over many. Enter thou into the joy of the Lord" (Matthew 25:23).

SCRIPTURE TO INTERNALIZE FOR THIS CHAPTER:

Hebrews 10:25 – not forsaking the assembling of ourselves together, as is the manner of some, but exhorting one another, and so much the more as you see the Day approaching.

1 Peter 4:10 – As each one has received a gift, minister it to one another, as good stewards of the manifold grace of God.

CHAPTER 8

INTENSE DEVOTION TO ONE'S FAMILY, ESPECIALLY ONE'S SPOUSE

The family was the first institution established by God on earth – even preceding the government and the church. I am confident that the family was instituted first because it is first in importance in bringing human life into existence and then nurturing that life to become what a holy and loving God intended it to be – to conform to the image of Christ (Romans 8:29) in character and conduct. God began the home by instituting marriage between one man and one woman and pronouncing them to be "one flesh" in a relationship to be ended only by death (Genesis 2:24-25). God did not leave the home without a government to assure its continuance and welfare. The husband was ordained as the head of the home and the wife was to complement him in that role. Later with the coming of the Son of God, Jesus Christ, to this earth, marriage and the family were recognized as paramount in God's plan for His people. Jesus reiterated the same rule set forth by His Father in the Garden of Eden when He said, "For this cause (of marriage) a man shall leave his father and mother and cleave to his wife, and the two shall become one flesh. Consequently, they are no more two but one flesh. What therefore what God has joined together, let no man separate" (Matthew 19:5-6, NASB).

The Apostle Paul underscored the mutual responsibilities of both the wife and husband in his last word to the church in the Ephesians epistle, Ephesians 5: 22-31. "Wives, submit to your own husbands, as to the Lord. For the husband is head of the wife, as also Christ is head of the church; and He is the Savior of the body. Therefore, just as the church is subject to Christ, so let the wives be to their own husbands in everything. Husbands, love your wives, just as Christ also loved the church and gave Himself for her, that He might sanctify and cleanse her with the washing of water by the word, that He might present her to Himself a glorious church, not having spot or wrinkle or any such thing, but that she should be holy and without blemish. So husbands ought to love their own wives

as their own bodies; he who loves his wife loves himself. For no one ever hated his own flesh, but nourishes and cherishes it, just as the Lord does the church. For we are members of His body, of His flesh and of His bones. For this reason a man shall leave his father and mother and be joined to his wife, and the two shall become one flesh."

In the light of the centrality of the home and its indispensable place in the plan of God for the human race, what role should the husband play in the home:

1. He should assume the role of being the head of the wife and home (Ephesians 5:23).

2. He should realize that next to God his obligations to his home is the most important call upon his life.

3. He should heed the admonition of the Lord "not to provoke his children to anger; but to bring them up in the nurture and admonition of the Lord" (Ephesians 6:4).

4. While certainly not ignoring his children, the husband should make his wife his first love even before his children.

5. The husband's love for his wife should know no limits but should be as sacrificial as was Christ's love for the church, expressed in the cogent words of the Apostle Paul, "Husbands, love your wives, just as Christ loved the church and gave Himself (in death on the cross) for her" (Ephesians 5:25).

6. Moreover, the husband should know that the spiritual welfare of his wife was also his responsibility, as expressed by Paul "that he might sanctify her" through his example, and teaching (Ephesians 5:27).

7. In a word, the husband should "mentor" his wife even as he has been mentored in our mentoring schools.

To discharge his responsibility to his wife, the husband must become a life-long student of his wife so he will know her needs and how to meet those needs. Such is the specific command of God through the Apostle Peter in 1 Peter 3:7, "You husbands likewise live with your wives in an understanding way, as with a weaker vessel, since she is a woman; and grant her honor as a fellow-heir of the grace of life, so that your prayers may not be hindered." (NASB) Just how can a husband

"understand his wife" as commanded by God? I trust the following words will answer this question:

BE A LIFELONG STUDENT OF YOUR WIFE AND MINISTER TO HER NEEDS
1 PETER 3:7

Men, how are you treating your bride? The most important aspect of a man's life, except his relationship to Jesus, is the way he treats his wife. In fact no man's life is completely right if things are not right at home. Moreover, for a husband to treat his wife right, he must be a lifelong student of his wife in order to understand her needs and how he can meet those needs. To do the above, a husband must die to self and become Christ-like. In doing so, he may discover that he himself is his wife's chief problem.

A great man of God and friend of mine, Rev. Ray Gilder, Bivocational Ministries Specialist, revealed to me that he asked himself this question for many years, "What is my wife's problem?" One day he discovered that he was the problem. Then God burned a special word in his heart over a period of several months:

"Likewise, husbands, live together according to knowledge, giving honor to the wife as to the weaker vessel, the female, as truly being co-heirs together of the grace of life, not cutting off your prayers" – 1 Peter 3:7 – NKJV.

"Similarly, you husbands should try to understand the wives you live with, honoring them as physically weaker yet equally heirs with you of the grace of life. If you don't do this, you will find it impossible to pray together properly" 1 Peter 3:7 – Philips.

I. Try To Understand The Wives You Live With

Do you know your wife? Have you ever heard her say "you do not understand me?" Refuse to hide behind the false statement, "Nobody can understand a woman." We are commanded by God to "understand the wife you live with." This means *we are to be lifelong students of our*

wives – Evaluate Yourself (from 1-10 with 10 being highest) in the Following Areas:

WHAT IS IT THAT WE NEED TO KNOW?

1. You need to know Her Weaknesses – 1-10 _____

   (a) Does she have a tendency to over commit herself?

   (b) Does she have a problem saying "no"?

   (c) Does she have a tendency to procrastinate?

   (d) Does she get busy and let time slip up on her?

   • You need to protect her from these.

2. You need to Know Her Strengths – 1-10 _____

   (a) What does she do well?

   (b) What energizes her?

   (c) What gives her a sense of accomplishment?

   • Encourage her to operate in these areas.

3. You need to know Her Fears – 1-10 _____

   (a) Is she afraid of snakes, spiders, storms, rats, high speed ?

   (b) Never tease or make fun of her fears.

   (c) What makes her feel insecure?

   • Seek to protect her from and relieve her of her fears.

4. You need to know Her Basic Needs – 1-10 _____

   (a) She needs spiritual leadership. She needs to believe that God is leading you to lead the family.

   (b) She needs affection—Become emotionally sensitive to your wife. She needs a lot of hugs, kisses and "I love yous", not always connected to sex.

(c) She needs communication. She needs to talk, she needs details. Women speak 25,000 words a day, men speak 12,500 a day. Make sure you save some for her.

(d) She needs undivided attention. She needs you to look at her, not the TV or newspaper or a book. She needs you to intelligently respond.

(e) She needs financial support. She needs to know that you will take care of her and the children.

(f) She needs family commitment. She needs to know you are faithful to her and committed to the well-being of the family.

(g) She needs romance and sexual expression. In the Old Testament sexual relations was described as "he knew his wife." Men are interested in their sexual needs. Wives need to know they are really loved.

5. You need to know Her Moods – 1-10 _____

(a) Her chemistry is different from yours. She is subject to mood swings.

(b) Some days even she does not know why she is in a bad mood.

(c) She does not need rejection, correction or a lecture. She needs to be held and loved unconditionally.

At times I have asked my wife, "Honey, what's wrong?" and have preached a whole sermon on this question.

6. You need to know what is Important to Her – 1-10 _____

(a) This means talk a lot.

(b) Encourage her to talk about what she really wants.

7. You need to know Her Ability to Visualize – 1-10 _____

(a) She can see how things will look in advance. Like decorating a home. Men cannot even see it after it is done.

(b) She visualizes a car wreck. If she says "your driving scares me, slowdown."

8. You need to know that She has Built-in Radar – 1-10 _____

   (a) She is usually a good judge of character.

   (b) Listen to her when she warns you about other people. Especially women.

9. You need to know why God made Her Different from You – 1-10 _____

   (a) He gave her to you to complete you.

   (b) Her strengths and unique traits are to be used to balance your life.

   (c) Actually, you are to blend and balance each other.

10. You need to know Her Love Language – 1 -10_____

    (a) Read Gary Chapman's book—*The Five Love Languages*.

    (b) Decide what your wife's love language is.

    (c) Speak to her in her love language.

11. You need to know Her Past – 1 -10 _____

    (a) What kind of family did she have as a child?

    (b) Did she experience any abuse as a child?

    (c) What traumatic experiences impacted her life?

    (d) Especially know her relationship with her father.

II. Give Honor To Her

How do your honor her?

A. Honor her by placing her above other people and things – 1-10 _____

   1. Place her above the church—not God, but the church. You are married to her not the church. For the layman, this means placing her above your work. But do not use her or your children as an

excuse not to pray, study, or attend important meetings.

2. Place her above the children—If you do not, when they are gone you will be living with a stranger.

3. Place her above your favorite past time: be it sports on TV, golf, or other hobbies.

4. Place her above your parents—especially your mother. The Bible tells us to leave before we cleave (Genesis 2:24).

B. Honor her by *showing* her she is special – 1 -10 _____

We are to cherish our wives. Genesis 3:16 tells us she is built with a strong desire for your acceptance and appreciation.

C. Honor her by *serving* her – 1-10 _____

Bring her breakfast in bed; give her a foot massage, open doors for her, take her weekly to the beauty parlor.

D. Honor her by *surprising* her with gifts, trips and, outings that she was not expecting – 1-10 _____

This lets her know you have been thinking about her.

E. Honor her by *spending* more on her than she expects – 1-10 _____

She is worth the investment.

F. Honor her by *shielding* her from unnecessary harshness – 1-10 _____

Protect her from crude language, vulgarity, blasphemy. Treat her like a lady and insist others do the same.

G. Honor her by having eyes for her only – 1-10 _____

She notices when your eyes follow that shapely young blonde. Burn Job 31:1 in your heart.

H. Honor her by valuing her opinion – 1-10 _____. Give her credit for her ideas.

I. Honor her by bragging on her – 1-10 _____. Proverbs 31:28 tells us that a godly woman is to be praised by her husband.

J. Honor her by spending time with her – 1-10 _____ This proves that you enjoy her presence and highly value her.

K. Honor her by making her your best friend – 1-10 _____. Look forward

to sharing you life with her.

L. Honor her as God's precious gift to you – 1-10____ (Proverbs 18:22).

When you decide to honor your wife, don't tell her you are going to do it, just do it. Let your actions speak for themselves. She has heard too many empty promises that never came true.

A husband can give honor to his wife and still disagree with her. As the spiritual leader in the home, he must sometimes make decisions that are unpopular, but he still can act with courtesy and respect.

III. Become Her Protector

A. Understand what "weaker vessel" means.

1. It does not mean weaker mentally, spiritually or emotionally.

2. The word "vessel" refers to an instrument in the hand of God.

3. She is just as important to God's work as you are.

4. Weaker refers to her physical strength.

B. God made wives to need protection from dangers, abuse and overwhelming pressure.

C. God designed husbands and fathers to find fulfillment in providing protection for wives and children.

D. This is where the term chivalry comes into the picture. This is one of the characteristics of a knight. Webster describes it as "special courtesy and consideration to women."

E. We should protect our wives from dangerous situations, heavy-duty physical work, physical and verbal abuse and more pressure than they can handle.

F. The husband should treat his wife like an expensive, beautiful, fragile vase, in which is a precious treasure.

IV. Develop A Partnership

A. You are heirs together of the grace of life (1 Peter 3:7).

B. One thing this teaches is that men and women are equal spiritually.

C. The grace of life is the grace given by God to live this life. It is given to you as a team or partnership.

D. Your greatest effectiveness is as a partner with your wife.

E. This should lead you to discover ways to work together.

V. Put Power In Your Prayer Life

A. A key to spiritual power is harmony with your wife (1 Peter 3:7b).

B. A husband's spiritual health depends to a large degree in the way he treats his wife.

C. Discover the power of praying together. There is a tendency to try to act spiritual when conflict arises between you and your wife. We throw ourselves into our work, we pray a lot more and we spend extra time reading the Bible. The Lord's answer is probably like what He told a man who brought a gift to the altar and had problems with a brother. He would say, "Get up and go get things settled with your wife."

Conclusion

Some of you may say, this study has been awfully one sided. My first response would be that this is the typical reaction to any call to dying to self.

Secondly, I am convinced that the man is called to take the lead role in the relationship.

Thirdly, don't use the excuse "I will do my part when she does her part."

Lastly, becoming the husband this verse teaches frees your wife to respond to you properly.

*The above was adapted from Ray Glider's article, "Giving Honor to Your Wife."

In conclusion I am happy and humbled to be able to say that we have seen many husbands grow into godly husbands and fathers through our mentoring emphasis on devotion to the home until quite

a few wives have said to me, "Dr. Bennett, I don't know what you are doing to my husband in your Mentoring School, but whatever it is, keep it up; for I have a new husband." Some wives have flatly remarked to me, "Before going to Mentoring School, my husband gave no spiritual leadership in our home, but after attending Mentoring School, he has become our spiritual leader." *Deo Soli Gloria.*

22 WAYS TO STAY SEXUALLY PURE:

If a husband is to be devoted to his wife, he must first of all be sexually pure. Such purity is more and more difficult because of the sensual and immoral environment which surrounds us today, especially reflected on television, the internet, music, movies, and spoken vulgarities. Thus, I urge you to take all precautions to be sexually pure.

1. **Be sure you are born again, possess a new nature, and have the power of the Holy Spirit on the inside of you, enabling you to overcome sexual lust** (Gal. 5:16). If you are not born again, make an appointment with me or my assistant immediately.

2. **Be convinced that all sex outside of marriage is exceedingly sinful in the sight of God and should not be tolerated at all.** God's command could not be clearer: "Ye shall not commit adultery" (Exodus 20:14; Heb. 13:4). Adultery includes every act of sexual sin as forbidden by this commandment: fornication before marriage, adultery after marriage, homosexuality, lesbianism, incest, child abuse, bestiality, pornography stimulating mental adultery.

3. **Take radical action to prevent mental adultery, which is plain adultery according to Jesus** (Matthew 5:28; 2 Cor. 10:5-6). "Sexual impurity begins in the desires of the heart. Again, Jesus is not saying that lustful desires are identical to lustful deeds, and therefore a person might just as well go ahead and commit adultery. The desire and the deed are not identical, but, spiritually speaking, they are equivalent. The "look" that Jesus mentioned was not a casual glance, but a constant

stare with the purpose of lusting. It is possible for a man to glance at a beautiful woman and know that she is beautiful, but not lust after her. The man Jesus described looked at the woman for the purpose of feeding his inner sensual appetites as a substitute for the act. It was not accidental; it was planned.

How do we get victory? By purifying the desires of the heart (appetite leads to action) and disciplining the actions of the body. Obviously, our Lord is not talking about literal surgery; for this would not solve the problem in the heart. The eye and the hand are usually the two "culprits" when it comes to sexual sins, so they must be disciplined. Jesus said, "Deal immediately and decisively with sin! Don't taper off – cut off!" Spiritual surgery is more important than physical surgery, for the sins of the body can lead to eternal judgment. We think of passages like Colossians 3:5 and Romans 6:13; 12:1-2; 13:14."[32]

4. **Renew your mind by continually internalizing the Word of God** (Romans 12:1-2; Psalm 119:11).

5. **Be absolutely committed to one woman or one man for life.** Humor: It is alleged that after Adam and Eve were married, they were walking in the Garden of Eden, and Eve said to Adam, "Adam, do you really love me?" Adam replied, "Honey, as far as I'm concerned, you are the only woman in the world." You should be able to say this to your wife. I never dated but one girl – Doris. I never wanted to marry but one girl – Doris. I never think of another woman, never compare Doris with another, she is the one and only, now, forever and always.

6. **Make it a rule and never break it under any circumstances:** Never be alone with any woman except your wife (Ephesians 4:27; 1 Thess. 5:22). I had one secretary for 19 ½ years and during all that time I was careful never to be alone with no one else around.

---

[32] Warren Wiersbe, *Bible Exposition Commentary*, p.24

7. **Be careful to guard your eyes and mind.** "The first look is inevitable; the 2nd look is sin" (Billy Graham). Sex begins in the mind. Sex is mental before it becomes physical (Matthew 5:27-28).

8. **Love your wife for who she is today – not when you married her or whom you have wanted her to become.** Remember you married her for "better or for worse" until death do you part.

9. **Do not believe the devil's lie** – "The sexual grass is greener on the other side." 70% of second marriages fail.

10. **Do not make plans to sneak around to enjoy evil.** "Be sure your (sexual) sins will find you out" (Numbers 32:23). Avoid like a plague going to wrong places, seeing wrong people, viewing immoral movies, reading salacious materials, and even talking or joking about immoral sexual activity. "...There must not be even a hint of sexual immorality, or any kind of impurity...nor should there be obscenity, foolish talk, or coarse joking...for this you can be sure: No immoral...person has any inheritance in the kingdom of God" (Ephesians 5:3-5).

11. **Be cleansed from past sexual sins and then do not replay the tapes of past sexual sins** which have been forgiven and removed from you as far as the east is from the west provided you have truly repented and trusted Jesus as Lord and Savior and Him alone (Psalm 103:12; Isaiah 1:18; Phil. 3:13).

12. **Don't Let the Devil Deceive You by The Deception of Gradualism.** Few if any persons plunge into sexual immorality. It is a gradual process consisting of four steps:

    a. **It begins with Distraction** – suppose you are working in an office and suddenly you are distracted by a beautiful woman, and she keeps distracting you for days to follow.

b. **Attraction – Distraction leads to Attraction.** Now you are attracted to her desk and begin to make sweet comments to her – how nice she looks, how sweet she smells, how beautiful her hair.

c. **Interaction** – Next, you invite her to eat lunch with you.

d. **Finally Interaction leads to Transaction.** No longer are you contended to talk to her at her desk, say sweet comments, invite her to lunch. Now you find yourself not with her at lunch but with her in the bed. "You have crossed the Rubicon, and there is no turning back."

13. **Be Certain That You Can't Get Away With Sexual Sin.** Men are deceived in thinking they can keep sexual sin secret. Sexual sin is the most serious sin against God, except the unpardonable sin. Listen to this word from God, "You have sinned **against the Lord; and be sure your sins will find you out**" (Num. 32:23). Illus.: John Doe, my friend and pastor of an enormous church, concealed his sin for 10 years. He was involved with several woman in his church, believing not one of them would divulge it. Then one day one woman squealed, and the whole group came forward. He was forced to resign, and thereafter he founded another church, and another, and another and all failed. He died of a brain tumor at 53 years of age. Just prior to his death, he asked his best friend, "Can I ever be forgiven of such a horrible sin?" My friend replied, "Yes, if you truly repent, but your ministry can never be restored" Read Hebrews 13:4; Prov. 6:32-33.

14. **Do not rationalize any sexual sin but know that all sexual sin is ultimately against a holy God.** Until we see sexual sin this way, we can call it weakness, or what everyone else is doing, but when we see it as offending our holy God and Father, then we can deal with it. Illus.: David sinned sexually and concealed it for one year, after which he cries out "Against thee and against thee only have I committed this sin" (Psalm 51:5). Joseph was hounded for some time by Potiphar's wife to get in bed with her. Finally, he ask her this question, "How can I do this wicked thing and sin against God" (Gen. 39:9).

15. **Remember and never forget this fact:** It is possible for anyone, including yourself, to fall into sexual sin. **Recognize the real possibility of being tempted.** If Jesus, God's Son, could be tempted, that should be clue that you are not bigger than He. Remember 1 Cor. 10:12, "Therefore let him who thinks he standeth take heed lest he fall." Remember the advance billing of the Titanic, "Even God couldn't sink it." If you drift into arrogance, not even God can get you through. I have noted that pastors who fell into sexual immorality have often been filled with pride. Read Daniel 4:37.

16. **Know without a doubt, based upon the experience of millions, that sex cannot meet the deepest longings of your heart and soul.** Only God can do this. Listen: "God has made us for himself, and we are restless until we find our rest in Him." The most miserable souls on this planet are those who sought satisfaction in sex only to learn that it does not satisfy. Like drinking salt water, the more you partake, the more you need. Finally, many not finding fulfillment in natural sex revert to all kinds of perversion. In fact our culture today has descended to the depths of pagan immorality. Illus.: Recently a speaker was invited to the UNC Greensboro, to speak on "Anal Sex." I grew up on a farm and observed animals and never saw one sink so low as this.

Let me speak frankly to you men: The body of your wife is yours only in the natural expression of sex, not in using her body to meet your selfish, ungodly desires. Sexual toys, anal sex, oral sex are all abominable and have no place in sexual relations. God commanded us husbands "Husbands, love your wives even as Christ loved the church and gave Himself for us." (Ephesians 5:25). Can you imagine Christ treating the church with ungodly, selfish, vulgar treatment? Perish the thought, and if any of you are guilty, fall before the Lord and ask His mercy and forgiveness before tragedy descends upon you.

17. **Make yourself accountable to somebody, especially in the area of internet pornography.**

    1. Call pornography what it is – adultery

    2. Genuinely repent and receive God's forgiveness

120

3. Receive the forgiveness of your wife if possible.

4. Get a "Big Dog" filtering system and give the code to your wife or some other person.

5. Don't be on the internet in the absence of your wife or late at night.

6. If losing the battle with sexual lust, check out on the website "covenanteyes.com." Recommended by Promise Keepers and Focus on the Family. This program will send your accountability partner every week the sites you have visited.

7. Or get rid of the internet in your home – as Jesus commands "take radical action to avoid physical and mental adultery."

18. **Make friends and associate often with a couple with a strong marriage.** "Do not be misled: bad company corrupts good character" (1 Cor. 15:33). But good company will encourage you in your marriage and convince you that you can have a good marriage yourself. "If you lie down with dogs, you will get up with fleas" (old adage).

19. **Be willing to make the sacrifices necessary to enjoy intimacy with your wife on all levels** – emotional, intellectually, socially, financially, physically. "Husbands, love your wives as Christ loved the church and gave Himself (in death) for her." "If husbands obeyed Ephesians 5:25, the modern feminist movement would collapse in 24 hours," said John Haggai.

20. **Please, please, please don't kid yourself or be a fool and go to hell.** But know this: If you live in sexual sin, you can say "Good Bye" to heaven. The Bible makes it crystal clear that the person living in sexual sin cannot enter God's kingdom but is destined to the "lake of fire" (Rev. 21:8). One may commit an act of adultery, fornication, etc and still be saved. But one cannot practice sexual sin and expect to enter heaven. This fact is set forth in Galatians 5:21; 1 Cor. 6:9; Rev. 21:8.

21. **Be assured that because of God's grace, and through your sacrificial obedience, your marriage can be a "little piece of heaven on earth,"** for that is what God intends. To quote the late Peter Marshall, "Marriage is the highest hall of human happiness." I beg you, plead and implore you, to make it just that.

22. **Finally, be encouraged by the example of your mentor.** Few people were more unprepared for marriage than myself. My home did not prepare me. My church did not prepare me. My pre-marriage counselors did not prepare me. My church did not prepare me. Duke University and Wake Forest University did not prepare me, even though I took "Marriage and the Family" courses. So to be brutally frank: The first two years of our marriage were rocky. When asked if Doris and I had ever fussed, I replied, "I would not say we ever fussed, but we have had some intense moments of fellowship." But one day I saw that BB was the chief problem in our marriage. I repented and began to live to satisfy Doris not myself. Now – 57 years later – we find ourselves still married and increasingly more happy as our anniversaries roll by. If not already, this can be your experience, too, provided you will die to self, live for Jesus, and the welfare of your spouse. Will you?

Humor:

1. On our 50th anniversary, I asked Doris if she would love me when I'm old and ugly and she replied, "Yes, I do, Bill."

2. On our 58th anniversary, I said to Doris, "Honey, I love you so much that I would like you to remarry me," she replied, "I'll have to pray and think about this first."

SCRIPTURE TO INTERNALIZE FOR THIS CHAPTER:

Ephesians 5:25 – Husbands, love your wives, just as Christ also loved the church and gave Himself for her.

1 Peter 3:7 – Husbands, likewise, dwell with them with understanding, giving honor to the wife, as to the weaker vessel, and as being heirs together of the grace of life, that your prayers may not be hindered.

CHAPTER 9

INTENTIONAL DISCIPLINE OF THE PHYSICAL BODY –
1 COR. 9:27

The Greeks looked upon the physical body as evil and taught that the body would only be delivered from its corruption at death. Even the brilliant Plato embraced this regrettable view of human kind in regarding the physical body. On the other hand, Christianity views the body to be as sacred as the soul and was, therefore, to be "presented to God, as a living sacrifice, holy and acceptable unto God" (Romans 12:1). The body would one day die because of sin (Romans 5:12), but by Christ's resurrection power, it would be raised "a glorious body, even like unto the body of Christ Himself." (Phil. 3:20; 1 Cor. 15:41ff).

If anyone would think the body is evil, he should ask himself the question, "Why would Jesus, the sinless Son of God, have come to this earth and incarnated Himself in a human body like that of man? And why would Jesus have risen from the grave in this same body, glorified, and today sits in heaven in that body at the right hand of God?

There are those who say, "All God requires of us is to keep our souls and spirit in shape and not bother about the body." The Apostle Paul surely kept his soul and spirit in top notch shape, but he asserts that he had to make his body his slave or he would be worthless in the kingdom of God. Listen to his drastic testimony "…I buffet my body and make it my slave, lest possibly, after I have preached to others, I myself should be disqualified." (1 Cor. 9:27).

Permit me to share a testimony regarding the discipline of my body. I disciplined my spirit and soul from the time of my salvation at nine years of age, and 27 years later discovered that my body was deteriorating so greatly that I was feeling very tired and declining in energy and feared I may not be able to continue my ministry. At this point I began to jog three days a week and now daily, until I feel stronger 40 years later and able to work as hard as ever. Where would I be if I had not learned to discipline my body? Perhaps in a rocking chair or even a wheel chair, or maybe in my grave, where many of my peers are. God forbid that I

would overstate the place of physical discipline in one's life, but I am compelled to say that physical discipline is as much a part of my life today as is prayer or Bible reading. When I have not been able to jog (very rarely), I am affected psychologically, emotionally, and spiritually. For your soul, body, spirit and ministry, if you do not have a program of physical discipline, begin one now. You'll be glad you did.

The following material enforces the need of physical discipline:

TAKING CARE OF ALL OF YOU –
I COR. 6:19-20; I COR. 9:26FF

Obesity is now the number two killer in America. Also the number one killer of the children of God. Of all religious groups, Baptists are the fattest! What is the answer to this devastating problem? The discipline of the total person. The Bible speaks clear and loud about "Taking Care of all of You."

I. **Taking Care Of Your Body:**

Eat Right. Eat in Moderation. If you feel a need to eat till you are full, try this:

- Stock up on raw vegetables. They're filling, nourishing, and they won't put on fat.

- Eat more slowly. Psychologically, if we'd just eat more slowly and wait before taking that second helping, we'd feel better with less. Fast eaters actually consume more than they need because they don't give their bodies time to feel full.

- Don't keep lots of junk food around. If it 's not there, you can't eat it!

- Make a treat a treat. Give yourself a bonus on occasion so that a special treat is really something special. That way it never loses its great taste.

The famous psychologist Dr. Frank Minirth observed: "God never intended food to become a compulsion for any of us. The cycle can

124

be broken, but it must be approached the same way it began, step by step, little by little. Take it a day at a time and you will succeed."

1. Above all, eat breakfast. Why? Researchers have repeatedly proven that breakfast is the most important meal of the day. Why? Because at breakfast – literally "breaking the fast" – we get the nourishment that sustains us through most of the day. What we eat at lunch and dinner really doesn't benefit us until the day is almost over.

2. Get the right amount of sleep. Some people need more; some need less. The key is consistency.

3. Have a physical checkup at least once every two years.

4. Exercise. Choose an exercise routine that fits you and that you can fit in your daily schedule.

5. Flee from sexual sins. "Run away from sexual sin! No other sin so clearly affects the body as this one does. For sexual immorality is a sin against your own body. Or don't you know that your body is the temple of the Holy Spirit, who lives in you and was given to you by God? You do not belong to yourself, for God bought you with a high price. So you must honor God with your body" (I Cor. 6:18-20 TLV). There is a sense in which sexual sin destroys a person like no other, because it is so intimate and entangling, corrupting on the deepest human level. But Paul is probably alluding to venereal disease, prevalent and devastating in his day and today. No sin has greater potential to destroy the body, something a believer should avoid because of the sacredness of the body as affirmed in 1 Cor. 6:19-20.

6. Avoid Internet pornography like a plague.

II. Taking Care Of Yourself Emotionally:

Solomon said "As a man thinketh in his heart, so is he" (Proverbs 23:7). How we think about God, ourselves, others, our lives, yourselves is the key to our behavior.

1. Memorize and Meditate on Scripture

   • It sharpens your mind and concentration.

   • It teaches you to think logically and redemptively.

- It raises your capacity to learn and stay alert.
- It helps us to combat the lies of the world, the flesh and the devil.

There are multitudes of falsehoods out there from "I'm worthless" to "God can't love me like He loves others" to "some sins just can't be overcome." As we memorize and meditate on Scripture we are exposed to God's truth. Isaiah said God's Word [His truth] never returns void without accomplishing what it was sent out to do(Isaiah 55:11).

2. Learn to love everybody. Through love we reach out, give, share, care, open our hearts to others, become vulnerable, and sacrifice – in fact love makes possible every positive trait of Christian character.

3. Especially love those who won't love you even when you love them. Paul states the Christian approach in 2 Cor. 12:15. "And I will very gladly spend and be spent for you, though the more abundantly I love you, the less I be loved." Every minister must do this.

4. Learn to Laugh. "A merry heart doeth good like a medicine" (Proverbs 17:22). "Laughter is a tranquilizer with no side effects." (Arnold Glasgow)

5. Overcome your fears by letting God love you. "There is no fear in love; perfect love casts out fear" (1 John 4:18). How is this so? When we know the omnipotent God loves us, we realize there is nothing that can overcome us. We may even be killed in this world, but we know we have a permanent home in the next.

6. Learn not to worry. "I have learned in whatsoever state I am therewith to be content (Phil. 4:11). How? Learn to pray, to praise and refuse to entertain worry, think worry, believe worry, tolerate worry, talk worry, write worry "And we know that God causes all things to work together for good to them that love God, to them who are the called according to his purpose" (Romans 8:28).

7. Give everyone, including you, a break. Don't require perfection from your friends, family, your spouse, your children, your boss, your parents, yourself.

8. Give problems time.

9. Watch carefully how you allow yourself to be entertained. TV is the major source of our modern lifestyle. I urge you to assess your television viewing habits. Are you throwing your life away by watching sitcoms and soaps? A capital "T" followed by a "V" spells victim. Don't become a victim in front of the boob tube.

III. Taking Care Of Yourself Spiritually.

I see a very troubling condition among Christians today: Many are talking about being Christians but are doing little to live like Christians. To such Paul gives this sobering word, "They profess they know God; but in works they deny him, being abominable, and disobedient, and unto every good work reprobate" (Titus 1:16).

A leading Rabbi said some years ago, "We Jews deny Christ by our teaching, but you Christians deny him by your living." Looking Billy Graham in the eye, Mahatma Gandhi allegedly said, "Mr. Graham, I will become a Christian when I see a Christian." What is the trouble? One serious trouble is that the average Christian is prayerless. A recent survey shows he prays only three minutes per day and the average pastor only seven minutes. Another problem is biblical illiteracy. Most Christians don't even know they are to "internalize" the Word, and when most are confronted with this need, they seem to think it is only for the super-spiritual and refuse to do so.

However, I believe the most serious problem among Christians is their failure to understand the seriousness of sin. Most professing believers certainly believe that Jesus Christ paid the penalty for their sins on the cross and they are forgiven. But they to do not believe Jesus broke the power of sin and they do not have to continue to practice and live in sin. Yet Scripture makes it crystal clear that when we came to Christ we were united in His death to sin and made alive to God through Jesus. After stating this truth in Romans 6, verses 1 – 10, Paul then says, "Likewise reckon ye also yourselves to be dead indeed unto sin, but alive unto God through Jesus Christ our Lord. Let not sin therefore reign in your mortal body, that ye should obey it in the lusts thereof. Neither yield ye your members as instruments of unrighteousness unto sin: but yield yourselves unto God, as those that are alive from the dead, and your members as instruments of righteousness unto God. For

sin shall not have dominion over you: for ye are not under the law, but under grace" (Romans 6:11-14).

The results of thinking we must sin are devastating. Example: The foremost problem in our churches today is the unforgiveness and bitterness of professing Christians toward their fellow Christians. Yet many Christians live in this state, either believing God will understand or that they cannot overcome such an attitude.

So if you would take care of yourself spiritually, you must claim the victory of Christ over all sin in your life. Until you do, you have not taken care of yourself spiritually. How do you do this? You cannot do so alone, so God in His graciousness has given the Holy Spirit to us to enable us to crucify indwelling sin. This glorious truth is stated in Romans 8:13. "For if you live according to the flesh you will die; but if by the Spirit you put to death the deeds of the body, you will live."

COLLATERAL MATERIAL FOR THE 9TH "I"
THE BATTLE OF THE BULGE

Perhaps the bloodiest battle of World War II was called, "The Battle of the Bulge." The allies won this battle on the ground in Germany 65 years ago. But a "Battle of the Bulge" rages as never before in the stomachs of most Americans. Sixty seven percent of Americans are obese, and obesity is the second greatest cause of death in the USA. How can we win this battle over our flesh? After much soul searching, since I am caught in the battle myself, I have concluded from studying God's Word and based upon my experience and research, that there are four stages we can take to win the "Battle of the Bulge" in our stomachs.

I. **Acknowledge Your Present Weight.** 67% of Americans are obese. Obesity is the second or third cause of death in the USA. How about you? As to weight, there are 7 categories into which men fall:

1. Proper weight – consult a scientific chart.

2. Proper weight within 5 pounds, more or less.

3. Under weight.

4. Yo-Yo weight – up and down.

5. Over Weight

6. Heavy Weight

7. Heaven's Gate or Hell awaits.

II. **Activate Eight Steps That Will Reduce Your Weight If Needed.**

1. Be Honest

2. Admit your present status based on the 7 categories. Don't overlook number 7.

3. Begin to take *drastic* action either to increase your weight if you need to, maintain your weight as it is if you have proper weight, or reduce your weight if you are overweight. Remember the 4 G's of good health: *God, Genes, Grub* and *Gym*. The last two are up to you and are a must if you would possess proper weight. Therefore:

    a. Change your eating habits. Consult "A Healthy Nutrition Plan." And read "Taking Care of All of You" on page 122.

    b. Chose some kind of physical regimen which fits your temperament and schedule, and engage in it three times a week or more. As to myself I chose jogging or power walking and I will celebrate my 49th exercise anniversary December 2009. My proper weight is 160. I weight 160 but desire to lose 10 pounds in six weeks. My accountability partner is my assistant.

4. Enlist the cooperation of your wife: Her words of encouragement, her cooking, her prayers.

5. Ask your accountability partner to hold you brutally accountable.

6. Do not cease in Shaping Up Your Body, Physically, until you can present it to the Holy Spirit spiritually as commanded in Romans 12:1. Illus: A 13 year old boy on TV weighed 555 pounds. Would he dare present this much "lard" to the Holy Spirit? Of course

not. Suppose you are so heavy that you find it hard to get up early to pray? Or to attend vital meetings? Or you have high blood pressure or shortness of breath? Or can't wear your clothes? Illus: An optimist is the man who picks up his trousers at the cleansers, can't put them on and complains that the "Cleansers are shrinking my pants every time they clean them."

7. Heed this Warning. You will either make your body your slave to yourself, or you will be a slave to your body. This is literally what Paul feared when he wrote 1 Cor. 9:27 which says, "I will treat my body severely and lead it as a slave *(doulagogo)* lest after I have preached to others God will put me on the shelf." Thus keeping our bodies in shape is not just desirable or cosmetic but imperative. It is a shame that of all religious groups, Baptists are the most obese. Do you know of some whom God may have put on the shelf and can use no more? God forbid that it happen to anyone who reads this warning.

III. Accept the Fact That Your Body Belongs to The Holy Spirit and you are to surrender it to Him without reservation (Romans 12:1-2)

IV. Some Food Fun

1. According to scientists, the 2nd day of a diet is the easiest. By that time, you are off of it.

2. The only thing rougher than being on a diet is listening to someone else who is.

3. My favorite food is "Sea Food-All the Food I see."

4. The Agriculture Department says the average American eats 1148 pounds of food a year. Of course, a lot of it goes to waist.

5. Health Rule: Eat like a king for breakfast, A prince for lunch, a pauper for dinner.

6. Recipe from Hippie Cook Book: Cut up lettuce, cucumbers, green peppers, and tomatoes. Add a little marijuana and let the salad toss itself.

7. An apple a day keeps the doctor away, an onion a day keeps everybody away.

8. A chef (not Lee Grossman) is a man with a big enough vocabulary to give the soup a different name every day.

9. An old gentlemen in the hospital refused to eat jello. Pressed for an explanation by the nurse, he replied, "I'm not going to eat anything more nervous than I am."

10. When asked if you have had enough to eat, the educated answer would be "My gastronomic satiety admonishes me that I have reached a state of deglutition consistent with dietetic superfluity."

11. Being diplomatic to the heavy weights: Example – I had a deacon named Howard Leverett, a dear brother indeed, who weighted 400 pounds plus. I used to say to him, "Brother Howard, I need your opinion on such and such a matter, because you carry "more weight" than any member of our church of 3000 members." Example: I baptized a Mrs. Lewey who weighted 400 pounds plus. I weighed about 140 pounds and doubted if I could lift the dear lady out from under the water. So I asked three other guys to assist me, saying to Mrs. Lewey, "Mrs. Lewey, do you realize how important you are?" "No," she replied, and I said, "You are so important that it takes four men to baptize you." I really can't be sure I said these words, but looking back I wish I had.

12. The best way to lose weight is to eat everything you don't like.

13. If you want to know what you ought not to eat, if it tastes good, spit it out.

14. To feel as fit as a "fiddle," you must tune down your middle.

15. A husband who calls his wife the "little woman" very likely hasn't looked lately.

A Healthy Nutrition Plan

There are small things you can do as far as making nutritional choices that can yield BIG RESULTS. Below you will find a nutritional strategy that will help you make smart, tasty choices that will help you shed those stubborn pounds, feel better, look better, and become healthier. This is not about drastically changing your eating habits, but making a few minor substitutions and compromises so that you can still enjoy the foods that

you like, but in a healthier way. Open your mind to the possibility of trying different foods and different ways of preparing them.

Some Basic Guidelines

The quantities listed below are the maximum amounts that you should have at one sitting. If you want to eat less than the maximum amounts shown, you're allowed to do that. But don't skip meals! Remember, avoid eating fried foods as much as possible and watch how much salt you eat. Try not to consume more than a teaspoon of salt per day.

Breakfast	Quantity
Eggs	2
Cold Cereal	1.5 cups
Hot Cereal	
Oatmeal	1 cup
Farina	1 cup
Grits	1 cup
Cream of Wheat	1 cup
Pancakes	2 (no more than 5 inches across)
Waffles	2 (no more than 5 inches across)
Yogurt (low fat)	6 oz. (in regular package)

Instructions:

Choose only one of the items above to have for breakfast. Always eat one piece of fruit in the morning. Pay attention to the quantities listed for each item. Don't skip breakfast. Even if you're not hungry, try to at least have a piece of fruit in the morning. You can add berries or sliced fruit to your low-fat or fat-free yogurt and sprinkle it with some granola. The hot cereal should measure only 1 cup AFTER it's cooked. You're allowed to have a small amount of butter (1 pat size) and 2 tbsp of syrup.

More about cereals: The best to eat: Bran, Corn Flakes, Cherrios (plain), Shredded Wheat (not frosted), Total, Puffed Rice, Puffed Wheat, Oatmeal, Farina, Cream of Wheat, Grits.

Avoid: Those cereals that have sugar added to them or have the word frosted in their title.

FRUITS

Instructions:

Fruits are full of powerful vitamins and minerals that can help fight disease and make you feel better as well as increase your energy. Eat as much fruit as you like. There are, however, some fruits that are better than others when trying to lose weight.

Best to eat: Strawberries, blueberries, apples, oranges, cherries, plums, grapefruit, pears, grapes, peaches, cantaloupe, and honeydew melons

Eat less of these: watermelon, pineapple, avocado and those juices that are marked "made from concentrate."

BREADS

The best to eat: whole grain, wheat, whole wheat, multi-grain or Rye Pita Bread.

Avoid: White and sour dough

Instructions:

Breads can be high in something called the Glycemic Index (for more about this, read Extreme Fat Smash Diet). You should limit the amount you consume per day to no more than 2 regular slices.

Milk Products	Quantity
Milk: Skim, 1%, 2%, Fat-free	2 cups
Low-fat Cottage Cheese	3 tbsp.
Yogurt: Low-fat plain yogurt, Low-fat fruited yogurt	12 oz.

Meats	Quantity
Chicken (not fried)	4 oz.
Turkey	4 oz.
Sirloin	4 oz.
Beef	4 oz.
Ham	4 oz.

Instructions:

Meats when eaten in proper quantities are part of a healthy nutritional plan. You should consume no more than two servings of meat in one day. Please pay attention to the quantities that have been listed. 4 oz is approximately the size of one-and-a-half decks of playing cards. Remember, try to limit your fried foods. Grilling, baking, sautéing are healthier ways to prepare your meats and they can be just as tasty!

VEGETABLES/GRAINS

Good to eat: All vegetables except those listed below. Don't fry your veggies. Bake, grill, boil (not too long), sauté, steam. Don't cook with bacon or other fats. Use a small amount—1 tbsp—of butter if you like. Add some spices for flavor.

What to avoid: white rice, white potato (white is the color of the pulp, not the skin. A red-skinned potato is still a white potato, because the pulp is white). Instead, have brown rice and sweet potatoes/yams.

BEVERAGES

Best to drink: natural juices, freshly-squeezed juices, water, flavored water, unsweetened tea, herbal tea, diet soda

Try to avoid or reduce your consumption of: regular soda, alcohol, sweetened drinks, drinks that are marked "made from concentrate."

If you'd like to learn more about a healthy diet or discover tasty, healthy recipes, read Dr. Ian's Extreme Fat Smash Diet or The Fat Smash Diet. They are both available in paperback in bookstores throughout the country or online at www.amazon.com or www.barnesandnoble.com.

10 Smart Swaps that Save Calories

One of the keys to achieving long-term weight loss success is to find ways to continue enjoying your favorite types of foods while you save calories. Whether you're snacking or grabbing lunch on the go, these 10 easy swaps will save calories and satisfy your cravings.

1. In the mood for a crunchy snack? Swap an ounce of Harvest Cheddar Sun Chips for two cups of air-popped popcorn to save 78 calories.

2. Instead of splitting a Chili's Awesome Blossom and sauce with three friends, snack on one medium order of Burger King onion rings to save 357 calories.

3. Swap a cup of strawberry ice cream for a Yoplait Whips, Strawberry Mist flavor, to save 114 calories.

4. Chicken isn't always the best choice when it comes to saving calories. Swap a Wendy's Chicken Club Sandwich for a Jr. Cheeseburger to save 300 calories.

5. Swap a 1.7-oz. package of M&M's Plain Chocolate candies for a half cup of Kozy Shack Real Chocolate pudding to get a chocolate fix while saving almost 100 calories.

6. Wraps sound diet-friendly, but often they are not the best choice. Swap an Au Bon Pain Chicken Caesar Wrap for one 8-oz. low-fat chicken noodle soup to save almost 500 calories.

7. It's not a fiesta for your waistline if you order Applebee's Fiesta Lime Chicken. Swap it for a Tortilla Chicken Melt from the appetizer menu to save a whopping 805 calories.

8. Swap a Wendy's Garden Sensations Southwest Taco Salad for a Garden Sensations Caesar Chicken Salad and save 250 calories.

9. Take your own treat to the mall. Swap one Mrs. Field's semi-sweet chocolate chip cookie for 13 (yes, 13!) Miss Meringue Chocolate Chip Minis to save 170 calories.

10. Chicken is a great salad topper, but fried or crispy chicken ups the fat and calories. For example, at Burger King, if you swap a Tendercrisp Garden Salad for a Tendergrill Garden Salad, you will save 180 calories.

SCRIPTURE TO BE INTERNALIZED FOR THIS CHAPTER:

1 Corinthians 9:27 – But I discipline my body and bring it into subjection, lest, when I have preached to others, I myself should become disqualified.

Romans 12:1 – I beseech you therefore, brethren, by the mercies of God, that you present your bodies a living sacrifice, holy, acceptable to God, which is your reasonable service.

CHAPTER 10

INSTANT REPENTANCE AND CLEANSING FROM ALL SIN

When one truly repents and trust Jesus Christ as Lord and Savior, all His sins are forgiven – past, present and future. Not only is that person forgiven, but at the same times he trust Christ and Him alone to forgive and save him from all sins, Christ imputes to him His total righteousness (2 Cor. 5:21). Simultaneously, the Holy Spirit enters the life of that person and imparts to him a new, even "divine nature" (2 Peter 1:4), making him a "new creation" with a new lifestyle (2 Cor. 5:17). Moreover, such a person cannot and will not continue to practice sin because of the "seed of God" which remains within him. "He who is born of God does not practice sin, for the seed of God is in him, and he cannot practice sin because the seed of God remains in him" (1 John 3:9). The Apostle Paul thunders forth this same truth in those convicting words in Romans 6:1 "What shall we say then? Shall we continue in sin that grace may abound? Certainly not! How shall we who died to sin live any longer in it?"

However, the saved, though forgiven and delivered from the practice of sin, may be tempted to sin and even fall into acts of sin. The Apostle John categorically commands God's children in these words, "My little children, these things I write unto you that you sin not," meaning a single act of sin. Then the apostle immediately allows for the possibility of and individual act of sin when he says, "And if any man sin (commits an act, not practice) we have an advocate with the Father, Jesus Christ the righteous" (1 John 2:1-2). Because Jesus is the believer's advocate (attorney) with the Father, the believer's sin is forgiven, provided he will confess his sins. "If we confess our sin, He is faithful and just to forgive us of all our sins and to cleanse us from all unrighteousness." Illus: I read of a pastor who was preaching a series of messages on sin to his people. One of the members said, "I wish you would not preach so much on sin for sin is not serious for Christians as it is for the lost. To which the pastor replied, " Sin is much more serious for the Christian than for the lost, for the Christian knows it is wrong and should not tolerate it." Amen and amen.

Certainly no one can "conform to the image of Christ" unless he keeps his sins "confessed up to date," forsakes them, and is cleansed by the blood of Christ. It is so easy to "cover" our sins, but those who do so shall not prosper, but those who confess and forsake their sins shall find mercy" (Proverbs 28:13). And the promise of God is that if we will walk constantly in the light – in this case the knowledge of constant brokenness and repentance – that "the blood of Jesus Christ His Son will keep on cleansing us from all sin" (1 John 1:7). Illus.: I read that some miners in Kentucky departed from a mine with their faces blackened with soot, except their eyes which were perfectly clean. Why? Because of the flow of the tear glands which protected their eye balls. There is scarcely a greater promise that God gives to His children than that if they will walk in obedience to Him – in instant repentance and cleansing from all sin – a "built in" spiritual gland, the Holy Spirit, will keep applying to their souls the cleansing blood of Jesus. Hallelujah what a Savior!

Since the "instant" repentance from all known sin depends upon our honest and specific confession of same, let us take a "Soul Search through the Scriptures."

COLLATERAL MATERIAL FOR THE 10ᵀᴴ "I"

SOUL SEARCH THROUGH THE SCRIPTURES
FOR CLEANSING AND THE SPIRIT'S INFILLING

Psalm 139:23-24: "Search me, O God, and know my heart; test my thoughts. Point out anything you find in me that makes you sad, and lead me along the path of everlasting life."

Repentance is necessary for salvation, and for fellowship with god, and revival among God's people. Prayerfully consider the following questions. Every "yes" answer means sin in your life.

In reading these questions, as you are convicted of sin, confess it and repent at once to God. Be willing to make it right. Then you can claim cleansing and forgiveness. I John 1:9, "If we confess our sins, He is faithful and just to forgive us our sins and to cleanse us from all unrighteousness."

Be sure to name your sin to God, as..."Lord, I have not put thee first in my plans." Or, "I have neglected thy Word and prayer." Do not make the least excuse for sin of any kind in your life. Proverbs 28:13, "He that covereth his sins shall not prosper; but whoso confesseth and forsaketh them shall have mercy."

No mater what others do, or do not do, Christian: leave nothing undone on your part. God wants to work through you to bring about a great spiritual awakening. He can begin by your fulfilling every requirement shown by the Lord through the Holy Spirit and His Word. A revival from the Presence of the Lord begins today **if you desire it.** (Read the Scripture first. Ask the question. Give a truthful answer – "yes" or "no.")

1. **Matt. 6:14-15**

   Is there anyone against whom you hold a grudge? Anyone you haven't forgiven? Anyone you hate? Anyone you do not love? Are there any misunderstandings that you are unwilling to forget? Is there any person against whom you are harboring bitterness, resentment, or jealously? Anyone you dislike to hear praised or well spoken of? Do you allow anything to justify a wrong attitude toward another?

2. **Matt. 6:33**

   Is there anything in which you have failed to put God first? Have your decisions been made after your own wisdom and desires, rather than seeking and following God's will? Do any of the following, in any way, interfere with your surrender and service to God: Ambition, pleasures, loved ones, friendships, desire for recognition, money, your own plans?

3. **Mark 16:15**

   Have you failed to seek the lost for Christ? Have you failed to witness consistently with your mouth for the Lord Jesus Christ? Has your life not shown to the lost the Lord Jesus?

4. **John 13:35**

   Are you secretly pleased over the misfortune of another? Are you secretly annoyed over the accomplishments or advancements of another? Are you guilty of any contention or strife? Do you quarrel, argue or engage in heated discussions? Are you a partaker in any divisions, or party spirit? Are there people whom you deliberately slight?

5. **Acts 20:35**

   Have you robbed God by withholding His due of time, talents, and money? Have you given less than a tenth of your income for God's work? Have you failed to support mission work either in prayer or in offerings?

6. **I Cor. 4:2**

   Are you undependable so that you cannot be trusted with responsibilities in the Lord's work? Are you allowing your emotions to be stirred for things of the Lord, but doing nothing about it?

7. **I Cor. 6:19-20**

   Are you in any way careless with your body? Do you fail to care for it as the temple of the Holy Spirit? Are you guilty of intemperance in eating or drinking? Do you have habits, which are dwelling in the body?

8. **I Cor. 10:31**

   Do you take the slightest credit for anything good about you, rather than give all the glory to God? Do you talk of what you have done rather than of what Christ has done? Are your statements mostly about "I"? Are your feelings easily hurt? Have you made a pretense of being something you are not?

9. **Eph. 3:20**

   Are you self-conscious rather than Christ-centered? Do you allow feelings of inferiority to keep you from attempting things you should do in serving others?

10. **Eph. 4:28**

    Do you underpay? Do you do very little where you work? Have you been careless in the payment of your debts? Have you sought to evade payment of debts? Do you waste time? Do you waste time for others?

11. **Eph. 4:31**

    Do you complain? Do you find fault? Do you have a critical attitude towards any person or thing? Are you irritable or cranky? Do you ever carry hidden anger? Do you get angry? Do you become impatient with others? Are you ever harsh or unkind?

12. **Eph. 5:11**

    Do you listen to unedifying radio or TV programs? Do you read unworthy magazines? Do you partake in worldly amusements? Do you find it necessary to seek satisfaction from any questionable source? Are you doing certain things that show that you are not satisfied in the Lord Jesus Christ?

13. **Eph. 5:20**

    Have you neglected to thank Him for all things: the seemingly bad, as well as the good? Have you virtually called God a liar by doubting His Word? Do you worry? Is your spiritual temperature based on your feelings instead of on the facts of God's Word?

14. **Phil. 1:21**

    Are you taken up with the cares of this life? Is your conversation or heart joy over "things" rather than the Lord and His Word? Does anything mean more to you than living for and pleasing Christ?

15. Phil. 2:14

Do you ever by word or deed, seek to hurt someone? Do you gossip? Do you speak unkindly concerning people when they are not present? Do you carry prejudice against true Christians because they are of some different group than yours, or because they do not see everything exactly like you do?

16. Phil. 4:4

Have you neglected to seek to be pleasing to Him in all things? Do you carry any bitterness toward God? Have you complained against Him in any way? Have you been dissatisfied with His provision for you? Is there in your heart any unwillingness to obey God fully? Do you have any reservations as to what you would, or would not do concerning anything that might be His will? Have you disobeyed some direct leading from Him?

17. Col 3:9

Do you engage in empty and unprofitable conversation? Do you ever lie? Do you ever exaggerate? Cheat? Carefully consider – do you overcharge?

18. II Tim. 2:22

Do you have any personal habits that are not pure? Do you allow impure thoughts about the opposite sex to stay in your mind? Do you read that which is impure or suggest unholy things? Do you indulge in any entertainment that is unclean? Are you guilty of the lustful look?

19. Heb. 10:25

Do you stay away from the meetings or preaching the Gospel? Do you whisper or think about things while God's Word is being read or preached? Are you irregular in attendance at services? Do you neglect to attend or participate in meetings for prayer? Have you neglected or slighted daily or private prayer? Have you neglected God's Word?

Do you find the Bible and prayer uninteresting? Have you neglected thanksgiving at meals? Have you neglected family devotions?

20. Heb. 13:17

Do you hesitate to submit to leaders in the church or elsewhere? Are you lazy? Do you rebel at requests given to you in the work of the Gospel? Do you in any way, have a stubborn or unteachable spirit?

21. James 1:27

Have you allowed yourself to become "spotted" by the world? Is your manner of dress pleasing to God? Do you spend beyond what is pleasing to God on anything? Do you neglect to pray about things you buy?

22. James 4:6

Do you feel that you are doing quite well as a Christian? That you are not so bad? That you are good enough? Are you stubborn? Do you insist on your own way? Do you insist on your "rights?"

23. James 4:11

Have you dishonored Him and hindered His work by criticizing His servants? Have you failed to pray regularly for your pastor or other spiritual leaders? Do you find it hard to be corrected? Is there rebellion toward one who wants to restore you? Are you more concerned about what people will think, than what will be pleasing to God?

+ + + + + + + + + + +

If you have been honest and true in the matter of repenting of your sins, then you are ready for God's cleaning. Remember these things:

1. If the sin is against God, repent to God, and make things right with God.

2. If the sin is against another person, repent to God and make things right with the other person.

3. If the sin is against a group, repent to God, and then make it right with the group. *If there is full confession and repentance, there will be full cleansing.* Then the joy of the Lord will follow.[33]

TEN DESPERATE STEPS TO PERSONAL REVIVAL

Some years ago a noted theologian said in effect "Revival does not come to nice people but to the desperate." Dr. J. Edwin Orr, the world's foremost authority on revival, was asked by a student, "Dr. Orr, besides praying for revival, what can I do to help to bring it about?" He then replied, "You can let it begin with you."

If it would begin in me or you, you must be desperate for it enough to take the following 10 Desperate Steps to Personal Revival:

1. Get thoroughly dissatisfied with yourself. Complacency is the deadly enemy of spiritual progress. The contended soul is the stagnant soul. Amos 6:1. When speaking of earthly goods Paul could say, "I have learned…to be content"; but when referring to his spiritual life he testified, "I press toward the mark." So stir up the gift of God that is in thee.

2. Set your face like a flint toward a sweeping transformation of your life. Gen. 32:20. Timid experimenters are tagged for failure before they start. We must throw our whole soul into our desire for God. "The kingdom of heaven suffereth violence, and the violent take it by force."

3. Put yourself in the way of the blessing. It is a mistake to look for grace to visit us as a kind of benign magic, or to expect God's help to come as a windfall apart from conditions known and met. There are plainly marked paths which lead straight to the green pastures; let us walk in them. To desire revival, for instance, and at the same time to neglect prayer and devotion is to wish one way and talk another. 2 Chronicles 7:14.

---

[33] Material for Soul Search adapted from one used by Ms. Bertha Smith, long time missionary.

4. Do a thorough job of repenting. Do not hurry to get it over with. Hasty repentance means a shallow spiritual experience and lack of certainty in the whole life. Let godly sorrow do her healing work. Until we allow the consciousness of sin to wound us we will never develop a fear of evil. It is our wretched habit of tolerating sin that keeps us in our half-dead condition. Mt. 3:8; Psa. 57.1

5. Make restitution wherever possible. If you owe a debt, pay it, or at least have a frank understanding with your creditor about your intentions to pay, so your honesty will be above question. If you have quarreled with anyone, go as far as you can in an effort to achieve reconciliation. As fully as possible make the crooked things straight. Mt. 5:23-24.

6. Bring your life into accord with the Sermon on the Mount and such other New Testament Scriptures as are designed to instruct us in the way of righteousness. Titus 2:11-14. An honest man with an open Bible and a pad and pencil is sure to find out what is wrong with him very quickly. I recommend that the self- examination be made on our knees, rising to obey God's commandments as they are revealed to us from the Word. Matt. 5:28; 5:4; 5:23; 5:44; 6:19-25; 7:12; 7:1; 6:33; 5:8; 5:13; 5:14. There is nothing romantic or colorful about this plain downright way of dealing with ourselves, but it gets the work done. Isaac's workmen did not look like heroic figures as they digged in the valley, but they got the wells open, and that was what they had set out to do.

7. Be serious-minded. You can well afford to see fewer comedy shows on TV. Unless you break away from the funny boys, every spiritual impression will continue to be lost to your heart, and that right in our own living room. The people of the world used to go to the movies to escape serious thinking about God and religion. You would not join them there, but you now enjoy spiritual communion with them in your own home. The devil's ideals, moral standards and mental attitudes are being accepted by you without your knowing it. And you wonder why you can make no progress in your Christian life. Your interior climate is not favorable to the growth of spiritual graces. There must be a radical change in your habits or there will not be any permanent improvement in your interior life. I Pet. 5:8

8. Deliberately narrow your interests. The Jack-of-all-trades is the master of none. The Christian life requires that we be specialists. Too many projects use up time and energy without bringing us nearer to God. If you will narrow your interests God will enlarge your heart. Phil. 3:17; Psa. 27:4. "Jesus only" seems to the unconverted man to be the motto of death, but a great company of happy men and women can testify that it became to them a way into a world infinitely wider and richer than anything they had ever known. Christ is the essence of all wisdom, beauty and virtue. To know Him in growing intimacy is to increase in appreciation of all things good and beautiful. The mansions of the heart will become larger when their doors are thrown open to Christ and closed against the world and sin. Try it.

9. Begin to witness. Find something to do for God and your fellow men. Refuse to rust out. Philemon 1:6 Make yourself available to your pastor and do anything you are asked to do. Do not insist upon a place of leadership. Learn to obey. Take the low place until such time as God sees fit to set you in a higher one. Back your new intentions with your money and your gifts, such as they are.

10. Have faith in God. Mark 11:22. Begin to expect. Look up toward the throne where Your Advocate sits at the right hand of God. All heaven is on your side. God will not disappoint you. (Adapted from *Rut, Rot Or Revival* by A. W. Tozer)[34]

SCRIPTURE TO BE INTERNALIZED FOR THIS CHAPTER:

1 John 2:1-2 – My little children, these things I write to you, so that you may not sin. And if anyone sins, we have an Advocate with the Father, Jesus Christ the righteous. And He Himself is the propitiation for our sins, and not for ours only but also for the whole world.

Luke 13:3 – I tell you, no; but unless you repent you will all likewise perish.

---

[34] Stephen F. Olford, Heart-Cry for Revival, quoted A. W. Tozer, Westwood, New Jersey: Fleming H. Revell, Company, pp. 30-31